T0149449

To Save the Earth from Global Warming and Nuclear War

WITH KNOWLEDGE AND VIRTUE

THEMI H. DEMAS, PhD

WITH KNOWLEDGE AND VIRTUE TO SAVE THE EARTH FROM GLOBAL WARMING AND NUCLEAR WAR

iUniverse books may be ordered through booksellers or by contacting:

iUniverse
1663 Liberty Drive
Bloomington, IN 47403
www.iuniverse.com
1-800-Authors (1-800-288-4677)

Because of the dynamic nature of the Internet, any web addresses or links contained in this book may have changed since publication and may no longer be valid. The views expressed in this work are solely those of the author and do not necessarily reflect the views of the publisher, and the publisher hereby disclaims any responsibility for them.

Any people depicted in stock imagery provided by Thinkstock are models, and such images are being used for illustrative purposes only. Certain stock imagery © Thinkstock.

ISBN: 978-1-5320-3224-0 (sc)
ISBN: 978-1-5320-3223-3 (e)

Library of Congress Control Number: 2017916144

Print information available on the last page.

iUniverse rev. date: 11/20/2017

CONTENTS

DEDICATION

This book is dedicated to my wife Christina for her patience and understanding.

INTRODUCTION

GENERAL

I feel great awe in inquiring into the genius of human spirit that developed our civilization from ancient times to today. We can marvel at great people and their astonishing achievements, their literature, their gems of art, and industry: the pyramids of Egypt, the Parthenon, philosophy, democracy, Romanesque and Gothic cathedrals, Renaissance art, the classical music of Beethoven and Mozart, the discoveries of Galileo and Newton, the Industrial Revolution, the novels of Victor Hugo and Leo Tolstoy, the instruments used to gaze at the universe, medicines, the transistor, and the Internet, to name just a few. Humanity has achieved an excellence of which it can be proud.

While the world is constantly reaching new levels of technical excellence in many endeavors, people have not cultivated enough ethical excellence or virtue. Science fiction writer Isaac Asimov's observation is timelier than ever: "The saddest aspect of life right now is that science gathers knowledge faster than society gathers wisdom."[1]

Since the beginning of the seventeenth century, Western culture has experienced a dazzling explosion in science and technology that unleashed an enormous potential of power for humanity. In the last century and a half, scientific and technical progress has followed an exponential rather than an arithmetical curve that is becoming almost vertical.

Unfortunately, along with this great technical genius, we face many challenges: the unchangeable human mind with the curses of immaturity and irrationality. This is testified to by our constant abuse of the environment, wars, and the use of technology for destructive applications with the ultimate of building tens of thousands of nuclear weapons. The continuous human strife in North Africa in the last ten years, in the Middle East, and in other areas of the world brings back war scenes over the last

---

[1] Isaac Asimov and Jason A. Shulman, *Isaac Asimov's Book of Science and Nature Quotations*, Blue Cliff Editions (New York: Weidenfeld & Nicolson, 1988), 281.

five centuries and the crusades 700–900 years ago: terrorism, invasions, big-power interventions, civil and religious wars, violence, poverty, migration, and chaos.

The Industrial Revolution created a need for energy that came from fossil fuels and created global warming. Along with its great benefits, technology has allowed us to create weapons of unparalleled power for terrorism and conventional and nuclear wars.

In this book, I shall discuss technological progress and the progress of the human mind toward achieving happiness, as this is the ultimate purpose of humanity and the conflict between the progression of the two. In addition, I will discuss how intellectual, technical, and moral excellence can address the two threats capable of annihilating life on earth: global warming and all-out nuclear war.

Leaving aside all technical progress, we need to look at these two great problems hovering over humanity. Humanity has acquired immense powers; nine nations possess nuclear weapons, and that number may increase. In the last century, 187 million perished in wars and by man-made causes.

The second is that we have been abusing nature and releasing so much carbon dioxide, methane, and other greenhouse gases that cause global warming with all the associated climate change issues. The 2015 United Nations Climate Change Conference held in Paris established that global warming is a major threat to the planet and that nations can and must control it. These two problems threaten our existence and make lives miserable.

Observing the terrorism and wars going on in the world today, we can think that the beliefs and philosophies developed to tame humanity are inadequate. We must gain knowledge and cultivate virtue in our intellects and hearts to solve these two threats.

Some of the secondary problems will be addressed along with global resources—primarily energy, as it plays a major role on war and global warming.

The fundamental problems mentioned above are created by the imbalance in humans between their technical and moral progress.

Because we are what we know, we are a synthesis of experience and knowledge. We receive information from our senses and synthesize it with what we already know; only knowledge can make us change our behavior. This is where knowledge and virtue come into consideration.

Many geniuses, from Socrates, Plato, and Aristotle to St. Paul, Kant, Archimedes, Einstein, and others, glorified these two subjects with their words and deeds to improve human existence. So many other famous and humble people from many civilizations labored on this task. It is only through the bond of knowledge and virtue that real, useful progress can take place, and no real progress takes place when the bond between the two is broken.

I shall review the ascent of humanity from the beginning and through the ages to our time. I shall review the glory and defeat of the human spirit, the times when humanity was glorified with what it said, did, and created and the times it shamed itself.

Our ascent can be characterized sometimes by brilliance that made great leaps forward and sometimes by stupidity that sank us to the lowest levels of knowledge and virtue and took a while to recover from.

I am very optimistic that despite the issues we are facing, we can overcome them as expressed in *The Progress of the Human Mind* by the Marquis de Condorcet (1743–1794), written when he was hiding from political prosecution during the French Revolutionary Reign of Terror. He foresaw the world enjoying a much higher standard of living, more leisure, and more equality among people in general and between the sexes in particular. War would be given up as irrational, and disease would be so effectively conquered by medicine that the average life span would be greatly lengthened. He stated,

> Such is the aim of work that I have undertaken, and its result will be to show by appeal to reason and fact that nature has set no bounds to the improvement of the human faculties: that the perfectibility of man is absolutely indefinite; and that the progress of this perfectibility, from now onwards independent of any power that might wish to halt it, has no other limit than the duration of the globe upon which nature has placed us. This progress may doubtless vary in speed, but it can never be reversed as long as the earth occupies its present place in the system of the universe, and as long as the general laws of the system produce neither a general cataclysm nor such changes as will deprive the human race of its present faculties and its present resources. [2]

I shall start by reviewing the ascent of humanity from its primitive state to today and put things in a historical perspective so we can learn from the past. As the ancient historian Polybius (c. 200–c. 118 BC) stated as his didactic motive for studying history,

> What is really educational and beneficial to students of history is the clear view of the causes of events, and the consequent power of choosing the better policy in a particular case … There are two roads to reformation for mankind; one is through their own disasters, and one through those of others. The former is the most unmistakable, the latter the less painful. One should never therefore voluntarily choose the former, for it makes reformation a matter of great difficulty and danger; but we should always look

[2] M. de Condorcet, *The Progress of the Human Mind*, 1794, Internet.

out for the latter, for thereby we can without hurt to ourselves, gain a clear view of the best course to pursue. It is this, which forces us to consider that the knowledge gained from the study of true history is the best of all educations for practical life. For it is history, and history alone, which, without involving us in actual danger, will mature our judgment and prepare us to see correctly, whatever may be the crisis or the posture of affairs.[3]

CHAPTER SYNOPSES

The issues I will address are complex and interrelated; they are global issues that require global cooperation. Technology has had an enormous influence on humanity, and it can be used for its benefit or destruction. I will discuss how knowledge bonded with virtue can address these issues.

Chapter 1 includes a review of the ascent of human knowledge that led to our current civilization. The review covers the social, political, and economic improvements—technical progress from the Paleolithic times, when humanity was living in caves, to today—and examines how civilizations advanced through the ages. We will draw lessons from them and establish goals for the future. This history offers a perspective of the past so we can evaluate human progress and learn from human disasters so we do not repeat them.

In chapter 2, I discuss the trinity of happiness, virtue, and knowledge, as they are required for self-perfection and reaching the pinnacle of human existence. Knowledge and virtue are key factors to reaching the material goods and with ethics to reach true happiness.

In chapter 3, I discuss the various issues associated with the two most horrific problems of today: global warming and war of all types, including nuclear war. There is still time to avoid these threats and improve life for all humanity. I offer detailed suggestions for resolving these issues. Global warming includes the interrelated issues of energy, resources, population growth, and pollution.

In chapter 4, I discuss the issues of energy and renewable energy alternatives to address the issues of pollution and global warming that have detrimental effects on our climate and all life. I offer a detailed proposal for combating climate change, building a more robust economy by creating jobs, eliminating oil imports, stabilizing energy prices, and eliminating pollution and its detrimental effects on society. This is achieved by switching the energy infrastructure to run on clean, renewable energy. It may sound utopian, but technology makes it practicable and economically viable today.

In chapter 5, I discuss the issues of overpopulation and its effects on the

---

[3] Polybius, *The Histories of Polybius*, vol. 1, 1. 35, Perseus Project, Internet.

environment, pollution, and climate change due to the greenhouse effect; food, water, and other resources require energy, land, water, and fertilizer and have a major impact on the environment and population.

In chapter 6, I discuss the causes of war, such as the desire for energy and other resources. Self-sufficiency in energy will go a long way to eliminating this major cause of war.

Chapter 7, the epilogue, contains my closing remarks.

In the following four sections, progress, civilization, knowledge explosions, virtue, and cumulative and noncumulative knowledge are defined, as they are very important concepts, before we delve into the main chapters later.

IDEA OF PROGRESS

The perennial questions for humanity have been, are now, and will be as follows: Where do we come from? Where are we now versus the past, and why? Where are we going? What can we do to make the future better? Are we making progress?

These questions have been asked by common people but primarily by futurists, philosophers, and societies to varying degrees and have resulted in various opinions, plans, and rituals. We shall define the ideas of progress and knowledge, the main ingredient of progress that makes up a civilization. Given that knowledge or the lack of it drives all societies, we shall get into the main topic of how knowledge and what types of knowledge can be applied to form better individuals, better societies, and a better world.

Throughout humanity's existence, we have been advancing or moving backward in knowledge at different rates, times, and places. Progress is constant activity toward achieving happiness, an ideal we pursue without always achieving it but always with hope we will.

In his seminal work *History of the Idea of Progress*, sociologist Robert Nisbet asserted,

> No single idea has been as important as the idea of progress in Western Civilization for nearly three thousand years ... the idea of progress holds that mankind has advanced in the past-from some aboriginal condition of primitiveness, barbarism, or even nullity-is now advancing, and will continue to advance through the foreseeable future.[4]

---

[4] Robert Nisbet, *History of the Idea of Progress* (Basic Books, 1980), 4.

The following paragraphs contain famous scholars' and philosophers' definitions of progress. Mike Salvaris, of the Australian Bureau of Statistics Directions in Measuring Australia's Progress, defined the idea of progress as

> a firm belief that it is given to humanity to pass from a qualitatively inferior to a qualitatively higher stage, in a sequence that will ensure a radically better spiritual and material life for not just a part but the whole of the human community ... Progress therefore means continuous and indefinite improvement of man's faculties and growing success in pursuit of the greatest possible individual and collective happiness, by means of a harmonious integration of rational enquiry, scientific research, technology, economic development, political and social institutions, and private and public ethics.[5]

According to Aristotle, progress occurs when humans and their societies are self-perfecting—they fulfill their purposes and cannot be improved any further. The goal of self-perfection is to make people happy. Happiness or what determines the best life is defined in chapter 2.

DEFINITION OF CIVILIZATION

What follows are various views stated by notable people to expose the reader to various definitions of civilization; each gives different weight to the various aspects and tenets of civilization.

Marquis Mirabeau seems to have been the first to use the word *civilization*; he did so in 1757. At the time, the word for him and philosophers of the Enlightenment had a narrower meaning than it does today: "It denoted humane laws, limitations on war, a high level of purpose and conduct, gentle ways of life; in brief the qualities considered the highest expressions of humanness in the eighteenth century."[6]

In his *Adventures of Ideas*, Alfred North Whitehead (1861–1947) stated,

> Civilization consists of four elements, Patterns of Behavior, of Emotion, of Belief and Technologies ... and a civilized society is exhibiting the five qualities of Truth, Beauty, Adventure, Art, Peace ... To sustain a civilization with its intensity of its first ardor

[5] Mike Salvaris, Australian Bureau of statistics *Directions in Measuring Australia's Progress*, 2010.
[6] Rene Dubos, *Celebrations of Life* (New York: McGraw-Hill, 1981), 196.

requires more than learning. Adventure is essential, namely, the search for new perfections.[7]

Edward Burnett Tyler's (1832–1917) book *Primitive Culture* is one of his most widely recognized contributions to anthropology and the study of religion. He defined culture this way: "Culture or Civilization, taken in its wide ethnographic sense, is that complex whole which includes knowledge, belief, art, morals, law, custom, and any other capabilities and habits acquired by man as a member of society."[8]

Civilization and its technical aspects—writing, medicine, industry, applied science, and produced goods—are the primary intellectual and spiritual activity that give us real life, happiness, and the desire to keep improving. This improvement includes the acquisition of material things as well as intellectual and spiritual ideas and actions.

In *Philosophy of Civilization*, Albert Schweitzer (1875–1965) emphasized the development of humanity to a state of higher organization and the ethical perfecting of the individual and his or her society. Ethics is humanity's attempt to secure inner perfection. Schweitzer outlined the idea that there are dual opinions in society,

> one regarding civilization as purely material and another civilization as both ethical and material. He stated that the current world crisis, back in 1923, was due to a humanity having lost the ethical conception of civilization. In this same work, he defined civilization, saying that it "is the sum total of all progress made by man in every sphere of action and from every point of view in so far as the progress helps towards the spiritual perfecting of individuals as the progress of all progress."[9]

Very little has changed in the ethics area since 1923, when Schweitzer wrote his book on the ethical aspects of civilization. He stated,

> If there is any sense in ploughing for the thousand and second time a field which has already been ploughed a thousand times and one times? Has not everything which can be said about ethics already been said by Lao-tse, Confucius, and Buddha, and Zarathustra by Socrates, Plato, Aristotle? by Epicurus and the Stoics? by Jesus and Paul: by the thinkers of the Renaissance, of the Enlightenment and of Rationalism? by Locke, Shaftesbury

[7] A. N. Whitehead, *Adventures of Ideas* (Middlesex: Penguin Press, 1948), 273, 257, 283.
[8] Edward Burnett Tyler, *Primitive Culture*, vol. 1, 1871, 17.
[9] Albert Schweitzer, *The Philosophy of Civilization* (Macmillan, 1960), 69.

and Hume? by Spinoza and Kant? by Fichte and Hegel? by Schopenhauer, Nietzsche, and others? Is there a possibility of getting beyond all these contradictory convictions of the past to new beliefs which will have a stronger and more lasting influence? Can the ethical kernel of the thoughts of all these men be collected into an idea of the ethical, which will unite all the energies to which they appeal? We must hope so, if we are not the despair of the fate of the human race.[10]

Fundamentally I remained convinced that ethics and the affirmation of life are interdependent and the precondition for all true civilization ... A deepened ethical will to progress that springs from thought will lead us back, the, out of our poor civilization with its many faults to true civilization. Sooner or later the true and final renaissance must dawn, which will bring peace to the world.[11]

In *The Classical Tradition: Greek and Roman Influences on Western Literature*, Gilbert Highet (1906–1978) commented on civilization and put emphasis on the mind.

Many of us misunderstand civilization. We live in a materialistic world. Most of us think incessantly about making money, or about gaining power-expressed in material-terms for one group or one nation, or about redistributing, wealth between classes, countries, or continents. Nevertheless, civilization is not chiefly concerned with money, or power, or possessions. It is concerned with the human mind. The richest state in the world, or a world-society of unlimited wealth and comfort, even although every single one of its members had all the food and clothing and machines and material possessions he could possibly use, would still not be a civilization. It would be what Plato called "a swine," eating, drinking, mating, and sleeping until they died.[12]

Historian and classical scholar J. B. Bury (1861–1927) wrote,

[10] Ibid., 103.
[11] Albert Schweitzer, *Out of my Life and Thought*, rev. ed. (Henry Holt and Co., 1990), 153, 159.
[12] S. Bertman, *Eight Pillars of Greek Wisdom* (New York: Barnes and Noble, 2003), 175.

To the minds of most people the desirable outcome of human development would be a condition of society in which all the inhabitants of the planet would enjoy a perfectly happy existence … from the point of view of increasing happiness, the tendencies of our progressive civilization are far from desirable. In short, it cannot be proved that the unknown destination towards which man is advancing is desirable. The movement may be Progress, or it may be in an undesirable direction and therefore not Progress … Progress of humanity belongs to the same order of ideas as Providence or personal immortality. It is true or it is false, and like them it cannot be proved either true or false. Belief in it is an act of faith. The idea of human Progress then is a theory, which involves a synthesis of the past and a prophecy of the future.[13]

Thus Mirabeau, Schweitzer, Bury, Highet, and other intellectuals emphasized the significance of perfection of the human mind as the primary determinate for the advance of citizens; material wealth is essential but secondary for living. These four scholars considered ethics or morality one of their key factors for progress; ethics implies moral virtue, which is the key reason for people's happiness. The answer to Schweitzer's question and those of others above is that we need some universal thoughts, activities, or actions a substantial majority if not all people believe lead to some universally accepted goals. Only this way can civilization make uniform progress across the globe.

KNOWLEDGE EXPLOSIONS

The great English critic John Ruskin (1819–1900) set three criteria for assessing the historical achievements of a civilization: "Great nations write their autobiographies in three manuscripts; the book of their deeds, the book of their words, and the book of their art. Not one of this can be understood unless we read the two others." [14] The achievements comprise works on history, philosophy, science, government and law, literature, visual and performing works of art, drama, oratory, medicine, public buildings and housing, roads, and other activities. This high level of achievements is demonstrated with works that Edith Hamilton described in her book *The Greek Way*.

Great literature, past or present, is the expression of great knowledge of the human heart; great art is the expression of a solution of

---

[13] J. B. Bury, *The Idea of Progress: An Inquiry into Its Origin and Growth* (Echo Library, 1920), 1.

[14] https://en.wikiquote.org/wiki/John_Ruskin

a conflict between the demands of the world without and that within; and in the wisdom of either there would seem to be small progress.[15]

Let us apply Ruskin's three criteria in this endeavor and examine the level of the prototype and sublime achievements, the quantity of visual and performing arts, the history describing what they achieved, and the voluminous literature in all areas of human activity. We can conclude that there have been two great knowledge explosions in the historical ascent of humanity. The first started around 600 BC in Greece, its islands, and its territories in Ionia and colonies in southern Italy, and it continued there till Alexander the Great's death in 323 BC. It continued and gradually expanded to include major cities such as Alexandria, Antioch, and Pergamum, and continued there until the death of Archimedes in 212 BC.

Looking at the archaeological finds, the Parthenon and its sculptures there and in the British Museum, the temples of southern Italy and western Turkey, the Delphi bronze statue of the charioteer, the statue of Hermes of Praxiteles at Olympia, the tomb finds of King Philip of Macedonia, the golden masks from Mycenaean tombs, the golden miniatures and paintings at Knossos, Venus de Milo, and the Winged Victory of Samothrace in the Louvre are all unsurpassed examples of great art. Great literature was produced in history, philosophy, law, drama, comedy, oratory, medicine, and other activities. In battle, the Greeks defeated the Persians on land and sea and saved Western civilization.

The second knowledge explosion started around AD 1320 with the dawn of the Renaissance in Italy. From Italy, it expanded into northern Europe and eventually reached most of the developed world. It continues today at an ever-increasing rate.

This knowledge explosion includes the Enlightenment and the industrial and postindustrial ages. If the past seven hundred years are any guide, we can predict progress will continue as far as we can see into the future unless we continually and relentlessly abuse nature or resort to nuclear weapons and bring humanity to an age of unprecedented misery and chaos—back to the Stone Age.

Yet there are still places in the world that civilization as we in the northern hemisphere know it has not touched. People in these areas live primitive lives resembling those of ancient times or no better than those of medieval Europe.

Between these two knowledge explosions, progress was slow, at times static, and at times retracted. Wars, invasions, barbarism, famines, pestilence, plagues, and mass movements of peoples created devastation; it took hundreds of years for the flame of progress to reignite. Religion played a major role—positive and negative—in many of these conflicts.

China reached a high level of civilization by the twelfth century AD while the West in the Middle Ages was not as advanced.

---

[15] Edith Hamilton, *The Greek Way* (W. W. Norton, 1942), 17.

Up to now, we have accumulated an immense amount of technical knowledge and are still acquiring more at an ever-increasing rate. But our increase in virtue—meaning technical and moral excellence—and wisdom has not kept up with the increase of technical knowledge. Our evolution in the moral area is lacking; we need to increase our excellence (virtue) and balance our technical virtue with moral virtue. It is up to us to make the future a golden age or an age of darkness. God gave us the greatest faculty: reason. We can achieve a better future with today's and tomorrow's technology and more virtue, which will lead to greater happiness for all people. Our existence can be assured for an additional 5 billion years until our sun burns out or an asteroid or comet pulverizes our planet.

Progress requires knowledge, and with knowledge, we may not make enough progress. But without knowledge, we will fail.

Progress in technology and acquisition or abundance of material things does not necessarily bring more happiness and improvement to our quality of life. Progress in science and technology may increase the wealth for some people but not affect others' lives at all. Progress in technology has brought many destructive wars and more deterioration to the environment. R. Dubos stated,

> Progress no longer means a higher degree of education, more enlightened tastes, nor even better health; rather it has gotten to mean how many manufactured goods people can own, how many destructive weapons a nation possesses, or at best, how many space vehicles a nation can put into orbit, or deposit on celestial bodies.[16]

We may possess much scientific knowledge, but we may be unable to improve society. Following science and technological achievements blindly may lead us to economic, political, and moral disaster and grief.

Some recent war misadventures with high-tech weapons have brought neither peace nor happiness to several areas particularly in the Middle East and northern Africa; they have destabilized governments and created chaos. Wars and injustices do not make friends; they sow hate, continuous strife, and the desire for revenge.

Vestigial problems complicated by history and recent actions make issues complex and difficult to address as they affect the environment and society's needs for natural resources such as oil, gas, and water. We must achieve real, measurable improvement in many areas such as government, freedom, conflict resolution, avoidance of war, perpetual peace that Kant dreamed about two centuries ago, environment, health, work conditions, morality, and goodwill among nations. We must focus on values, virtues, responsibility, reason, and the great divine, eternal, and unchangeable qualities.

---

[16] R. Dubos, *Reason Awake: Science for Man* (New York and London: Columbia University Press, 1970), x.

CUMULATIVE AND NONCUMULATIVE KNOWLEDGE

Humanity has been accumulating knowledge since primitive times when humans started using tools for hunting, killing, and skinning animals and started domesticating animals, cultivating plants, building homes, etc.

Progress is based on knowledge, whose usefulness is undisputed in performing any task. Knowledge is the single key ingredient to progress, but at times, it can be detrimental to human progress especially with the unwise use of technology. Knowledge without wisdom is not beneficial; wisdom is a major factor in guiding humans on how to use knowledge.

All of humanity's knowledge can be categorized as two types: cumulative and noncumulative. In *Ideas and Men*, Crane Brinton wrote, "Cumulative knowledge is best exemplified by the knowledge we call commonly natural science, or just science."[17] The natural sciences include physics, chemistry, astronomy, all branches of engineering, and life sciences (medicine, biology, zoology, botany); it is what the ancients called *techne*. They enable us to know how to perform practical tasks—build a house, teach, use computers, and so forth.

We know much more than we did 2,500 years ago about astronomy and physics. Over time, ideas have accumulated and gradually became the physics and astronomy of today. Since ancient times, humans have been studying the discoveries of the past; each generation builds on the knowledge and abilities of its predecessors, it adopts and continuously improves on them. Some are discarded as they are proven false.

As an example, the geocentric concept of our solar system in which Earth was central (supported by Aristotle and others) competed with the heliocentric concept, in which all the planets revolved around the Sun (supported by Aristarchus of Samos). Ptolemy improved the geocentric view through his calculations and made it acceptable despite some problems. Thanks to the efforts of Copernicus, Brahe, Kepler, and especially Galileo, who provided the proof and almost lost his life over it, the heliocentric system replaced the geocentric system, which had been in use for over 2,200 years.

Noncumulative knowledge is exemplified by the knowledge of humanities and social sciences including philosophy, literature, visual and performing arts, religion, economics, sociology, psychology, and education. As Brinton wrote,

> Noncumulative knowledge can here be illustrated best from the field of literature. Men of letters make certain propositions, entertain certain ideas, about men, about right and wrong action, about beautiful and ugly things. Over two thousand years ago, men of letters were writing in Greek on these matters ... Our contemporary men of letters write about the same things the

---

[17] Crane Brinton, *Ideas of Man, the Story of Western Thought* (Prentice Hall, 1950), 12.

Greek men wrote about, with no clear or certain increase in knowledge.[18]

The distinction between cumulative and noncumulative knowledge is obvious, but that is the only distinction between them. All knowledge is good and useful.

Knowledge is an accumulation of not only facts but also of valid interpretations of those facts. In cumulative knowledge, we possess the great literature and philosophy of the past containing brilliant ideas, immutable and eternal, and we can benefit from it.

The other major distinction between cumulative and noncumulative knowledge is constant change—we hear almost daily of new inventions and capabilities in technical areas, and yet there is silence in other areas. New technical inventions and their applications have immense implications for people's lives and more likely require immense adjustments.

In the cumulative side of things, we continuously add to previous knowledge, which is passed on in its totality. Every generation builds on the previous generation's knowledge, knowledge continuously accumulates and expands, and humanity progresses primarily in the natural sciences. A modern college physics graduate is not wiser than one of the sages of antiquity and has no better taste than an artist in antiquity, but he or she knows much more physics than any ancient scientist and probably more than Newton (1642–1727), the greatest physicist ever, whose discoveries have had more influence on humanity than anyone else's.

The rate of knowledge acquisition is accelerating. It took thousands of years to reach the knowledge of analytic geometry and calculus discovered in the seventeenth century, but these two subjects are taught in college courses today. We learned more about the universe in the last century than we had since the beginning of history.

Cumulative knowledge has increased to the point that no one can master it all. Knowledge became highly specialized, and people became specialists in single areas. The fields of knowledge were subdivided into branches such as physics, chemistry, botany, zoology, mathematics, medicine, and so on. Aristotle (384–323 BC), the most learned man in his time, may have been the last person to know everything there was to be known in his time.

The last man to possess all the knowledge in mathematics and mechanics was Archimedes of Syracuse (c. 287–c. 212 BC). The last man to possess all the knowledge in physics was Hermann von Helmholtz (1821–1894). The last man to possess all the knowledge in atomic physics was Niels Bohr (1885–1962). No one knows all about atomic physics anymore. Similarly, no one knows all the details of the design and fabrication of complex semiconductor chips, which were invented only about fifty years ago. We have become a society of specialists. The field of medicine itself contains more than thirty specialties. Big social, scientific, and religious traditions are challenged so we can continue ascending to higher levels of happiness and well-being.

---

[18] Ibid., 13.

To assess where we are going and what constitutes a happy life, we shall first review the major milestones of the history of knowledge in philosophy, art, science, and history itself that we have gained from the time prehistory ended—when humanity started writing—to today. We will try to define what is good, what constitutes the happiness humans strive for, what should be our future, noble goals, and what challenges we face in accomplishing them.

The experience and knowledge we have accumulated can be used to reach a higher level of development with a balance between us and our environment and to lessen world conflicts. We will review the great achievements and follies of humanity over the centuries.

People and nations cause all the problems mentioned above, but they act slowly, partially, or not at all to solve them. Some do not even realize the problems, or they expect the very rich nations to address them. These are problems to be addressed by all.

To examine the issues in a rational manner, we need to answer certain questions: What are people striving for? What is happiness? What is progress? Are there limits to our quest for what we think we need? The problems and the solutions are interconnected, so it will require national as well as global coordinated efforts. Addressing one problem while ignoring others will result in no progress. Religious and national biases and ethnic boundaries play a major role, and there is too much suspicion and ignorance. The issues are very complex; they require interdisciplinary approaches and international cooperation.

The situation is not hopeless yet, but now is the time to act. Technology takes time to develop, and worst of all, changing human attitudes and getting humans to act is a much more difficult task. But I am optimistic that the solutions I propose are practical and achievable. I will offer details that may stimulate discussion that may lead to action.

These issues must be addressed in their totality because they are interrelated. What makes people happy? Can we live in a world people are not taking responsibility for? Can we address environmental issues without addressing energy and overpopulation? How do we address war, terrorism, and their effects?

We need to do something different; we must engage all human faculties—knowledge, virtue, and reason—in all our activities to confront issues. We need to change our attitudes and our understanding of ethics, and we must elevate ourselves through education and knowledge to a higher level of understanding and concern for ourselves, our societies, and our world. If we stop trying, we are doomed.

Let us try. As Kazantzakis stated in his *Report to Greco*, "Joy to the courageous young who thinks that he has a duty to change the world; to make it more in line with virtue and justice; more in line with his heart. Woe to which starts life without insanity."[19]

---

[19] Nikos Kazantzakis, *Report to Greco.*

A SHORT HISTORY OF KNOWLEDGE

From time immemorial, humanity has pursued knowledge out of a sense of wonder and to improve human life. People built houses for protection from the weather and wild animals and to store food. The increase of knowledge led to human progress. Humanity went through many stages of gradual development as described in this chapter.

The history of knowledge extends from the creation of the universe to today. It covers a period of 13.7 billion years, but the history of humanity dating from the invention of writing is only about 5,300 years.

I separate the periods of human progress into ten periods that will be reviewed in the following sections, specifically the knowledge and progress of humanity through the ages including its glories and disasters.

In this chapter, besides describing humanity's technical achievements, I provide a concise description of the intellectual human development through the ages. I focus on humanity's attempts to improve its life in ethical terms—the best the human spirit dreamed to accomplish. This is for comparison with our thoughts today with those of the past and how they turned out.

I shall provide some of the great thoughts of the brilliant minds of the past that we have inherited from those who wanted to make the world better. I hope some of those thoughts will find a place in readers' hearts and minds.

CREATION OF THE UNIVERSE TO 8000 BC: BEGINNING OF THE NEOLITHIC AGE

According to the big bang theory, the universe was created about 13.7 billion years ago. This determination was an accomplishment of the scientific community during the twentieth century; the major conclusions were arrived at about fifty years ago. They came about after cosmologists' observations using optical and radio telescopes and theoretical evaluations that confirmed the various theories.

The theory is widely accepted, but there is debate about the existence of multiple universes, whether there have been other big bang explosions or if this was the first one, and what triggered it. This would not have been possible if physics had not produced spectacular discoveries starting in the seventeenth century and especially since the beginning of the twentieth century. Understanding of gravity, of the space-time relationship, atomic physics, fusion, and fission were the essential knowledge drivers for the development of the big bang theory and its credibility. The coincidence of man landing on the moon about the same time as the unfolding of the big bang theory provided an additional impetus for us to wonder and explore further the universe (*cosmos* in Greek).

We now know that the big bang produced by a gigantic flash of energy and from that energy all matter was created—all that has been, is, and will ever be.

We now know that the universe is expanding and consists of about 200 billion galaxies each comprising about 200 billion stars like our own star, the Sun. Each sun may or may not have planets. Our galaxy, the Milky Way, has about 400 billion stars and many more planets.

Our solar system was formed about 4.6 billion years ago, and Earth was formed about 4.5 billion years ago. Life itself in a primitive form was formed in the earth's oceans about 3.5 billion years ago, and humanity around 2 million years ago. Our solar system contains planets some of which have moons as Earth does. Our solar system contains many small comets and asteroids. All planets, comets, and asteroids circle the sun at different speeds in full harmony.

The discovery of gravity by Newton in the latter part of the seventeenth century provided the explanation that the force of gravity keeps all heavenly bodies in harmonic, predictable motion. Since ancient times, time and the calendar were determined from the time of the basic rotations of the moon or earth due to this harmonic planetary motion.

Man entered the so-called Paleolithic Age, which started about 2.6 million years ago and lasted until about 10000 BC, the beginning of the Neolithic Age. The Paleolithic Age is subdivided into three successive divisions of the period, the Lower, Middle, and Upper Paleolithic.

The people of this age had no houses, roamed for food, and hunted animals with stone tools; they were called hunter-gatherers. They developed language, and discovered fire, hunting methods, and weapons. At that stage of development, man started using primitive stone tools to chip other stones into useful instruments. Man's progress, exceedingly slow at this age, lasted a very long time; they endured a continuous struggle for survival.

By far the most outstanding feature of the Paleolithic period was the evolution of the human species from near-human, apelike creatures to true *Homo sapiens* (modern man). *Homo sapiens* evolved first in Africa around 160,000 years ago. They moved out of Africa around 100,000 years ago and appeared in Europe about 37,000 years ago.

One of the oldest man-made objects of aesthetic value of this period is the Venus (or now Woman) of Willendorf discovered in a village near Krems, Austria, in 1908; it dates to about 28,000 years ago. The oldest cave paintings in Lascaux, France, discovered in 1940 depict deer, bison, and horses and date to around 15000 BC. The Altamira caves in Spain discovered in 1879 depict bison and date to around 18000 BC. The oldest pottery, the so-called Jōmon, discovered in Japan, dates to about 11000 BC.

In his tragedy *Prometheus Bound*, Aeschylus (c. 525–c. 456 BC) described man's state of being and how man lived in the Paleolithic Age this way.

> First, though they had eyes to see, they saw to no avail; they had ears but understood not; … They did not know how to build houses of brick facing the sun, not yet of work in wood; but lived beneath the ground like swarming ants in the dark and sunless recesses of caves. They had no sign, either, of winter nor of flower fragrant spring, nor of fruitful summer, but they carried on entirely without any rational thought, until I, showed them the star's risings and settings, difficult to discern. And more: number, that mental feat par' excellence, I discovered and gave them, and the combining of letters, memory's helper hand working mother of the Muse.[20]

In Plato's homonymous work *Protagoras* (c. 490–c. 420 BC), he related the early development of man.

> Prometheus came to inspect the state of men and found the other animals well off for everything, but men naked, unshod, un-bedded, and unarmed, and already the appointed day had come when man too was to emerge from within the earth into the daylight. Prometheus therefore being at a loss to provide any means of salvation for man stole from Hephaestus and Athena the gift of skill in the arts, together with fire—for without fire it was impossible for anyone to possess or use this skill—and bestowed it on man. In this way man acquired sufficient resources to keep himself alive, but had no political wisdom … men soon discovered articulate speech and names, and invented houses and clothes and shoes and bedding and got food from the earth. Thus, provided for, they lived at first in scattered groups; there were no

---

[20] Aeschylus, *Prometheus Bound*, trans. W. K. C. Guthrie, 442–52.

cities. Consequently, wild beasts devoured them, since they were in every respect the weaker, and their technical skill, though a sufficient aid to their nurture, did not extend to making war on the beasts. They sought therefore to save themselves by coming together and founding fortified cities, but when they gathered in communities, they injured one another for want of political skill, and so scattered again and continued to be devoured. Zeus therefore fearing the total destruction of the human race sent Hermes to impart to men the qualities of respect for others and a sense of justice, so as to bring order into the cities and create a bond of friendship and union.[21]

Protagoras insisted that justice was at the foundations of a society, and that was how he implied humanity gained reason.

Hermes asked Zeus how he should bestow these gifts to men, equally to all men or to some experts: Shall I distribute justice and respect for their fellows in this way, or to all alike? "To all," said Zeus. "Let all have their share. There cannot be any cities if only a few shared in these virtues as in the arts."[22]

NEOLITHIC AGE: 8000 BC-3300 BC, THE BEGINNING OF HISTORY

The term *Neolithic* derives from Greek that means "new stone age"; it was invented by Sir John Lubbock in 1865 as a refinement of the three-age system.

The Neolithic period was a time of human development beginning about 10000 BC in some parts of the Middle East and later in other parts of the world. Man left the nomadic life, built primitive homes or small huts, settled down, and domesticated animals for food, milk, and clothing. He started developing farming, used more-sophisticated stone tools, and created advanced pottery. He moved from the state of food gatherer to food producer. He started using wool apparel and fewer and fewer animal skins. He settled on pieces of land in common with others; communities were formed.

The first cultivation appears to have taken place in western Asia about 8000 BC or earlier in the Fertile Crescent area in present-day Iraq from the Persian Gulf between the Tigris and Euphrates Rivers (called Mesopotamia) down the eastern

---

[21] Plato, *Protagoras*, 321c, d, e, 322a-b, *Plato the Collected Dialogues, including the letters*, ed. Edith Hamilton and Huntington Cairns, trans. W. K. C. Guthrie (1961), 319.

[22] Ibid., Plato, *Protagoras*, 322c, d, 320.

Mediterranean coast and reaching the Nile valley. This place, called Sumeria, is credited as the first civilization.

The Neolithic period ended between 4500 and about 2000 BC depending on different developments of civilization in different areas when metal tools became widespread in the Copper and Bronze Ages. All these civilizations were distinguished by their organization of society, laws, customs, forms of government, and above all, their art. We know very little about some of them, but we know a lot about their art as earth kept their secrets secure until they were dug up primarily in the last 200 years.

The first major prehistoric civilizations include the Chinese along the Yellow River, Indians along the Hindus River, Egyptians along the Nile River, Sumerians between the Tigris and Euphrates Rivers, Hittites in Hattusas in the middle of Turkey, and Greeks in Greece, Aegean and the coast of Turkey. The North and South American ancient peoples moved in during the Paleolithic Age from Alaska to reach the tip of South America and became domesticated around 11000 BC.

The Copper and Bronze Ages, which followed the Neolithic Age, started around 4000 and 3100 BC respectively. Bronze is copper with the addition of tin, which makes the amalgam harder, and more than likely, it was discovered by accident. The Iron Age followed the Bronze Age; iron was a much harder metal that allowed for stronger and more-enduring tools.

The most important inventions of this period were the wheel and axle, plow, sickle, ax, sail, earthenware pottery, basket making, stone grinders for grain, terracotta structures, and more-advanced, harder, sharper, and longer-lasting tools. Stones and primitive, unfired adobe bricks were used to construct houses.

HISTORIC PERIOD: 3300 BC TO 825 BC, ALPHABETIC WRITING WITH VOWELS

The history of every civilization begins with the invention of writing, which differed from people to people. Around the end of the Neolithic period—at the beginning or shortly thereafter of the Bronze Age—five major civilizations invented writing. The Sumerians in Mesopotamia were the first to be credited for discovering writing, cuneiform, in 3300 BC. Thus, humanity's history starts at Sumer.

The Sumerians were followed by the Egyptians, who developed hieroglyphic writing around 2700 BC; the Indians in the Indus River valley did so around 2500 BC, and the Chinese in the Yellow River valley created pictorial type writing in 1400 BC. Ancient Minoans in Greece invented the so-called Linear A writing used around 2500–1450 BC. The Indian writings and the Greek Linear A writing discovered in Crete have not yet been deciphered.

The Greek Mycenaean civilization created Linear B writing around 1450 BC. The Hittites in Anatolia developed cuneiform-type writing around 1500 BC. The Phoenicians discovered alphabetic writing around 1100 BC.

Besides writing, other inventions and achievements during this period were irrigation, the wheel and cart, which were invented around 3500 BC, and others. Bronze casting in China reached its peak before 1200 BC, and its level of quality was not achieved in the West until the Renaissance. Silk and tea were invented in China around 2500 BC and 2200 BC respectively. The Babylonians figured out the solar year based on the hexadecimal system consisting of 360 days.

This period, 3300 BC–825 BC, began with the invention of writing and ended with the invention of alphabetic phonetic writing. Writing became an extension of the human brain and its memory. The invention of writing is one of humanity's most important inventions of all times—maybe the greatest of them all. With the invention of writing, civilizations moved from prehistoric to historic eras, prehistory being the time before the invention of writing systems.

Writing gave those who lived in that period and subsequent peoples the concept of memory, and we can assess their level of civilization by deciphering their writing. It was a tool to disseminate information and preserve knowledge about their civilizations. Writing preserved on stone or on tablets lasts; it becomes memory that can travel distances and survive the ravages of time. From their writings, we can tell what they did, thought, and believed. Writing is the key component to maintaining and spreading knowledge. With writing, communication among people increased and civilizations accelerated their development.

Without their written words, we would know much less about certain civilizations; we would have to theorize about them through only their objects of utility and their art, and we could guess wrongly. Writing was one of the key factors for developing trade and eventually industrialization. The early writing systems were primitive and the tools rather crude for writing and reproduction. Writing on rocks, turtle bones, wet clay tablets that had to be baked, and reeds that were not as stable with primitive inks were not the ideal media. Reproduction of writing was relied on hand copying only.

Sumerians were writing with wedge-shaped pens made of reeds or other sharp items on wet clay tablets that had to be baked. This type of writing is called cuneiform from the Latin *cuneus*, "wedge." The epic poems of Gilgamesh and the law code of Hammurabi were preserved on this cuneiform type of writing.

The Sumerians also invented bronze, an alloy of copper and tin that could be cast in molds to produce tools and weapons; they are credited with bringing about the Iron Age around 1600 BC.

Linear B, the first Greek writing to be deciphered, was invented around 1400 BC and used by the Mycenaean civilization, which flourished 1600–1200 BC. Greek Linear B writing tablets were discovered in 1900 in many locations in the Greek mainland as well as on some of the islands including Crete. It was deciphered in 1952. It was a major milestone; it pushed back the beginning of Greek history by about 600 years to 1400 BC.

The geographic closeness of the Sumerians, Egyptians, Hittites, and Greeks allowed some cross-pollination of these civilizations in the area of astronomy and subsequently the calendar and ways of calculating time. The Sumerians invented the twenty-four-hour day-night system, which was adopted by the Egyptian and Greeks and is still in use today.

The notable archeological findings from this era include the pyramids of Egypt, one of the seven wonders of the ancient world and the only one in existence today. All others have succumbed to the passage of time. Egyptian tombs reveal burial sites of the pharaohs with gold masks such as the famous one of King Tut. Other famous findings are jade, pottery, and bronze objects from China; Scythian gold from southern Russia; the gold of Troy; the Minoan palaces in Crete with pottery and gold objects; Mycenaean gold, bronze, and pottery findings; and pottery and large, carved stone objects from Mesopotamia.

GREEK PERIOD: 825 BC–323 BC, THE FIRST KNOWLEDGE EXPLOSION

Around 825 BC, a monumental event took place: the invention of the first phonetic alphabet. The Greeks made significant changes to the Phoenician alphabet, which had been invented around 1100 BC. They took certain consonants to which no consonant sound corresponded in Greek and employed them as vowels. The alphabet, with only twenty-four letters, was easily understood and memorized; it was highly phonetic—every letter is pronounced, and thus phonetic ambiguity is reduced if not eliminated. The first true alphabet in this sense is believed to be the Greek alphabet. This was a major simplification and improvement of expressing the verbal word in written form.

The alphabet and thus writing is the medium of storing and transmitting knowledge. Simplicity of writing and precision of meaning are very essential for the efficient transmission of knowledge.

With writing, humanity took a giant leap forward in its progress. French economist and statesman Turgot (1727–1781) wrote,

> Genius, whose course is at first slow, unmarked, and buried in the general oblivion into which time precipitates human affairs, emerges from obscurity with them by means of the invention of writing. Priceless invention!—Which seemed to give wings to those peoples who first possessed it, enabling them to outdistance other nations. Incomparable invention! Which rescues from the power of death the memory of great men and models of virtue, unites places and times, arrests fugitive thoughts and guarantees them a lasting existence, by means of which the creations,

opinions, experiences, and discoveries of all ages are accumulated, to serve as a foundation and foothold for posterity in raising itself ever higher! [23]

Alphabetic writing was clear and simple; that proved to be a valuable factor in the invention of printing in the fifteenth century AD. Alphabets use a standard ordering of their letters; that makes them useful for collation specifically by allowing words to be sorted in alphabetical order.

B. F. Cocker characterized language's importance in this way.

> Language is unquestionably the highest creation of reason, and in the language of a nation we can see reflected as in a mirror the amount of culture to which it has attained. The rare balance of the imagination and the reasoning powers, in which the perfection of the human intellect is regarded as consisting, the exact correspondence between the thought and the expression.[24]

The role alphabetic writing played in the history of humanity was detailed by Marquis de Condorcet.

> From the period that alphabetical writing was known in Greece, history is connected by an uninterrupted series of facts and observations, with the period in which we live, with the present state of mankind in the most enlightened countries of Europe; and the picture of the progress and advancement of the human mind becomes strictly historical. Philosophy has no longer anything to guess, has no more suppositious combinations to form; all it has to do is to collect and arrange facts, and exhibit the useful truths which arise from them as a whole, and from the different bearings of their several parts ... there remains a third picture to form-that of our hopes, or the progress reserved for future generations ... by what ties nature has indissolubly united the advancement of knowledge with the progress of liberty, virtue, and respect for the natural rights of man.[25]

Writing proved to be an extremely valuable contribution judging by what happened after the development of the ancient Greek civilization that followed. The

---

[23] Turgot, *A Philosophical Review of the Successive Advances of the Human Mind*, 325, Internet.

[24] B. F. Cocker, *Christianity and Greek Philosophy*, 90, Internet.

[25] Marquis de Condorcet, *Sketch for a Historical Picture of the Progress of the Human Mind*, Internet.

alphabet spread with Western civilization, and eventually, many nations of the West adopted alphabetic writing. The Latin alphabet was derived from the Greek alphabet used by Greek colonies in southern Italy and Sicily. All the alphabets of Western languages were derived from Latin, such as French, Italian, Spanish, and the other Germanic and Romance languages.

About two millennia later, around AD 850, the Slavic nations adopted the Cyrillic alphabet from the Greeks as well with the addition of some letters. More languages adopted the Latin alphabet in more-recent times with the addition of diacritical marks; these included the Turkish, Vietnamese, and Malaysian/Indonesian languages.

According to the *Encyclopedia Britannica*,

> The invention of the alphabet is a major achievement of Western culture. It is also unique; the alphabet was invented only once, though it has been borrowed by many cultures. It is a model of analytic thinking, breaking down perceptible qualities like syllables into more basic constituents. And because it can convey subtle differences in meaning, it has come to be used for the expression of a great many of the functions served by speech.[26]

But there were always skeptics of innovation. Plato expressed concern about the invention of writing and its effect on people's memory.

> This invention will produce forgetfulness in the minds of those who learn to use it, because they will not practice their memory. Their trust in writing, produced by external characters, which are no part of themselves, will discourage the use of their own memory within them. You have invented an elixir not of memory, but of reminding; and you offer your pupils the appearance of wisdom, not true wisdom, for they will read many things without instruction and will therefore seem to know many things, when they are for the most part ignorant and hard to get along with, since they are not wise, but only appear wise.[27]

This is a concern voiced by some about the Internet today.

Despite Plato's concerns, writing was the right tool not only for the ease of dissemination of knowledge but also for the historical preservation of the written word. What a miracle! The alphabet was responsible for preserving the greatest

---

[26] *The Britannica Guide to Inventions That Changed the Modern World*, ed. Robert Curley, "The Greek and Latin Alphabets" (2010), 29.
[27] Plato, *Phaedrus*, 275b, Loeb translation.

poetry ever written and the first Western literature, the *Iliad* and the *Odyssey*. In his monumental book *The Advancement of Learning*, Francis Bacon (1561–1626) wrote,

> We see how the monuments of wit and learning are more durable than the monuments of power of the hands. For have not the verse of Homer continued twenty-five-hundred years, or more, without the loss of a syllable or letter; during this time infinite palaces, temples, castles, cities, have been decayed and demolished?[28]

The alphabet provided humanity the capability of eternal memory of what it inherited. The alphabet preserves it all if the numerous copies are correct. And the invention of printing in the fifteenth century solved the problem of hand copying and eliminated copying mistakes.

The alphabet immortalized humanity's words. "Writing allowed complex information to be stored outside the human mind and transmitted over great distances in space and time."[29] And today with the Internet, all information in the public domain can be instantly available anywhere in the planet.

The history of humanity is about 5,300 years old. However, written, phonetic, alphabetic history is about less than half of that, about 2,800 years. This period of history is a tiny period out of the approximately 200,000 years since the appearance of *Homo sapiens*.

The period between 585 BC—the beginning of European philosophy and science—and 212 BC—the death of Archimedes, the greatest ancient physicist and mathematician—marks the first of the two greatest knowledge explosions in world history. The Western intellectual values and cultural ideals were originated, and they are as relevant today as they were in the fifth century BC. What were the cultural ideals? Werner Jaeger wrote, "Virtue, or excellence, was the central ideal of all Greek culture. It was the creation of a higher type of man with the belief that education embodied the purpose of all human effort."[30]

According to Jaeger, "without Greek cultural ideals, the Greco-Roman civilization would not have been a historical unity and the culture of the Western world would never have existed."[31] Other scholars, historians, and philosophers provided a description of the Greek knowledge explosion as follows. H. D. F. Kitto stated,

---

[28] Basil Montagu, *The Works of Francis Bacon: Lord Chancellor of England*, Vol. 1, 183.
[29] Paul Ehrlich, *Human Natures, Genes Cultures, and the Human Prospect* (Penguin Books, 2000), 267.
[30] Werner Jaeger, *Paideia: The Ideals of Greek Culture* (New York: Oxford University Press, 1945), vol. 1, xvii, 15.
[31] Ibid., xvii.

The contribution made to Greek and European culture by this one city is quite astonishing, and, unless our standards of civilization are comfort and contraptions, Athens from about 480 to 380 BC was clearly the most civilized society that has yet existed ... Never again, until the Greek spirit intoxicated Italy at the Renaissance, do we find such superb self-confidence in humanity a self-confidence that, in Renaissance Italy, was not restrained by the modesty imposed on the Greek by his instinctive religious outlook ...

That which distils, preserves and then enlarges the experience of a people is Literature. Before the Greeks the Hebrews had created religious poetry, love-poetry, and the religious poetry of the Prophets, but literature in all its other forms (except the novel) was created and perfected by the Greeks.[32]

Rousseau provided a picture of ancient Athens and its flourishing arts, beauty, and impact on future cities.

Athens became the seat of refinement and taste, the country of orators and philosophers. The elegance of its buildings equaled that of its language; on every side might be seen marble and canvas, animated by the hands of the most skillful artists. From Athens emanated those remarkable works, which will serve as models to every corrupt age.[33]

Bertrand Russell stated,

The rise of Greek Civilization that produced this outburst of intellectual activity is one of the most spectacular events in history. Nothing like it has ever occurred before or since. Within the short space of two centuries, the Greeks poured forth in art, literature, science and philosophy, an astounding stream of masterpieces which have set the general standards for Western civilization.[34]

---

[32] H. D. F. Kitto, *The Greeks* (Penguin Books, 1951), 96, 61, 8.
[33] Jean-Jacques Rousseau, *Discourse on the Arts and Sciences*, The Collector's Library of Essential Thinkers (London, 2005), 36.
[34] B. Russell, *Wisdom of the West* (1959), 10.

G. Lauren wrote,

> How many today realize that the Greeks invented Grammar,
> Geography, Oratory, Rhetoric, Logic, Poetry, Theatre, History,
> Philosophy, Political Science, Democracy, Architecture, Natural
> History, Economics, Gastronomy, Law, Science, and made vast
> improvements in the Arts and Crafts? Why did this people
> produce so many great leaders and thinkers in just two centuries?
> The more I learned about the Greeks, the better I understood
> the genius of Western civilization, and the more I learned about
> Western civilization the wider the distance between Western and
> Eastern thought became.[35]

Edith Hamilton (1867–1963), a German-American educator and author
"recognized as the greatest woman classicist," described the achievement of this
period.

> Of all that the Greeks did, only a very small part has come down
> to us and we have no means of knowing if we have their best. It
> would be strange if we had. In the convulsions of that world of
> long ago there was no law that guaranteed to art the survival of
> the fittest. But this little remnant preserved by the haphazard of
> chance shows the high-water mark reached in every region of
> thought and beauty the Greeks entered.
>
> No sculpture comparable to theirs; no buildings ever more
> beautiful; no writings superior.
>
> Prose, always late of development, they had time only to touch
> upon, but they left masterpieces.
>
> History has yet to find a greater exponent than Thucydides;
> outside of the Bible there is no poetical prose that can touch Plato.
>
> In poetry, they are all but supreme; no epic is to be mentioned with
> Homer; no odes to be set beside Pindar; of the four masters of the
> tragic stage three are Greek. Little is left of all this wealth of great
> art: the sculptures, defaced and broken into bits, have crumbled
> away; the buildings are fallen; the paintings gone forever; of the
> writings, all lost but a very few. We have only the ruin of what was;

---

[35] G. Laurén, *The Stoic's Bible & Florilegium for the Good Life*, Internet.

the world has had no more than that for well on to two thousand years; yet these few remains of the mighty structure have been a challenge and an incitement to men ever since and they are among our possessions today which we value as most precious. There is no danger now that the world will not give the Greek genius full recognition. Greek achievement is a fact universally acknowledged.[36]

Erwin Schrödinger (1887–1961), a physicist and Nobel Prize winner for key developments in quantum mechanics, wrote,

I am of the opinion that for this reason the philosophy of the Greeks is so attractive to us today, for nowhere in the world, before or after, did there arise such a progressive and harmonious structure of knowledge and thought, without the fatal fragmentation which has been at work for centuries and has become unbearable in our time.[37]

Author and art historian Kenneth Clark (1903–1983) commented on the ideals established in the Greek knowledge explosion.

Western Europe inherited such ideal. It had been invented in Greece in the fifth century before Christ and was without doubt the most extraordinary creation in the whole history, so complete, so convincing, so satisfying to the mind and the eye that it lasted practically unchanged for over six hundred years.[38]

The famous poet Percy Bysshe Shelley (1792–1822), one of the major English Romantic poets, wrote around 1820 about the accomplishments and advancements made by the people of that time.

The period which intervened between the birth of Pericles and the death of Aristotle, is undoubtedly, whether considered in itself or with reference to the effects which it had produced upon the destinies of the civilized world, the most memorable in the history of the world.

[36] Edith Hamilton, *The Greek Way* (W. W. Norton 1942), 17.
[37] E. Schrödinger, *Die Natur und die Griechen*, 28.
[38] Kenneth Clark, *Civilization* (New York: Harper and Row, 1969), 3.

What was the combination of moral and political circumstances which produced so unparalleled a progress during that period in literature and the arts; why that progress, so rapid and so sustained, so soon received a check, and became retrograde, -are problems left to the wonder and conjecture of posterity ... The history of ancient Greece is the study of legislators, philosophers, and poets; it is the history of men, compared with the history of titles. What the Greeks were, was a reality, not a promise. And what we are and hope to be, is derived, as it were, from the influence and inspiration of these glorious generations.[39]

Johann Winckelmann (1717–1768), a German art historian and "the prophet and founding hero of modern archaeology"[40] as Daniel J. Boorstin called him, stated,

By no people has beauty been so highly esteemed as by the Greeks ... Every beautiful person sought to become known to the whole people by this distinction, and above all to approve himself to the artists, because they awarded the prize of ... The universal dominant characteristic of the Greek masterpieces, finally, is noble simplicity and serene greatness in the pose as well as the expression.[41]

Winckelmann made these remarks in 1764, before the archeologist's spade had unearthed the Venus de Milo, the Winged Victory of Samothrace, and other beautiful archaeological findings.

Homer and Hesiod

Homer and Hesiod, two eloquent poets, marked the beginning of European literature. Homer composed the *Iliad* and *Odyssey* around 775–750 BC. These two poems are the greatest epics of Western civilization and are considered two great if not the greatest poems. According to Werner Jaeger, Homer was the representative of the early Greek civilization as we have his great poems and can evaluate them.

The *Iliad* describes the last six months of the Trojan War that took place around 1200 BC. The Trojan War was fought for ten years and ended with the destruction of Troy. Heinrich Schliemann (1822–1890) located and excavated ancient Troy, and in 1873, he discovered Priam's gold and jewels, which are now on display at the Pushkin Museum in Moscow. Besides Troy, Schliemann also discovered Mycenae and Tiryns

---

[39] Shelley, Internet book.
[40] Daniel J. Boorstin, *The Discoverers* (New York: Random House, 1983), 584.
[41] Johann Winckelmann, *The History of Ancient Art Among the Greeks*, Internet.

in 1876. The *Odyssey* describes the ten-year adventure of Odysseus returning from the Trojan War to his native kingdom of Ithaca.

Both are epic poems dealing with bravery of heroes and involvement of the gods in their favoring parties. In these poems, Homer introduced the concept of virtue or excellence—the ideal of perfection of the epic heroes' bravery, cunning, strength, nobility, and achieving immortal glory. The virtue of courage and competition is also introduced with the famous phrase derived from the sixth book of Iliad translated as "to strive always for the highest virtue, and to excel all others" or "ever to excel and be better than the rest."

Homer, per Kitto,

> enshrined all wisdom and all knowledge … combined with his hopeless fatalism, with the fierce joy in life and the exultation in human achievement and in human personality. We hear in the Iliad and in most Greek literature, the tragic note produced by the tension produced by two forces: passionate delight in life and clear apprehension of its unalterable framework.[42]

The following few lines of Homeric poetry in the *Iliad* describe humanity's generations on earth and their fate.

As is the generation of leaves, so is that of humanity,
The wind scatters the leaves on the ground, but the live timber;
Burgeons with leaves again in the season of spring returning;
So, one generation of men will grow while another dies.[43]

Homer showed the two sides of man—humility and heroism. Shelley commented on Homer.

> Poetry is the record of the best and happiest moments of the happiest and best minds … The poems of Homer and his contemporaries were the delight of infant Greece; they were the elements of that social system which is the column upon which all succeeding civilization has reposed. Homer embodied the ideal perfection of his age inhuman character … Homer was the first and Dante the second epic poet: that is, the second poet, the series of whose creations bore a defined and intelligible relation to the knowledge and sentiment and religion of the age in which

---

[42] Kitto, *The Greeks*, 44.
[43] Homer, *Iliad*, VI.111, *stoicsbible*, Internet.

he lived, and of the ages which followed it: developing itself in correspondence with their development.[44]

Per Jaeger, "The spiritual lifeblood of the Iliad is the pathos and the heroic doom of man's struggle; the Odyssey is inspired by human character, shown in aristocratic culture and morality ... Homer sees life as governed by universal laws."[45]

Homer's poetry was followed by Hesiod's poetry in two major works: *Theogony* (Genealogy of the Gods) and *Works and Days*. The *Theogony* details the descent of the gods. *Works and Days* is didactic in that it describes how and when to plant crops and how to run a household.

Works and Days introduced the concept of wisdom and the acquisition of knowledge.

> Those that lack wisdom themselves, and still refuse to accept advice, are useless ... If you work, the idle will soon envy you, as you grow rich, for fame and renown attend on wealth. Whatever be your lot, work is best for you. Turn your misguided mind away from other men's property and attend to your livelihood. An evil shame is the needy man's companion, shame that both greatly harms and prospers men: shame is with poverty and confidence with wealth.[46]

Hesiod introduced explicitly the subject of ethics. On virtue, vice and hard work, Hesiod stated,

> The road to vice is smooth and she lives near us. But between virtue and us, the gods have put we find for the first time the sweat from the first step. Long and steep is the path that leads to her, and it is rough at the first; but when a man has reached the top, he finds tranquility.[47]

Hesiod mentioned, "Work is not disgrace but idleness is disgrace," and he praised the virtues of hope and moderation. He wrote,

> Poverty is native to Greece; but manly virtue is acquired as the fruit of wisdom and strong law; by using it Greece defends herself from poverty and tyranny ... Man cannot reach his goal by

---

[44] *A Defense of Poetry and Other Essays by Percy Bysshe Shelley*, Internet.
[45] Jaeger, *Paideia*, vol. 1, 39.
[46] Hesiod, *Works and Days*, verses 293–319, Internet.
[47] Ibid., vv. 286–92.

violence, strife, and injustice. All this striving must be adapted to the purpose that rules the world, if he is to profit from it. Once a man has understood that in his heart, another can instruct him to find the right way.[48]

Pre-Socratics

By the fifth century BC, humanity reached a point of intellectual development that was not unlike ours today. Morals, aesthetic activity, science, and philosophy flourished. This is illustrated in their literature, art, and the concept of humanism as we understand it. Sophocles, the fifth-century dramatist, as Aeschylus before him did in *Prometheus Bound*, praised humanity's achievements and evolution from the primitive to a mature stage in his tragedy *Antigone*.

> Many are the world's wonders, but none more wondrous than man.
> Under the south wind's gale, he traverses the gray sea,
> Knifing through its surging swells.
> Earth, eldest of the gods imperishable and everlasting,
> He erodes year after year with winding furrows
> Cut by his equine team.
> The winged flocks of birds,
> The wild herds of beasts,
> And the salt-sea schools of fish
> He entraps in the woven mesh of his devious net.
> With his devices, he overpowers the creatures of the wild,
> Reining in the shaggy-manned stallion
> and yoking the stubborn mountain bull.
> Speech he developed and wind-swift thought
> And the talent to dwell together, and learned
> how to evade the chilling frost and pelting rain.
> Ingenious, there is nothing that comes he cannot master.
> Only from Death can he not contrive an escape.[49]

In the beginning of the sixth century, after the invention of alphabetic writing, a group of people in Ionia, a Greek settlement in Asia Minor, on Samos, on other islands in the eastern Aegean Sea, and other colonies in southern Italy and Sicily started in a rather intense way the exploration of nature (Greek *physis*). They wondered

---

[48] Herodotus, *Histories*, 7.102.1, trans. A. D. Godley (Cambridge: Harvard University Press, 1920).

[49] Aeschylus, *Antigone*, in Stephen Bertman, *The Genesis of Science: The Story of Greek Imagination* (Prometheus Books, 2010), 341.

what the universe was made of and what forces were governing nature and how. They abandoned superstition, religion, and mythology and tried to understand the world through reason only. They believed global physical laws governed nature independently of higher authorities. Natural phenomena could be explained with human understanding and without mythical and divine inspiration. They theorized that all matter was made of small, microscopic particles called atoms, the Sun was a planet of the Earth, and that all stars were very far away.

These philosophers of nature, called pre-Socratic philosophers as they preceded Socrates (469–399 BC), introduced the humanistic philosophy concerning humanity and society, not nature. Pre-Socratic philosophy started in the beginning of the sixth century and ended in the middle of the fifth century BC.

The term *philosophy* was introduced by Pythagoras (c. 570–500 BC); it means love of wisdom or knowledge. It came into use as philosophers inquired into nature through speculation and observation to acquire knowledge of nature.

Philosophy is that intellectual capability of humans that drives them to a level of human existence with knowledge, perfection, divine wisdom, and virtue instead of ignorance and wickedness. And per A. Sidgwick,

> It is the primary aim of philosophy to unify completely, bring into clear coherence, all departments of rational thought; and this aim cannot be realized by any philosophy that leaves out of its view the important body of judgments and reasoning which form the subject matter of Ethics. And it seems especially impossible, in attempting the construction of a Theistic Philosophy, to leave Ethics on one side.[50]

Philosophy was invented in a continuous and eternal search to identify and define the special intellectual framework and level that guides human existence from primitive ignorance and vice to divine wisdom and virtue. Philosophy is that special intellectual capacity of human reason to lift humanity to a level of human existence with knowledge and perfection. Philosophy is the search for cosmic truths and first causes. The cosmic truths are basic universal laws of physics such as gravity and kinetic and potential energy. The first causes are the theories of cosmogony, the basic elements of matter, etc. It then moved to ethics, defining behavior for the perfection of humanity and society, which it has helped achieve the highest ideals of morality and inspired us to achieve many of our noblest achievements in science, art, and literature. The search continues.

The researchers of nature were eventually called physicists as they addressed nature. In ancient times, philosophy was concerned with all knowledge until

---

[50] Henry Sidgwick, *A Memoir*, The World's Great Thinkers (New York: Random House, 1947), 342.

knowledge increased too much for any one individual to comprehend in its totality, and thus specialization of the professions came to be. The Greek word *episteme* means knowledge in general, and later, it was to mean only knowledge of the physical phenomena or science.

We will start exploring the evolution of the Greek thought with the pre-Socratic philosophers. The first three were Thales (c. 625–545 BC), Anaximander (c. 611–546 BC), and Anaximenes (died c. 500 BC) all from Miletus, the most prosperous town in Ionia. They tried to determine the beginning of the universe. They believed the basis of all matter was stable, immutable, and eternal. Thales postulated that this primary substance was water, Anaximander, fire, and Anaximenes, the infinite. Per Aristotle, Thales was the founder of European philosophy and science. Thales was considered one of the seven ancient wise men or sages as well. Thales predicted a moon eclipse in 585 BC, which was a major event for that time. This milestone date is considered the beginning of philosophy. Diogenes Laertius commented on Thales's inscription on his tomb, which reads, "Here in a narrow tomb great Thales lies; Yet his renown for wisdom reached the skies."[51]

Along with the physicists or natural philosophers, the seven sages who flourished around the first part of 600 BC started asking how man should best live and established a moral base consisting of maxims on how to live the good, moral life. This was the dawn of ethical philosophy.

Per Plato, the seven sages were "Thales of Miletus, Pittacus of Mytilene, Bias of Priene, Cleobulus of Rhodes, Solon of Athens, Periander of Corinth, and Chilon of Sparta."[52] No texts of their discourses survived; all we have are quotes from them in the writings of others. Their answers were wise laws and maxims for civilizations and nations to live with the highest moral principles. They introduced laws and virtues—qualities of excellence—a code of ethics for human behavior.

Early in the fifth century, the ancient Greeks enshrined their accumulated knowledge and wisdom in 145 maxims to be passed on in the Temple of Apollo at the holy site of Delphi, the well-known place of the Delphic Oracle. The immortal words of these illustrious men were engraved in marble at the temple. The Temple of Apollo has partially survived, but only the floor and seven partial columns still stand. But the maxims have survived in literature after nine invasions of conquerors and plunderers such as the Celts, Romans, Heruli, Visigoths, Slavs, Normans, Franks, Turks, World War II, and a civil war.

As if by a miracle, having taken custody of the imperishable literary monuments, the Muses saved 145 of them from the ravages of time. After printing and now the Internet, their preservation is assured for eternity along with all other classic

---

[51] Diogenes Laertius, *Lives of the Eminent Philosophers*, Internet.

[52] Plato, *Protagoras*, 343b, *Plato the Collected Dialogues, including the letters,* ed. by Edith Hamilton and Huntington Cairns, trans. W. K. C. Guthrie, 1961, 336.

documents. We should feel lucky and sad—lucky that this knowledge survived and sad because the human spirit has hardly advanced in excellence since that time.

After Greece's classical age, this knowledge was transmitted to major Hellenistic cities of the east including Antioch, Alexandria, and Pergamum and later to the Arabs and Persians. The Romans adopted it, and from there, it provided the ethical basis of Western civilization.

The maxims at Delphi deal with knowledge, excellence, and happiness. The maxims are concise suggestions for living in virtue and piety. Surprisingly, they include the three Christian virtues of faith, hope, and love directly or by inference, which were to be revealed more precisely six hundred years later. They include some of the Ten Commandments.

The two most famous of the maxims, found at Delphi are "Know thyself" and "Nothing to excess." Know thyself is the most famous of all and is considered the motto of philosophy. Man, above all, should be well reasoned, must know his capabilities and limitations, and achieve success and happiness through self-knowledge. As Socrates said, this happiness is not a product of external or physical goods but is dependent on the individual living a life that is good for the soul. As Plato eloquently stated the words of Socrates, "The unexamined life is not worth living."

The maxim Nothing to excess embodies the virtue of temperance and the law of proportion to avoid extremes in life, in architecture, and in so many other areas. Other maxims are, Praise hope, Do not tire of learning, and Pray for happiness. The Greeks believed that civilizations and nations had to practice prudence and temperance and all other virtues if they wanted to live in harmony and prosper.

A rather concise series of instructions for life, these maxims were believed to have been inscribed in descending order. Though they were brief, they provided an understanding of a life well lived. And from these maxims, we see the continued emphasis on an attainment of virtue as a way of achieving happiness. This was almost without exception the consensus of every philosopher of ancient Greece who tried his or her hand at ethics. Some of the quotes that follow provide the spirit of the virtues in the society and stated the various qualities people should acquire.

Pittacus of Mytilene (650–570 BC) stated, "Acquire things which last forever: nobleness and goodness, care, faith, education, prudence, truthfulness, trust, experience, tact, comradeship, diligence, frugality, skill."[53]

Pythagoras

Pythagoras of Samos, famous for the Pythagorean theorem and other mathematic formulae, followed the three Milesians. Pythagoras claimed that ethics was a major

[53] Pittacus, *Demetrius, Stoicbible*, Internet.

factor in human life. He introduced the term *philosophy* and determined that the earth was a sphere rather than a circular disk.

John Lord, who provided a summary of the thoughts prevailing at the time of Pythagoras, wrote,

> It is also said, that Pythagoras cultivated the moderation of the passions, and mediocrity, and that by the conjunction of a certain precedaneous good, he rendered the life of each of his disciples happy … With respect to justice, however, we shall learn in the best manner, how he cultivated and delivered it to mankind … But besides all this, the best polity, popular concord, community of possessions among friends, the worship of the gods, piety to the dead, legislation, erudition, silence, abstinence from animals, continence, temperance, sagacity, divinity, and in one word, whatever is anxiously sought after by the lovers of learning, was brought to light by Pythagoras.[54]

Heraclitus

Heraclitus of Ephesus (c. 535–c. 475 BC), according to Carl Jaspers (1883–1969), was the most famous of the pre-Socratics. Heraclitus, a contemporary of Pythagoras, introduced the concept of reason (*logos*), the backbone of philosophy. Per Jon Lord, "Heraclitus was one of the greatest speculative intellects that preceded Plato, and of all the physical theorists arrived nearest to spiritual truth."[55] Heraclitus introduced several very crucial ideas that influenced his successors, Sophists, Plato and Aristotle. They were

> the concept of Reason (Logos in Greek, means speech, word). There is a Logos or Rationale, by which all things are one. Failure to understand the Rationale is the root of all evil.

> Change is the essence of the Cosmos, everything is in a state of flux, a continuous change. "Everything changes and nothing remains still … and you cannot step twice into the same stream."

> "Fire" was the primary matter from which all things were made. Fire he meant: "force" or "energy." This Cosmos [the same of all] did none of gods or men make. But it always was, and is, and

---

[54] John Lord, *Beacon Lights of History*, vol. 1, Internet, 89, 15, 146.
[55] Ibid.

shall be an ever-living Fire, kindling in measures and going out in measures.

Men who love wisdom must be inquirers into very many things indeed.

War is both king of all and father of all, and some he shows gods, others as men; some he makes slaves, others free.[56]

An analysis of these concepts follows.
According to Karl Jasper,

Logos can neither be translated into any other term nor defined as a concept. Logos can signify: word, discourse, content of discourse, meaning; reason; truth; law; even Being. In Heraclitus, it is not defined: it carries all these meanings at once and is never limited to any one of them.[57]

Reason is the noblest faculty of man, and as Friedrich Schiller (1759–1805) stated, "Reason is the source of ideas of moral feelings and of conceptions free from all elements taken up from experience."[58]

In modern days, the word *logical* comes from logos. In Latin, the word for logos is *ratio*, from which springs the words *reason* and *rationalism*.

Logos is the human faculty stimulating thoughts and knowledge; it is the moving force of all human activity and challenging opinions, an essential element of prudence. Logos is the second-best gift to humanity after the gift of life. The gift of logos is the gift of rationale and logic to invent and improve life. Individuals as well as groups use this gift not in the common interest of all but in their own interests to the detriment of the rest and sometimes to life itself.

The Christian concept of logos comes from the first chapter of the gospel of John, where logos is often translated as "word" as follows.

In the beginning was the Word, and the Word was with God, and the Word was God. He was with God in the beginning. Through him all things were made; without him nothing was made that has been made. In him was life, and that life was the light of men. The light shines in the darkness, but the darkness has not overcome

---

[56] K. Freeman, *Ancilla to the Pre-Socratic Philosophers, a complete Translation of the Fragments of Diels* (1948), 38.
[57] Karl Jasper, *The Great Philosophers*, vol. 2 (New York: Harcourt Brace, 1957), 11.
[58] Friedrich Schiller, *Aesthetical Essays of Friedrich Schiller*, Internet.

it … And the Word was made flesh, that dwelt among us, full of grace and truth.[59]

The gospel of John identified the logos through which all things were made as divine and further identified Jesus as the incarnate Logos.

Philo (ca. 20 BC–AD 50), a Hellenized Jew from Alexandria, adopted the term *logos* into Jewish philosophy. The Stoic philosophers who followed Aristotle identified the term with the divine animating principle pervading the universe.

Empedocles (484–424 BC) said the basic elements of nature were water, earth, air, and fire.

Leucippus (fl. fifth century BC) and Democritus (c. 460–c. 370 BC) of Abdera, Thrace, were pre-Socratic philosophers who formulated the universal theory of atomism: that all matter was made up of atoms, which were indivisible, imperishable particles, and that between atoms is empty space. This theory was to survive until the end of the nineteenth century. Actually, their theory is still good as they did define an atom that could not be divided. In that sense, the elementary particles making up an atom as we define it today is their proper meaning. Democritus was a polymath who wrote many books, but only his theory of atomism and many fragments of his ethics and political maxims survive. Epicurus and the Roman Lucretius adopted and expanded Democritus's atomic theory.

In his *Philosophy in the Tragic Age of the Greeks*, German philosopher Nietzsche (1844–1900) described the Greek interaction and influence from other cultures.

> Nothing would be sillier than to claim an autochthonous (indigenous) development for the Greeks. On the contrary, they invariably absorbed other living cultures. The very reason they got so far is that they knew how to pick up the spear and throw it onward from the point where others had left it. Their skill in the art of fruitful learning was admirable. We ought to be learning from our neighbors precisely as the Greeks learned from theirs, not for the sake of learned pedantry but rather using everything we learn as a foothold which will take us up as high, and higher than our neighbor … The Greeks themselves, possessed of an inherently insatiable thirst for knowledge, controlled it by their ideal need for and consideration of all the values of life … They forbore, trying to re-invent the elements of philosophy and science. Rather they instantly tackled the job of so fulfilling, enhancing, elevating and purifying the elements they took over from elsewhere that they became inventors after all, but in a higher sense and a purer sphere. For what they invented was *the archetypes of philosophic*

---

[59] John 1:1–14.

thought. All posterity has not made an essential contribution to them since.[60]

Nietzsche exalted the pre-Socratics for their philosophical achievements.

All other cultures are put to shame by the marvelously idealized philosophical company represented by the ancient Greek Pre-Socratics masters, along with Socrates. These men are monolithic. Their thinking and their character stand in a relationship characterized by strictest necessity. They are devoid of conventionality, for in their day there was no philosophic or academic professionalism. All of them, in magnificent solitude, were the only ones of their time whose lives were devoted to insight alone. They all possessed that virtuous energy of the ancients, herein excelling all men since, which led them to find their own individual form and to develop it through all its metamorphoses to its subtlest and greatest possibilities … Almost every age and cultural stage has at some time or another sought in an ill-tempered frame of mind to free itself of the Greeks, because in comparison with the Greeks, all their achievements, apparently fully original and admired in all sincerity, suddenly appeared to lose their color and life and were reduced to unsuccessful copies … Other nations have their Saints, the Greeks have Sages. Rightly it is said that a nation is characterized not only by her great citizens but rather by the way she recognizes and honors them.[61]

Not unlike Nietzsche, John Lord had nothing but praise for the pre-Socratics; he provided a description of the Greek intellect.

The progress of philosophy from Thales to Plato is the most extraordinary triumph of the human intellect. The reason of man soared to the loftiest flights that it has ever attained. It cast its searching eye into the most abstruse inquiries which ever tasked the famous minds of the world. It exhausted all the subjects which dialectical subtlety ever raised. It originated and carried out the boldest speculations respecting the nature of the soul and its future existence.[62]

---

[60] F. Nietzsche, *Philosophy in the Tragic Age of the Greeks*, in *The Nietzsche Reader*, K. Pearson, D. Large, eds. (Malden, MA: Blackwell, 2006), 102.

[61] Ibid., 103.

[62] Lord, *Beacon Lights of History*, vol. 1, Kindle locations 1419–1422.

Sophists

The Sophists were paid teachers of philosophy, rhetoric, and virtue; they followed the pre-Socratics. The primary Sophists were Gorgias, Hippias, Antiphon, Prodicus, and the most famous of them, Protagoras. Plato did not give the Sophists high marks as his teacher and mentor Socrates thought that knowledge was to be free. Protagoras (c. 490 BC–c. 420 BC) was a philosopher considered a Sophist by Plato. One of Plato's major dialogues was named after Protagoras. Protagoras is famous for his statement, "Man is the measure of all things"; there is no absolute truth but what individuals deem to be the truth.

Socrates

Till about end of sixth century BC, Greece had developed a society with ethical norms based on the aristocratic norms of the established order, the rule of the *aristoi* (best), and religious and ethical values. The evolution of democratic ideas had reached a rather advanced stage, and with it came the challenging of the new teachers of moral and intellectual relativism of the established order. Then Socrates came to define and clarify the new ethics derived through reason.

Socrates (469–399 BC) was one of the greatest philosophers of all times and one of the founders of Western philosophy who lived during the golden age of Greek civilization. He was the son of a stonemason and a midwife. He has been described as one of the most powerful, inspiring, truthful, virtuous, famous, and intriguing figures in the history of philosophy.

Up until Socrates's time, the primary inquiries of philosophy were directed at nature and cosmology. Socrates was not interested in nature, astronomy, and physics; he turned his inquiry to the study of man and his conduct, which we call ethics. He relentlessly pursued his desire to establish the concepts of truth, beauty, and justice. He argued that the most important philosophical questions of all were how we ought to live, how to tame ourselves, and how to achieve moral perfection. In his masterpiece *The Republic*, Plato offered the universal challenge of man's purpose on earth: "We must look closer at the matter, what is at stake is far from insignificant: it is how one should live one's life."[63] This was the key aim of Western world's greatest philosopher.

About four centuries later, Cicero (106–43 BC), in his *Tusculan Disputations*, provided the best description of the role of Socrates on philosophy.

> Socrates was the first who brought down philosophy from the heavens, placed it in cities, introduced it into houses, and made it necessary for inquires to be made on life and morals, good and

---

[63] Plato, *The Republic*, 352d, trans. Robin Waterfield (Oxford: OUP, 1993), 40.

evil. And his different methods of discussing questions, together with the variety of his topics, and the greatness of his abilities, being immortalized by the memory and writings of Plato, gave rise to many sects of philosophers. [64]

Socrates, the founder of scientific ethics, defined it as the study of ideal conduct. He was concerned about the values and virtues of humanity and society, and he devoted his life to teaching the "good"; he believed people would be good by knowing what good was. He regarded reflection on moral problems as the only inquiry worthy of philosophy. He believed that virtue was knowledge, that the highest knowledge was the knowledge of good and evil, and that all other goods that lead to happiness spring from virtue.

In Plato's *Apology*, Socrates stated, "the unexamined life is not worth living," and he pressed for definitions of the virtues or excellences. In the dialogue, he tried to reach the truth with his audience by asking, What is good, piety, wisdom, what is justice and injustice, what is temperance, courage? Know thyself was the proper maxim for humans to undertake seriously.

Socrates declared that the most important thing in life is how we live, and the pursuit of virtuous life is the highest good, or *summum bonum*, as the Romans called it. It was repeated by Plato and Aristotle, the Christian dogmatists, from the apostles to St. Augustine, to Thomas Aquinas through the Middle Ages, to Renaissance and modern times, and continues to the twenty-first century. It will continue as long as humans exist, The goal of every human being is to achieve virtue and lead a happy life. Socrates devoted his life to the pursuit of the virtuous life and truth; he tried to implant this ideal in all with no exceptions, and the struggle of humanity toward this ideal goal started. Socrates marked the beginning of ethics in a systematic way in human history. As Hegel said, "Socrates is celebrated as a Teacher of Morality, but we should rather call him the Inventor of Morality."[65]

Rousseau exalted Socrates for his exemplary life: "Socrates ... would leave to us, as he did to his disciples, only the example and memory of his virtues; that is the noblest method of instructing mankind."[66]

The famous historian Grote sang an encomium to Socrates.

No man has ever been found, strong enough to bend the bow of Socrates, the father of philosophy, the most original thinker of antiquity ... Socrates bases truth on consciousness, Uncertainty

---

[64] Marcus Tullius Cicero, *Cicero's Tusculan Disputations*, 4, 10, Internet.

[65] Georg Hegel, *The Philosophy of History* (New York: Cosimo Classics), 269.

[66] Jean-Jacques Rousseau, *Discourse on the Arts and Sciences*, The Collector's Library of Essential Thinkers (London: 2005), 37.

of physical inquiries in his day, Superiority of moral truth, Happiness, Virtue, Knowledge, —the Socratic trinity.[67]

In Socrates's *Apology*, Plato described Socrates discussing his function in Athenian society. His goal was to teach virtue to achieve perfection in the society. Without virtue, there is no harmony in society. Afterward, Socrates's students Plato and Aristotle expanded philosophy from ethics to cover logic, politics, aesthetics, epistemology, and metaphysics.

John Lord stated,

> Socrates learned his philosophy from no one, and struck out an entirely new path. He declared his own ignorance, and sought to convince other people of theirs. He did not seek to reveal truth so much as to expose error. And yet it was his object to attain correct ideas as to moral obligations. He proclaimed the sovereignty of virtue and the immutability of justice. He sought to delineate and enforce the practical duties of life. His great object was the elucidation of morals; and he was the first to teach ethics systematically from the immutable principles of moral obligation. Moral certitude was the lofty platform from which he surveyed the world, and upon which, as a rock, he rested in the storms of life. Thus, he was a reformer and a moralist. It was his ethical doctrines, which were most antagonistic to the age, and the least appreciated. He was a profoundly religious man, recognized Providence, and believed in the immortality of the soul.[68]

Socrates exalted many of the ethical virtues later adopted by the Stoic philosophers and Christianity—wisdom, temperance, courage, justice, nobility, and truth.[69] Moral philosophy began with Socrates and ethics, a new branch of philosophy. It is the study of the ideal conduct and the foundation of moral science. After Socrates, first Plato and later Aristotle expanded on these virtues and made them the cornerstones of Greek ethical philosophy.

In the *Academica*, Cicero attributed to Varro the following view.

> It is my view, and it is universally agreed, that Socrates was the first person who summoned philosophy away from mysteries veiled in concealment by nature herself, upon which all philosophers before him had been engaged, and led it to the subject of ordinary life,

---

[67] Lord, *Beacon Lights of History*, vol. 1, Internet.
[68] Ibid.
[69] Plato, *Phaedo*, 69b.

to investigate the virtues and vices, and good and evil generally, and to realize that heavenly matters are either remote from our knowledge or else, however fully known, have nothing to do with the good life.[70]

I am listing below some quotes from Socrates's *Apology* to show his temper during his trial: piety, calmness, and true to his principles, virtue.

> I respect and I love you but I shall obey the God rather than you; and so long as I draw breath and am able, I shall not cease to practice philosophy, to exhort you in my usual way, and warning any one of you I may happen to meet, saying: Most excellent man, are you who are a citizen of Athens, the greatest city with the greatest reputation for both wisdom and power; are you not ashamed of your eagerness to possess, as much wealth, reputation and honors as possible while you do not care nor give thought to wisdom or truth, or the perfection of your soul?

> Be sure that this is what the god orders me to do, and I think there is no greater blessing but persuading both young and old not to care about your body or your wealth in preference to or, as strongly as, for the perfection of your soul, as I say to you:

> Virtue does not come from wealth but from virtue comes wealth and all other good things to man, both to the individual and to the state ...

> For if you kill me you will not easily find another like me. I was attached to this city- though it seems a ridiculous thing to say-as upon a great and noble horse which was somewhat sluggish because of its size and needed to be stirred up by a kind of a gadfly; It is to fulfill some such function that I believe the god has placed me in the city.[71]

As was the case with Confucius, Buddha, and Christ, Socrates never wrote anything down. Everything we know about him is through the eyes and ears of his students Plato, Xenophon, and some of Aristophanes' work. Socrates believed his ideas on virtue, morality, and reason had universal applicability. Cicero said,

[70] Cicero, v .4.10, trans. Rackham, Routledge, *History of Philosophy Vol I: From the Beginning to Plato.*
[71] Plato, *Socrates's Apology* 29d-30a-b-d-31a.

"Socrates, indeed, when he was asked where he belonged to, replied, 'The world'; for he looked upon himself as a citizen and inhabitant of the whole world."[72]

His faithful students, particularly Plato, immortalized Socrates's teachings in their writings, and thus eternity was assured him. Humanity is fortunate to have all Plato's writings; most of the rest of the great ancient writings perished over time.

Socrates lived a humble, virtuous life and did not claim to possess knowledge and know the truth, but he said he was always a seeker of knowledge and truth. His humility was exemplified by his saying: "I know one thing, that I know nothing."

Xenophon (430–354 BC) was a historian and a student of Socrates; he described Socrates in his *Memorabilia*.

> This was the tenor of his conversation with Hermogenes and with the others. But amongst those who knew Socrates and recognized what manner of man he was, all who make virtue and perfection their pursuit still to this day cease not to lament his loss with bitterest regret, as for one who helped them in the pursuit of virtue as none else could … To me, personally, he was what I have myself endeavored to describe: so pious and devoutly religious that he would take no step apart from the will of heaven; so just and upright that he never did even a trifling injury to any living soul; so self-controlled, so temperate, that he never at any time chose the sweeter in place of the better; so sensible, and wise, and prudent that in distinguishing the better from the worse he never erred; nor had he need of any helper, but for the knowledge of these matters, his judgment was at once infallible and self-sufficing. Capable of reasonably setting forth and defining moral questions, he was also able to test others, and where they erred, to cross-examine and convict them, and so to impel and guide them in the path of virtue and noble manhood. With these characteristics, he seemed to be the very impersonation of human perfection and happiness.[73]

Dr. W. Windelband stated,

> Socrates teaches, indeed, even according to Xenophon, that man's true fortune is to be sought, not in outward goods nor in luxurious life, but in virtue alone: if, however, this virtue is to consist only in the capacity to recognize the truly useful and act accordingly, the

---

[72] Cicero, *Tusculan Disputations / Also, Treatises on the Nature of the Gods, And on the Commonwealth*, Internet.

[73] Xenophon, *Memorabilia*, Internet.

doctrine moves in a circle as soon as it maintains that this truly useful is just virtue itself. In this circle, Socrates remained fast; the objective determination of the conception of the good which he sought he did not find.[74]

Socrates was charged by Athens with corrupting the youth and impiety. The following is from Socrates's *Apology* as recorded by Plato.

Men of Athens, I respect you and I am your friend, but I shall obey God rather than you ... Wealth does not bring virtue, but virtue brings wealth and every other blessing, both to the individual and to the state ... Either acquit me or not; but whichever you do, understand that I shall never alter my ways, not even if I have to die many times ... I understand Socrates; it is because you say that you always have a divine guide. I mean, because I find it hard to accept such stories people tell about the gods?[75]

Speaking of his approaching death before drinking hemlock and referring to Crito, who was lamenting, Socrates said,

Thus, will Crito bear it more easily, and, when he sees my body burned or buried, will not grieve over me as if I had suffered some dreadful thing, nor say at the funeral that it is Socrates who is laid out on the bier or carried forth to the grave or buried. For you must know, dearest Crito, that this false way of speaking not only is wrong in itself, but also does harm to the soul. Rather you should be of good courage, and say that it is my body you are burying; and this you may do as you please, and in the way which you think most conformable to custom here.[76]

Socrates laughed and joked on the day of his death. Plato described in *Phaedo*, *Apology*, and *Crito* Socrates's last days. Per Karl Jaspers, "These are among the few irreplaceable documents of mankind. All through antiquity men of philosophical mind read it and learned how to die at peace by accepting their lot, however cruel and unjust."[77]

[74] W. Windelband, *A History of Philosophy*, 200.
[75] Plato, *Apology*, trans. H. Tredennick, *Plato the Collected Dialogues*, Hamilton and Cairns, eds. (Pantheon Books), 3.
[76] Ibid., 95.
[77] Karl Jaspers, *Socrates, Buddha, Confucius, Jesus, from the Great Philosophers*, vol. 1 (New York: Harcourt Brace, 1957), 15.

The words exchanged by Socrates's pupils immediately after his death were, "Such was the end, Echecrates, of our friend, who was, as we may say, of all those whom we knew in our time, the best and wisest and the most righteous man."[78]

The great Renaissance humanist, theologian, and social critic Erasmus (1466–1536) equated Socrates with a saint in his famous saying, "Sancte Socrates, ora pro nobis" (Saint Socrates, pray for us).[79]

Plato

Plato (428/427–347 BC) was an eminent philosopher and mathematician in classical Greece. Some call him the greatest philosopher of all times. He was a student of Socrates and a teacher of Aristotle.

In discussing philosophy, the great philosopher and mathematician Alfred North Whitehead wrote that Plato's contribution was widely recognized as he developed philosophy to the state of almost perfection unsurpassed to this day. He wrote on the importance of Plato's philosophy and relevance.

> The safest general characterization of the European philosophical tradition is that it consists of a series of footnotes to Plato. I do not mean the systematic scheme of thought, which scholars have doubtfully extracted from his writings. I allude to the wealth of general ideas scattered through them … Every problem that Plato discusses is still with us today.[80]

This may be slightly overstated, but there is little argument that the triad of Plato, Socrates, and Aristotle are at the top of the pyramid of philosophy and ethics and laid the foundation of Western philosophy. Of all the ancient writings except for Aristotle's, Plato's writings are the most voluminous. As far as it has been determined from other ancient writers' references, all of Plato's writings survived.

Per B. F. Cocker,

> The philosophy of Plato was but the ripened fruit of the pregnant thoughts and seminal utterances of his predecessors, —Socrates, Anaxagoras, and Pythagoras; whilst all of them do but represent the general tendency and spirit of their country and their times.[81]

Plato established a school of philosophy called the Academy, which lasted until

---

[78] Plato, *Phaedo*, 118a12.
[79] Jaspers, *Socrates, Buddha, Confucius*, 18.
[80] A. N. Whitehead, *Process and Reality* (Free Press, 1979), 165.
[81] B. F. Cocker, *Christianity and Greek Philosophy*, Internet.

Emperor Justinian closed it in AD 529. Plato's famous masterpiece is his *Republic*, a book on justice. It has been studied through the ages, and it is as modern today as it was when written. In the *Republic*, Plato wrote very highly of educating citizens: "Can anything be better than a commonwealth than to produce men and women of the best type?"[82]

About 2,200 years after Plato's *Republic* was written, Rousseau, in his book *Emile*, commented on the importance of the *Republic*.

> If you wish to know what is meant by public education read Plato's Republic. Those who merely judge books by their titles take this for a treatise on politics, but it is the finest treatise on education ever written ... Keep your children ever within the little circle of dogmas, which are related to morality. Convince them that the only useful learning is that which teaches us to act rightly.[83]

According to Jaeger,

> Law was the most universal and permanent form of Greek moral and legal experience. The culmination of Plato's work as a philosophical educator comes in his last and greatest book, when he himself turns lawgiver; and Aristotle closes his Ethics by calling for a legislator to realize the ideal he has formulated. Law is the mother of philosophy, for another reason-because of Greece law making was always the work of great individuals ... as Heraclitus had said, "the people must fight for their law as for their city walls."[84]

Whitehead stated,

> The creation of the world, or the creation of civilized order—said Plato—is the victory of persuasion over force ... Civilization is the maintenance of social order, by its own inherent persuasiveness as embodying the nobler alternative. The recourse to force, however unavoidable, is a disclosure of the failure of civilization, either in the general society or in a remnant of individuals ... Civilized

---

[82] L. P. Pojman, *Ethics Discovering Right and Wrong* (Belmont, CA: Wardsworth Publishing), 251.

[83] Rousseau, *Emile*, Free Press, 1979, 39, Internet.

[84] Jaeger, *Paideia*, vol. 1, 109–10.

order survives on its merits, and is transformed by its power of recognizing its imperfections.[85]

Per John Lord, what follows is Archer Butler's praise of Plato.

> No modern writer has written more enthusiastically of what he considers the crowning excellence of the Greek philosophy. The dialectics of Plato, his ideal theory, his physics, his psychology, and his ethics are most ably discussed, and in the spirit of a loving and eloquent disciple ... these sentences [of Plato] contain the culture of nations; these are the cornerstones of schools; these are the fountainhead of literatures. A discipline it is in logic, arithmetic, taste, symmetry, poetry, language, rhetoric, ontology, morals, or practical wisdom. There never was such a range of speculation. Out of Plato come all things that are still written and debated among men of thought.[86]

According to Diogenes Laertius, the following epitaphs were inscribed on Plato's tomb.

> Here lies the god-like man Plato, eminent among men for temperance and the justice of his character. And he, if ever anyone, had the fullest reword of praise for wisdom, and was too great for envy.

> Earth in her bosom here hides Plato's body, but his soul has its immortal station with the blessed, Ariston's son, whom every good man, even if he dwells afar off, honors because he discerned the divine life.

> a. Eagle, why fly you over this tomb? Say, is your gaze fixed upon the starry house of one of the immortals?

> b. I am the image of the soul of Plato, which has soared to Olympus, while his earth-born body rests in Attic soil.

> There is also an epitaph of my own which runs thus:

---

[85] Whitehead, *Adventures of Ideas*, 103.
[86] Lord, *Beacon Lights of History*, vol. 1, Internet.

If Phoebus did not cause Plato to be born in Greece, how came
it that he healed the minds of men by letters? As the god's son
Asclepius is a healer of the body, so is Plato of the immortal soul.[87]

B. Cocker wrote,

Independent of all other considerations, virtue is, therefore, to
be pursued as the true good of the soul. Wisdom, Fortitude,
Temperance, Justice, the four cardinal virtues of the Platonic
system, are to be cultivated as the means of securing the
purification and perfection of the inner man.[88]

In summary, Plato, after his teacher Socrates, established happiness as the
highest good for man. He passed the torch to his student Aristotle, who reached a
higher plateau in describing knowledge, virtue, and happiness. Aristotle along with
Plato laid the foundations of Western civilization, and Aristotle's scientific influence
continued to the sixteenth century.

Aristotle

Aristotle was the greatest and most famous student of Plato. He was born
in Stagira in 384 BC, and later was Alexander the Great's tutor. Aristotle was a
polymath; according to Diogenes Laertius, he wrote more than 360 works covering
many subjects of which 40 survive. He founded the Peripatetic school of philosophy
covering all subjects of knowledge. He carried the philosophic movement started by
Socrates and Plato to new heights. His surviving writings far exceed the writings of
any ancient writer, and his precious thought has had more influence on humanity
than any other person up until the seventeenth century.

He was the first, and in the words of D. Boorstin, the unexcelled organizer,
classifier and codifier of knowledge. His writings cover every branch of knowledge
of his time such as logic, ethics, law, politics, art, metaphysics, and natural science.

Per Ferngren,

No one in the history of civilization has shaped our understanding
of science and natural philosophy more than the great Greek
philosopher and scientist Aristotle, who exerted a profound and
pervasive influence for more than two thousand years.[89]

---

[87] Diogenes Laertius, Internet.
[88] Benjamin Franklin Cocker, *Christianity and Greek Philosophy*, Internet.
[89] G. B. Ferngren, *Science and Religion: A Historical Introduction* (JHU Press, 2002), 33.

Hegel wrote,

> Aristotle penetrated into the whole mass, into every department of the universe of things, and subjected to the comprehension its scattered wealth; and the greater number of the philosophical sciences owe to him their separation and commencement.[90]

In his three books on ethics, Aristotle was more than anyone the first and last to explore most of humanity's inner moral issues using reasoned principles. He taught the ultimate goal of men was *eudaimonia* (happiness), and he wrote on how to achieve it. His philosophical successors over the centuries could do little but add footnotes to his priceless writings.

Many of his writings were translated into Arabic and studied by Muslim philosophers, scientists, and other scholars. Aristotle was the most revered Western thinker in early Islamic theology. His writings, especially his *Ethics*, greatly influenced Middle-Age scholastic thinkers including St. Thomas Aquinas, who sought to reconcile Aristotelian philosophy with Christianity by bringing the thoughts of ancient Greece into the Middle Ages. As far as the constituents of matter were concerned, Aristotle adopted Empedocles's theory of the four elements—water, air, earth, and fire—that survived until the seventeenth century.

Hegel said,

> The development of philosophic science as science, and, further, the progress from the Socratic point of view to the scientific, begins with Plato and is completed by Aristotle. They of all others deserve to be called teachers of the human race ... The philosophic culture of Plato, like the general culture of his time, was not yet ripe for really scientific work; the Idea was still too fresh and new; it was only in Aristotle that it attained to a systematic scientific form of representation.[91]

Aristotle stated, "Man, by nature is a political animal" and man's distinction from other animals is "that he alone has any sense of good and evil, of just and unjust."[92]

Dante referred to Aristotle, Plato, and Socrates in his *Inferno* as being in his first circles of hell.

---

[90] Lord, *Beacon Lights of History*, vol. 1, Internet.
[91] Hegel, *Lectures on the History of Philosophy*, vol. 2.
[92] Aristotle, *Politics*, 1.1253a, trans. Benjamin Jowett.

I saw the Master there of those who know,
Amid the philosophic family,
By all admired, and by all reverenced;
There Plato too I saw, and Socrates,
Who stood beside him closer than the rest.[93]

According to John Lord,

> Aristotle ... is the father of the history of philosophy, since he gives an historical review of the way in which the subject has been hitherto treated by the earlier philosophers ... Says Adolph Stahr: Plato made the external world the region of the incomplete and bad, of the contradictory and the false, and recognized absolute truth only in the eternal immutable ideas. Aristotle laid down the proposition that the idea, which cannot of itself fashion itself into reality, is powerless, and has only a potential existence; and that it becomes a living reality only by realizing itself in a creative manner by means of its own energy ... There can be no doubt as to Aristotle's marvelous power of systematizing. Collecting together all the results of ancient speculation, he so combined them into a co-ordinate system that for a thousand years he reigned supreme in the schools. From a literary point of view, Plato was doubtless his superior; but Plato was a poet, making philosophy divine and musical, while Aristotle's investigations spread over a far wider range.[94]

Aristotle has been regarded as the father of logic, and Hegel and Kant think there has been no improvement upon it since his day. Kant said that since the age of Aristotle, logic, like pure geometry, since Euclid's day has been a complete and perfect science that has kept its place even down to the present day without attaining any further scientific improvements. This became to him the real organon of science. John Lord commented on Plato and Aristotle,

> He supposed it was not merely the instrument of thought, but the instrument of investigation ... Sensation thus becomes the basis of knowledge. Plato made reason the basis of knowledge, but Aristotle made experience that basis.[95]

---

[93] Will Durant, *Story of Philosophy,* Simon and Schuster, 180.
[94] Lord, *Beacon Lights of History*, vol. 1, published by VM ebooks.
[95] Ibid.

Athens

In 508 BC, Cleisthenes introduced Athens to the concept of democracy, the greatest political system in history; it had a great impact on Western civilization. It was adopted by the Romans but disappeared until modern ages. It has become the best system of governing people—not perfect, but no other has been proven better. Jakob Burckhardt stated,

> Throughout the seventh century Athens does not seem to stand out especially from the other Greek communities. But from the sixth century on, these words gradually come to apply to it: "However this city rears out its head among other cities as great as the cypresses are accustomed among the supple wayfaring trees."[96]

Besides Homer, Hesiod, Socrates, Plato, and Aristotle were many who made some of the most important contributions to Western civilization. These included statesmen such as Solon and Cleisthenes; poets including Pindar and Sappho; dramatists including Aeschylus, Sophocles, Euripides, and comedian Aristophanes; the historians Herodotus, Thucydides, and Xenophon; the orators Isocrates and Lysias; the physician Hippocrates famous for his Hippocratic oath that is still in use today; the sculptor Phidias; the architect Ictinus, the philosophers Heraclitus, Pythagoras, Xenophanes, Empedocles, Parmenides, Protagoras, Democritus, Anaxagoras, Zeno of Elea; the statesman Pericles; and generals Miltiades and Themistocles. Athens produced a pantheon of brilliant people who achieved excellence in the arts, philosophy, medicine, mathematics, and literature.

The followings are some of the most important references to their great writings.

> Athens reached its pinnacle in their democratic constitution and its arts during the fifth century. In Athens, there was a remarkable politician named Pericles. His famous "funeral oration," honoring fallen Athenian heroes, sounds almost American in its logic: "We have a form of government ... which, because in the administration it hath respect not to a few but to the multitude, is called a democracy. Wherein ... there be an equality amongst all men in point of law for their private controversies ... And we live not only free in the administration of the state but also one with another void of jealousy touching each other's daily course of life, not offended at any man for following his own humor ... So that conversing one with another ... without offense, we stand chiefly in fear to transgress against the public and are obedient always to

[96] J. Burckhardt, *On History and Historians* (New York: Harper Torchbooks, 1958), 10.

those that govern and to the laws, and principally to such laws as are written for protection against injury."[97]

In his funeral oration as recorded by the historian Thucydides, Pericles praised Athenian society and its ideals. He showed confidence, extolled democracy, justice, the ideal of the beautiful and the good, citizen's participation in government, courage, freedom, and happiness. He eloquently stated,

> Our form of government does not enter into rivalry with the institutions of others. Our government does not copy our neighbors, but we are an example to them. It is true that we are called a democracy, for the administration is in the hands of the many and not of the few. But while there exists equal justice to all and alike in their private disputes, the claim of excellence is also recognized; and when a citizen is in any way distinguished, he is preferred to the public service, not as a matter of privilege, but as the reward of merit. Neither is poverty an obstacle, but a man may benefit his country whatever the obscurity of his condition …

> And we have not forgotten to provide for our weary spirits many relaxations from toil; we have regular games and sacrifices throughout the year; our homes are beautiful and elegant; and the delight, which we daily feel in all these things, helps to banish sorrow. Because of the greatness of our city the fruits of the whole earth flow in upon us; so that we enjoy the goods of other countries as freely as our own …

> For we are lovers of the beautiful, yet simple in our tastes, and we cultivate the mind without loss of manliness. Wealth we employ, not for talk and ostentation, but when there is a real use for it. To avow poverty with us is no disgrace; the true disgrace is in doing nothing to avoid it. An Athenian citizen does not neglect the state because he takes care of his own household; and even those of us who are engaged in business have a very fair idea of politics. We alone regard a man who takes no interest in public affairs, not as a harmless; but as a useless character … Our natural bravery springs from our way of life, not from the compulsion of laws … I speak not of that in which their remains are laid, but of that in which their glory survives, and is proclaimed always and on every fitting occasion both in word and deed. For the whole earth is the tomb

[97] *Isocrates*, trans. N. George (Cambridge, MA: Harvard University Press), 1980.

of famous men; not only are they commemorated by columns and inscriptions in their own country, but in foreign lands there dwells also an unwritten memorial of them, graven not on stone but in the hearts of men ... and you may be sure that if we cling to our freedom and preserve that, we shall soon enough recover all the rest. But, if we are the servants of others, we shall be sure to lose not only freedom, but all that freedom gives.[98]

Referring to the golden age of Greece, Pericles considered the Athenians the greatest people in the world. They were first in war, first in freedom, and first to discover new ideas. The Athenians had discovered a new way to govern themselves; they believed it was a better way of life. The people of other cities and nations could enjoy this better way of life as well. To Greeks in other city-states at the time, the Athenians appeared arrogant. Their empire posed a threat. The Peloponnesian War that followed sapped all the Athenian energy, and its decline followed.

The great rhetorician Isocrates praised Athens.

For they established government by the people ... And so far, has our city distanced the rest of mankind in thought and in speech that her pupils have become the teachers of the rest of the world; and she has brought it about that the name Hellenes suggests no longer a race but an intelligence, and that the title Hellenes is applied rather to those who share our culture than to those who share a common blood ... Those who conducted the affairs of the city at that time established a constitution that was not merely in name most mild and impartial, while in reality it did not show itself such to those who lived under it,—a constitution that did not train its citizens in such a manner that they considered license democracy, lawlessness liberty, insolence of speech equality, and the power of acting in this manner happiness, but which, by hating and punishing men of such character, made all the citizens better and more modest.[99]

Thus, we come to a transition from Hellenic to Hellenistic civilization and its center moving from Athens to Alexandria and southern Italy. Whitehead stated the reason this transition took place.

---

[98] Thucydides, *The Peloponnesian War*, Jowett trans.

[99] Isocrates, *Panegyricus*, trans. N. George (Cambridge, MA: Harvard University Press, 1980).

The race was awakened into progress by a great ideal of perfection. This ideal was an immense advance upon the ideals, which the surrounding civilizations had produced. It was effective and realized in a civilization that attained its proper beauty in human lives to an extent not surpassed before or since. Its art, its theoretic sciences, its modes of life, its literature, its philosophic schools, its religious rituals, all conspired to express every aspect of this wonderful ideal. Perfection was attained, and with the attainment inspiration withered. With repetition of successive generations, freshness gradually vanished. Learning and learned taste replaced the ardor of adventure. Hellenism was stifled by the Hellenistic epoch in which genius was stifled by repetition … to sustain a civilization with the intensity of its ardor requires more than learning. Adventure is essential, namely, the search for new perfection.[100]

A thousand years later, the second knowledge explosion—the Renaissance—started in Italy. Its impetus came from the rediscovery of the literature and art of this classic era, and Greece's enduring contribution to Western civilization continued. Humanity rediscovered and appreciated the intellectual level of the ancients and became determined to surpass them. According to Brinton, "The Renaissance in Italy raised the Greek model into a highest level point it has ever attained."[101]

HELLENISTIC PERIOD: 323–31 BC, THE ROMAN TAKEOVER OF EGYPT

The time between Alexander the Great's death in 323 BC and 31 BC, the defeat of Cleopatra and Mark Anthony by the Roman Emperor Octavian, marked the Hellenistic period. The Greek civilization from Greece, southern Italy, and Sicily spread to the east, primarily Alexandria, Antioch, Ephesus, and Pergamum.

Alexandria with its famous library became the intellectual center, the depository and beacon of knowledge. The library undertook the task of collecting, copying, and editing all knowledge recorded to that date. They continued this task to the middle of the next millennium until the library was destroyed. Unlike Ephesus and Pergamum, little of ancient Alexandria survived.

The diffusion of knowledge in this period was accelerated and preserved with writing on parchment, a technique invented in Pergamum. Parchment is processed animal skins and is much more durable than papyrus. Parchment allowed writing

---

[100] Whitehead, *Adventures of Ideas*, 256.
[101] C. Brinton, *A History of Western Morals* (New York: Harcourt Brace), 73.

to survive the vicissitudes of time and preserved knowledge for thousands of years. Parchment was eventually replaced by paper in the Middle Ages.

After the sudden death of Alexander in Babylon in 323, all his ambitious plans came to an end. There was infighting among his generals, and the empire was divided into various chiefdoms; the Ptolemys in Egypt became the torchbearers of Hellenistic civilization. During Hellenistic times, famous people continued to produce masterpieces of literature, philosophy, and art, and great progress was achieved in mathematics and physics.

Stoicism and Epicureanism were philosophies introduced in the beginning of the third century BC; they were not too different from the classic Socratic, Platonic, and Aristotelian philosophies.

Zeno (334–262 BC) of Citium introduced Stoicism. The Stoics, not unlike Plato, adopted the four cardinal virtues—prudence, courage, temperance, and justice—and believed in using reason, logos, meaning not only using logic but also understanding the processes of nature, the universal reason inherent in all things.

According to Erasmus, not unlike Socrates and Plato, the Stoics were the staunchest supporters of virtue and equated wisdom with virtue and foolishness with unhappiness. They formed a synthesis of Greek moral thought to explore most of humanity's moral issues, live well according to reason and virtue, and strive to be in harmony with nature and the divine order of the universe.

Gilbert Murray stated this on Zeno's stoic answer.

> Consider the judgments of history. Do you ever find that history praises a man because he was healthy, or long-lived, or because he enjoyed himself a great deal? History never thinks of such things; they are valueless and disappear from the world's memory. The thing that lives is a man's goodness, his great deeds, his virtue, or his heroism.[102]

The successors of Zeno of the Stoa or the so-called Stoic school were Cleanthes (264–232 BC) and Chryssippus (232–206 BC).

Epicurus (341–270 BC) was an atomic materialist following in the steps of Democritus; he introduced Epicurean philosophy. Even though he defined pleasure as the key to human happiness, his theory meant more the absence of pain in the body and of trouble in the soul. He set the spiritual joys higher than those of the body.

Stoicism and Epicureanism dominated philosophy during the Hellenistic period. According to W. K. C. Guthrie, Stoicism in particular dominated the scene; it could be called the representative philosophy of the Hellenistic as well as the Greco-Roman

---

[102] Gilbert Murray, "The Stoic Philosophy," Conway memorial lecture delivered at South Place Institute on March 16, 1915, Internet.

ages lasting to the fifth century AD. Two of the most influential figures of Stoicism, Epictetus and the Roman emperor Marcus Aurelius, appeared in the second century AD. They will be discussed in the next section covering the Roman period.

Edward Zeller summarized the development of Greek philosophy over the period from Epicureanism to the pre-Socratics.

> Boldly almost impetuously Greek philosophy had in 6th Century BC trod the way, which leads from myth to the Logos. Trusting in the power of the human mind, the great pre-Socratic Ionians, Plato and Aristotle built up their systems on a basis of science and superseded the mythical ideas. Socrates, the minor schools which took their rise from him and the Hellenistic philosophy of the Stoa and Epicureanism were all united in maintaining that ethical conduct of man depends on his knowledge.[103]

During this period, besides the Stoic and Epicurean philosophies was an explosion of scientific knowledge in Hellenistic Alexandria as well as in southern Italy and Sicily. According to Gillespie,

> Albert Einstein once remarked that there is no difficulty in understanding why Indian or China did not create science. The problem is rather why Europe did, for science is a most arduous and unlikely undertaking. The answer lies in Greece. Ultimately, science derives from the legacy of Greek philosophy. The Egyptians, it is true, developed surveying instruments and conducted certain surgical operations with notable finesse. The Babylonians disposed of numerical devices of great ingenuity for predicting the patterns if the planets. But no Oriental civilization graduated beyond technique or thaumaturgy to curiosity about things in general. Of all the triumphs of the speculative genius of Greece, the most unexpected, the most truly novel, was precisely its rational conception of the cosmos as an orderly whole working by laws discoverable in thought.[104]

Aristarchus of Samos (c. 310–230 BC) in 270 BC challenged Aristotle's teachings by placing the sun, not the earth, at the center of our planetary system as it is accepted today. He asserted that the planets, including the earth, revolved around the sun.

---

[103] Edward Zeller, *Outlines of the History of Greek Philosophy*, revised by Dr. Wilhelm Nestle, trans. L. R. Palmer (New York: Meridian Books, 1955), 336.

[104] C. Gillespie, *The Edge of Objectivity: An Essay in the History of Scientific Ideas* (Princeton, NJ: Princeton University Press, 1960), 9.

His astronomical ideas were rejected at the time in favor of the geocentric theories of Aristotle and later on by Claudius Ptolemy (c. AD 90–c. 168). At the time, people were unaware of gravity, the force that attracts and keeps everything on the ground; they could not believe the earth could be moving. They thought such movement would scatter all earthly items into space.

Aristarchus's idea was picked up by Copernicus and was reintroduced and adopted 1,900 years later after further studies and proofs provided by Galileo's telescopic studies. Copernicus was fully aware of Aristarchus's idea. Archimedes preserved it in the following letter.

> You (King Gelon) are aware the "universe" is the name given by most astronomers to the sphere, the center of which is the center of the Earth, while its radius is equal to the straight line between the center of the Sun and the center of the Earth. This is the common account as you have heard from astronomers. But Aristarchus has brought out a book consisting of certain hypotheses, wherein it appears, as a consequence of the assumptions made, that the universe is many times greater than the "universe" just mentioned. His hypotheses are that the fixed stars and the Sun remain unmoved, that the Earth revolves about the Sun on the circumference of a circle, the Sun lying in the middle of it the Floor, and that the sphere of the fixed stars, situated about the same center as the Sun, is so great that the circle in which he supposes the Earth to revolve bears such a proportion to the distance of the fixed stars as the center of the sphere bears to its surface.[105]

Eratosthenes (c. 276–194 BC) was a man of knowledge who became the chief librarian at the library of Alexandria. He was also an astronomer, geographer, and mathematician. His greatest achievement was calculating the circumference of the earth with great accuracy. He also calculated the tilt of the earth to a greater accuracy than Oenopides had done about 200 years earlier (c. 450 BC) from an estimate of 24 degrees to the accepted value of 23 degrees. Eratosthenes established the term *geography* still being used today. He created the first map of the world incorporating parallels and meridians based on the available geographical knowledge of the era. Anaximander created the first map in the sixth century BC.

Around 200 BC, Apollonius of Perge (262–190 BC) developed such a great description and analysis of the conic sections of the ellipse, parabola, and hyperbola that it still dazzles mathematicians in modern times.

Archimedes (287–212 BC), the father of the science of mechanics, was

---

[105] Timothy Ferris, *Coming of Age on the Milky Way* (William Morrow, 1988), 37, Wiki.

indisputably the greatest mathematician of antiquity and one of the greatest engineers of his time. He lived in Syracuse, the capital of a Greek colony in Sicily.

M. de Condorcet stated,

> Archimedes discovered the quadrature of the parabola, and measured the surface of the sphere ... in a word, that very calculus which the moderns, with more pride than justice, have termed the calculus of infinities. It was Archimedes who first determined the proportion of the diameter of a circle to its circumference ... He may, in some respect, be considered as the father of rational or theoretical mechanics. To him we are indebted for the theory of the lever, as well as the discovery of that principle of hydrostatics, that a body immersed in any fluid, loses a portion of its weight equal to the mass of fluid it has displaced.[106]

After he discovered the famous hydrostatic principle, he became so excited that he ran into the streets exclaiming the famous "Eureka!" (I found it!). Archimedes also made a careful calculation of π, which was improved by Apollonius of Perge.

Plutarch said of Archimedes,

> He possessed such a lofty spirit, so profound a soul, and such a wealth of scientific theory, that although his inventions had won for him a name and fame for superhuman sagacity, he would not consent to leave behind him any treatise on this subject, but regarding the work of an engineer and every art that ministers to the needs of life as ignoble and vulgar, he devoted his earnest efforts only to those studies the subtlety and charm of which are not affected by the claims of necessity. These studies, he thought, are not to be compared with any others; in them the subject matter vies with the demonstration, the former supplying grandeur and beauty, the latter precision and surpassing power. For it is not possible to find in geometry more profound and difficult questions treated in simpler and purer terms.[107]

Jean Le Rond d'Alembert (1717–1783), a French polymath, a man of the Enlightenment, and a coeditor of an encyclopedia, stated,

---

[106] M. de Condorcet, *The Progress of the Human Mind*, 1794.

[107] Plutarch, *Plutarch's Lives*, trans. Bernadotte Perrin (Cambridge, MA: Harvard University Press, 1917).

Of all the great men of antiquity, Archimedes is perhaps the one who most deserves to be placed beside Homer. I hope that this digression by a geometer who loves his art will be pardoned, and that he will not be accused of being an excessive enthusiast; and I return to my subject.[108]

Euclid (fl. 300 BC), a Greek mathematician from Alexandria, is often called the father of geometry. His *Elements* is one of the most influential works in the history of mathematics; it served as the main textbook for teaching geometry from the time of its publication until the late nineteenth or early twentieth century. In the *Elements*, Euclid deduced the principles of what is now called Euclidean geometry from a small set of axioms. Euclid also wrote works on perspective, conic sections, spherical geometry, and number theory.[109]

Hipparchus of Nicaea (c. 165–c. 127 BC) was probably the greatest of Greek astronomers.

He discovered the precession of the equinoxes; he catalogued 1000 stars and is considered the inventor of trigonometry … invented the mathematical vocabulary still used in modern times and marked off the planet's surface into 360 parts, which became the "degrees" of modern geographers.[110]

He was likely the inventor of the astrolabe. It was three centuries before Claudius Ptolemy's synthesis of astronomy would supersede the work of Hipparchus.[111]

Attic Greek, a dialect of the language, became the lingua franca in the eastern Mediterranean area and facilitated the spread of ideas and literature west as well to Rome.

If there is a moral to be drawn from the Hellenistic age, this surely is it: the essential condition of the common people … had changed little between the coming of Alexander and the death of Cleopatra; nor it would it, until the advent of the Industrial Revolution.[112]

This is because no scientific discovery or industrial discovery was introduced. The water mill and windmill, though they were invented before Christ, were introduced

---

[108] Jean Le Rond d'Alembert, *Preliminary Discourse to the Encyclopedia of Diderot*, 52, Internet.
[109] Wiki.
[110] D. Boorstin, *The Discoverers* (New York: Random House, 1983), 96–97.
[111] Wiki.
[112] P. Green, *The Hellenistic Age* (New York: Modern Library), 130.

in the Middle Ages on s large scale. Nonetheless, most people were not affected by the Industrial Revolution; they would have to wait until the middle of the twentieth century for that. And still, some parts of the world remain untouched by any modern conveniences.

The Old Testament was translated from Hebrew into *koine* Greek, a simpler form of the language, in Alexandria between about 280 and 130 BC. These translations, commissioned by Ptolemy Philadelphus, were called the Septuagint (Latin for seventy) for the seventy scholars participating in the translation. This Septuagint translation remains the basis of the Old Testament in the Eastern Orthodox Church.

ROMAN PERIOD: 31 BC—AD 476, FALL OF THE WESTERN ROMAN EMPIRE

The Romans expanded their territory and occupied mainland Greece in 146 BC and Sicily around 212 BC. They adopted Greek civilization in philosophy, art, and engineering. So strong and overwhelming was the Greek civilization's impact on the Romans that the famous poet Horace (65–8 BC) in Epist. 2.1.156 said, "Captive Greece took her savage conqueror captive."[113]

Along this line, John Lord stated, "Grecian artists have been the teachers of all nations and all ages in architecture, sculpture, and painting … Without the aid of Greece, Rome could never have reached the civilization to which she attained."[114] So great was the Greek influence on Rome that many Roman philosophers wrote in Greek.

Lucretius (c. 99–c. 55 BC) was a Roman poet and Epicurean philosopher. His only known work is the epic philosophical poem *De Rerum Natura* (On the Nature of Things) about the tenets and philosophy of Epicureanism and atomism. He eloquently described the ascent of man through the ages—an ancient description and yet so modern.

> Hence is our age unable to look back
> On what has gone before, except where reason
> Shows us a footprint.
> Sailings on the seas,
> Tillings of fields, walls, laws, and arms, and roads,
> Dress and the like, all prizes, all delights
> Of finer life, poems, pictures, chiseled shapes
> Of polished sculptures- all these arts were learned
> By practice and the mind's experience …

---

[113] https://en.wikiquote.org/wiki/Horace
[114] Lord, *Beacon Lights of History*, vol. 1, Internet.

Grow clear by intellect, till with their arts
They've now achieved the supreme pinnacle.[115]

Lucretius based Epicurean philosophy on happiness, untroubled serenity, calmness, knowledge, and freedom from passion, care, and danger in the following.

> It is comforting to watch someone else's hardship from land,
> when the wind churns the waves on the great sea.
> This is not because there is a special pleasure in any man's pain
> but because to know what suffering you are avoiding is a comfort.
> It is also pleasant to gaze upon the great contests of war
> spaced out over the field when you have no part of the danger.
> but nothing is sweeter than to hold fast well-fortified temples–
> the serene teachings prepared by wise men …
> Don't you hear nature's wish, the body to be free of pain,
> And the spirit enjoys happiness, far from care and fear![116]

Marcus Tullius Cicero (106–43 BC) was one of Rome's most famous statesmen, jurists, and orators. Cicero's writings were heavily influenced by the Greek Stoic leader Panaetius of Rhodes (c. 185–110 BC).[117] As a young man, Cicero traveled there to study. But Stoicism spread to southern Italy before Cicero's time.

Romans accepted Stoicism through Cicero's translations. Other philosophers, including Seneca, Epictetus, the emperor Marcus Aurelius, praised Stoicism as one of the highest goods and adopted Greek virtues. They wrote extensively on it and left us some of the most memorable literature produced on Stoic philosophy and virtues.

Cicero praised philosophy in his *Tusculan Disputations*.

> O Philosophy, thou guide of life! Thou discoverer of virtue and expeller of vices! what had not only I myself, but the whole life of man, been without you? To you it is that we owe the origin of cities; you it was who called together the dispersed race of men into social life; you united them together, first, by placing them near one another, then by marriages, and lastly, by the communication of speech and languages. You have been the inventress of laws; you have been our instructress in morals and discipline; to you we fly for refuge; from you we implore assistance; and as I formerly

[115] Lucretius, *De Rerum Natura*, William Ellery Leonard (E. P. Dutton, 1916), Perseus project, Internet.
[116] Lucretius, *De Rerum Natura*, 2.1–16
[117] Gordon H. Clark, *Selections from Hellenistic Philosophy* (New York: Appleton-Century-Crofts, 1940), 51.

submitted to you in a great degree, so now I surrender up myself entirely to you ... if what is honorable be the only good, it must follow that a happy life is the effect of virtue: so that if a happy life consists in virtue, nothing can be good but virtue.[118]

Intellectual historian Murray N. Rothbard

praised Cicero as the great transmitter of Stoic ideas from Greece to Rome. Stoic natural law doctrines heavily influenced the Roman jurists of the second and third centuries A.D., and thus helped shape the great structures of Roman law which became pervasive in Western civilization.[119]

Rome was one of the first large multinational, multicultural, and multiracial societies. In the *Aeneid*, Virgil stated the rules of governing: "Remember, O Roman, to rule the peoples with power. These will be your arts: to impose the habit of peace, to spare the conquered and to cast down the proud."[120]

In term of human progress, law was the Romans' major achievement. In terms of science, they excelled at engineering. Romans introduced the arch and mastered road, aqueduct, and bridge construction, and they built many palaces, mausoleums, and the Coliseum and the Pantheon in Rome with its famous dome, a marvel of engineering. The Romans were great in the organization of armies. They had to fight the numerous hordes of barbarians, including Carthaginians under their leader, Hannibal, Celts, Vandals, Visigoths, Ostrogoths, Greeks, Egyptians, and others.

Seneca (c. 4 BC–AD 65), a Roman statesman, expressed the definition of the happy life based on Stoic ideals.

What is the happy life? It is peace of mind, and lasting tranquility. This will be yours if you possess greatness of soul; it will be yours if you possess the steadfastness that resolutely clings to a good judgment just reached. How does a man reach this condition? By gaining a complete view of truth, by maintaining, in all that he does, order, measure, fitness, and a will that is inoffensive and kindly, that is intent upon reason and never departs therefrom, that commands at the same time love and admiration. In short, to

---

[118] Cicero, *Tusculan Disputations*, VIII. A., Internet
[119] J. Powell, *The Triumph of Liberty: A 2,000 Year History Told through the Lives of Freedom's Greatest Champions* (Free Press, 2000).
[120] J. Burckhardt, *On History and Historians* (New York: Harper Torchbooks, 1958), 12.

give you the principle in brief compass, the wise man's soul ought to be such as would be proper for a god.[121]

Vitruvius (c. 80/70–c. 15 BC), a Roman author, engineer, and architect, produced a multivolume treatise on architecture and on all aspects of engineering including the first description of a water mill.

Plotinus (c. AD 204/5– 270), a Greek, invented Neoplatonism as defined by historians of the nineteenth century. His student Porphyry wrote his major opus, the *Enneads.* Having at his disposal all Greek philosophies from the past eight centuries, Plotinus created Neoplatonism as the culmination of all Greek philosophy.

Plato's and Plotinus's writings greatly influenced St. Augustine and Christian theology. St. Augustine combined Neoplatonism and Christianity in many philosophical themes; he wrote, "Plato made me to know the true God. Jesus Christ showed me the way to Him."[122]

The discovery of Cicero's writings encouraged people to pursue wisdom and had a significant effect on Augustine. John Lord stated,

> The Greeks themselves, after Grecian liberties were swept away and Greek cities became a part of the Roman Empire. The Romans learned what the Greeks created and taught; and philosophy, as well as art, became identified with the civilization which extended from the Rhine and the Po to the Nile and the Tigris.[123]

Burckhardt provided a short history of the Roman Empire.

> Rome shook the Gauls and the Etruscans, subdued the Samnites, and made its presence felt in lower Italy. Then the highest representative of the Diadochian warlords appears, Pyrrhus, and Rome is victorious and loses its fear of elephants. Then Rome wages its first war with Carthage for hegemony over Sicily ... Rome displays its initial veneration of Hellenism, considering itself the preserver and protector of the Greek tradition; the age-old Greek spirit stirs within the Romans. Rome Hellenizes itself, primarily under the leadership of Titus Quinctius Flamininus and the Scipios, who, for their part, had enforced Rome's political and military power in Greece ...

---

[121] Seneca, *Moral letters to Lucilius/Letter 92.3 On the happy life,* Internet.

[122] B. F. Cocker, *Christianity and Greek Philosophy,* Internet, 495.

[123] Lord, *Beacon Lights of History,* vol. 1, 184.

Just as Rome had once made Hellenistic culture its own and thus enabled Hellenism to live on for all time (and on this depended all knowledge and understanding of the Orient), Christianity now took over the Greco-Roman heritage, to salvage it beyond the time of the Germanic invasion.[124]

Burckhardt remarked on the first two centuries of the Roman Empire.

The confluence of the ancient lands of Greek civilization with Italy, Africa, and the West into one world empire is no mere accretion of flotsam. Its significance does not lie in its size, but in the fact that it benefited so many peoples, stopped the wars among the nations, and let the ancient world come to about as favorable an end as was possible … The character of the second century is determined by the Antonines … two great rulers and then two wholly virtuous ones, of whom Marcus Aurelius quite obviously seeks to tower above his enormous imperial office through his Stoic personality.

The influence of the Stoa makes itself felt among the jurists of the time and we get the beginnings of humane legislation; one direct consequence of this is that slaves are given some rights. But on the whole, "Roman law," for which Justinian's compilers were later given credit, is actually the work of the great emperors of the second century and the great jurists of the third.

To be sure, when Marcus Aurelius, who hated the amphitheater, sent the gladiators off to war against the Marcomanni, there was almost an uprising, as though the emperor wanted to force the people to philosophize.[125]

Besides Cicero and Seneca, two great Stoic philosophers flourished in the second century AD—Epictetus, a former slave, and Emperor Marcus Aurelius. Their extensive writings survived as eternal gifts to humanity.

Epictetus (AD 55–135) was a Stoic philosopher who flourished in the early second century AD, about four hundred years after the Stoic school was established in Athens. He lived and worked first as a student in Rome and then as a teacher with his own school in Nicopolis in Greece. Our knowledge of his philosophy comes to

[124] Burckhardt, *On History and Historians*, trans. Harry Zohn (New York: Harper & Row, 1965), 12–15.
[125] Ibid., 16–18.

us via two monumental works composed by his student Arrian, the *Discourses* and the *Handbook*, concentrating almost exclusively on ethics and emphasizing charity and humility.

Not unlike all other philosophers of the Hellenistic period, Epictetus considered moral philosophy's purpose as a guide for leading a better life. The aim was to live well and achieve happiness by learning to follow God and nature.

The numerous maxims of Epictetus are emphasizing virtues that lead to happiness. Here are some of his maxims.

> God is beneficial. Good is also beneficial. It should seem, then, that where the essence of God is, there too is the essence of good. What, then, is the essence of God? Flesh?—By no means. An estate? Fame?—by no means. Intelligence? Knowledge? Right reason?—Certainly. Here then, without more ado, seek the essence of good.

> The key is to keep company only with people who uplift you, whose presence calls forth your best.

> There is only one-way to happiness and that is to cease worrying about things that are beyond the power of our will ... The essence of philosophy is that a man should so live that his happiness shall depend as little as possible on external things ... Be careful to leave your sons well instructed rather than rich, for the hopes of the instructed are better than the wealth of the ignorant.

> If virtue promises happiness, prosperity and peace, then progress in virtue is progress in each of these for to whatever point the perfection of anything brings us, progress is always an approach toward it ... Ignorance, or lack of knowledge and instruction, is harmful in matters that are indispensable.[126]

Marcus Aurelius (AD 121–180) was chosen by Emperor Hadrian to succeed him, and he served as emperor of Rome from 161 to 180; he kept the empire safe from the Parthians and Germans. He was the last of the five good emperors; along with Epictetus, he is considered an important Stoic philosopher. Our knowledge of his philosophy comes to us via his *Meditations*, written in Greek; it is still revered as a great literary monument to a philosophy emphasizing service and moral duty.

The numerous aphorisms taken from his *Meditations* describe how to find and

---

[126] *Epictetus, The Stoic and Epicurean Philosophers, Discourses and Fragments*, ed. W. I. Oates (New York: Modern Library, 1957), 224.

preserve serenity in the middle of struggle and uncertainty by emphasizing nature and virtue as a source of guidance and inspiration. Marcus Aurelius emphasized moral contact, piety, universal brotherhood, rules for daily life, and law with justice. Listed below is a sample of his writings.

> The emperor selects justice as the virtue which is the basis of all the rest, and this had been said long before his time … Justice, or the giving to every man his due; fortitude, or the enduring of labor and pain; and temperance, which is moderation in all things … Some Greek poet long ago wrote: — "For virtue only of all human things takes her reward not from the hands of others. Virtue herself rewards the toils of virtue."

> The happiness of your life depends upon the quality of your thoughts: therefore, guard accordingly, and take care that you entertain no notions unsuitable to virtue and reasonable nature.

> If you find in human life anything better than justice, truth, temperance, fortitude, and, in a word, anything better than thy own mind's self-satisfaction in the things which it enables you to do according to right reason, and in the condition that is assigned to you without your own choice; if, I say, you seek anything better than this, turn to it with all your soul, and enjoy that which you have found to be the best.

> Keep thyself then simple, good, pure, serious, free from affectation, a friend of justice, a worshipper of the gods, kind, affectionate, strenuous in all proper acts. Strive to continue to be such as philosophy wished to make thee. Reverence the gods, and help men. Short is life. There is only one fruit of this terrene life, — a pious disposition and social acts.[127]

Matthew Arnold (1822–1888), an English poet, cultural critic, and sage, wrote an essay on Marcus Aurelius; while he discussed morality, he exalted Epictetus and Aurelius.

> A life without a purpose is a languid, drifting thing; Every day we ought to renew our purpose, saying to ourselves: This day let

---

[127] Marcus Aurelius, *The Thoughts of Marcus Aurelius*, trans. George Long, Internet.

us make a sound beginning, for what we have done previously is nothing; Our improvement is in proportion to our purpose.[128]

I have said that it is by its accent of emotion that the morality of Marcus Aurelius acquires a special character, and reminds one of Christian morality. The sentences of Seneca are stimulating to the intellect; the sentences of Epictetus are fortifying to the character; the sentences of Marcus Aurelius find their way to the soul.[129]

Marcus Aurelius summed up life: "The good life can be achieved to perfection by any soul capable of showing indifference to the things that are themselves indifferent."[130]

Christianity

Christianity has had immense influence on the history of humanity and especially on Western civilization. Today, Christianity counts the most followers of any religion. It withstood persecutions primarily in its first three centuries until Constantine the Great (c. 272–337) proclaimed the Edict of Milan that decreed tolerance for Christianity in the empire.

According to Whitehead,

Christianity rapidly assimilated the Platonic doctrine of the human soul. The philosophy and the religion were very congenial to each other in their respective teachings; although as was natural the religious version was much more specialized than the philosophic version … the fortunate coalescence of the initial Christian institutions with its philosophic Platonic doctrines provided the Western Races with a beautiful sociological ideal, intellectually expressed and closely allied with intermittent bursts of emotional energy.[131]

In his *History of Western Philosophy*, Bertrand Russel stated,

To the Christian, the Other World was the Kingdom of Heaven, to be enjoyed after death; to the Platonist, it was the eternal world of ideas, the real world as opposed to that of illusory

---

[128] Matthew Arnold, *Selections from the Prose Works of Matthew Arnold*, Internet.
[129] Ibid.
[130] John Passmore, *The Perfectibility of Man* (New York: Scribners, 1970), 55.
[131] Whitehead, *Adventures of Ideas*, 25.

appearance. Christian theologians combined these points of view, and embodied much of the philosophy of Plotinus ... Plotinus, accordingly, is historically important as an influence in molding the Christianity of the middle Ages and of theology.[132]

Platonism and Neoplatonism influenced St. Augustine. Edmond Pressensé (1824–1891) described the influence of Greek philosophy on Christianity.

If we regard this sublime philosophy as a preparation for Christianity instead of seeking in it a substitute for the Gospel, we shall not need to overstate its grandeur in order to estimate its real value ... Men like Socrates and Plato fulfilled amongst their people a really sublime mission. They were to the pagan world the great prophets of the human conscience, which woke up at their call. And the awakening of the moral sense was at once the glory and ruin of their philosophy; for conscience, once roused, could only be satisfied by One greater than they, and must necessarily reject all systems which proved themselves impotent to realize the moral ideal which they had evoked.[133]

Eduard Zeller added,

The whole attitude of mind on which Neo-Platonism rests is at bottom the same as that of its youthful and vigorous opponent, the Christian religion, which explains why it could offer no successful resistance to the latter. Nevertheless, the victory of the new religion was by no means complete; many ideas of the ancient wisdom of Greek philosophy passed into the speculative theology of the Christian faith and lived on in the dogmatism of the church.[134]

According to St. Justin, the philosophers had profited from the activity of the divine Logos, Jesus Christ.

The seed of the Logos planted in man's mind from the beginning, was the true source of philosophical truth. Between Philosophy then

[132] Bertrand Russell, *A History of Western Philosophy* (Simon and Schuster, 1945), 284–85.
[133] Edmond de Pressensé, *The religions before Christ, being an introduction to the history of the first three centuries of the Church*, Internet.
[134] Edward Zeller, *Outlines of the History of Greek Philosophy*, trans. L. R. Palmer (New York: Meridian Books, 1955), 286.

and Christianity there could not be any real and final opposition. All who have lived according to that light are Christians, Socrates, and Heraclitus, as truly as Abraham. Christianity, is the fulfilment of Philosophy, Jesus Christ of Socrates![135]

As discussed earlier, Heraclitus was the first to introduce the concept of Logos. Werner Jaeger stated, "Among the factors that determined the final form of the Christian tradition Greek civilization exercised a profound influence on the Christian mind."[136] Jaeger quoted historian Johann Gustav Droysen, who asserted,

> Without the post classical evolution of Greek culture the rise of a Christian-speaking world would have been impossible. Of course, this Christianization of the Greek-speaking world within the Roman Empire was by no means one sided, for at the same time it meant the Hellenization of the Greek religion.[137]

Whitehead continued, "The progress of humanity can be defined as the process of transforming society to make the original Christian ideals increasingly predictable for its individual members."

Eventually, Christianity triumphed despite its numerous schisms. As Whitehead stated, "In the Western Roman Empire, the Christian Church, armed with Hellenic and Hellenistic thought, captured the interest and the victorious barbarians and civilized Western Europe up to the Arctic Ocean."[138]

Before the end of the first millennium, the Eastern Roman Empire, Byzantium, Christianized all the Slavic peoples occupying Eastern Europe from the steppes of Russia to Bulgaria and the rest of the Balkans.

We can see parallel and compatible Christian ethics expressed by Socrates to his pupil Crito.

> Then we must do no wrong ... we ought not to retaliate or render evil for evil to anyone, whatever evil we may have suffered from him ... this opinion has never been held, and never will be held, by any considerable number of persons.[139]

The above statement is not unlike Christ's teachings: "But I tell you not to

---

[135] P. Hughes, *A History of the Church* (Sheed & Ward, 1935), 102.

[136] W. Jaeger, *Early Christianity and Greek Paideia* (Cambridge, MA: Harvard University Press, Cambridge 196, 4.

[137] Ibid., 5.

[138] Whitehead, *Adventures of Ideas*, 125.

[139] Plato, *Crito*, 49b7-d3, trans. B. Jowett.

resist an evil person. But whoever slaps on your right cheek, turn the other one too" (Matthew 6:39)[140] and "Love your enemies, do good to those we hate you" (Luke 6:27).

Guthrie stated,

> The first men to set down the new Gospel in writing not in their own vernacular but in the language of Plato and Aristotle as it had now adopted itself to its function as the "lingua franca" of the greatly enlarged Hellenic world.[141]

After Christ's apostles in the first two centuries, the major influential theologians who played a major role in preaching, organizing, and defending the church against heresies were Clement of Alexandria and Origen. Thereafter, in the first five centuries since the founding of the church, the major advocates were St. Athanasius, St. Gregory of Nyssa with his brother St. Basil, St. Gregory Nazianzus, and St. John Chrysostom in the East and St. Ambrose and St. Jerome in the West.

St. Augustine (354–430) is considered one of the most important church fathers in Western Christianity for his extensive writings in the Patristic era. His most important works are the *City of God* and *Confessions*. Augustine's influence in the Catholic Church is considered to be second only to that of St. Paul.

Augustine said that reading Cicero brought him closer to God indirectly by putting him on the hunt for truth, wisdom, and philosophy. He wrote in his *Confessions*,

> My spirit was filled with an extraordinary desire for the eternal qualities of wisdom. … I was on fire then, my God, I was on fire to leave created things behind and fly back to you, nor did I know what you would do with me; for with you is wisdom. But that book filled me with Philosophy … I was urged on by a passionate zeal to love and seek and obtain and embrace and hold fast wisdom itself, whatever it might be.[142]

St. Augustine was very aware of humanity's technical progress through the ages while lacking ethical progress. He blamed humanity's miseries on its propensity to make inventions for the benefit and injury of others and not keeping his faith to God. He wrote in *The City of God*,

---

[140] http://biblehub.com/matthew/5-39.htm

[141] W. K. C. Guthrie, *A History of Greek Philosophy: The Earlier PreSocratic and the Pythagoreans*, vol. 1 (Cambridge University Press, 1977), 23.

[142] Augustine, *Confessions*, III, 8.

For over and above those arts which are called virtues, and which teach us how we may spend our life well, and attain to endless happiness,—arts which are given to the children of the promise and the kingdom by the sole grace of God which is in Christ,—has not the genius of man invented and applied countless astonishing arts, partly the result of necessity, partly the result of exuberant invention, so that this vigor of mind, which is so active in the discovery not merely of superfluous but even of dangerous and destructive things, betokens an inexhaustible wealth in the nature which can invent, learn, or employ such arts? What wonderful—one might say stupefying—advances have human industry made in the arts of weaving and building, of agriculture and navigation! With what endless variety are designs in pottery, painting, and sculpture produced, and with what skill executed! What wonderful spectacles are exhibited in the theatres, which those who have not seen them cannot credit! How skillful the contrivances for catching, killing, or taming wild beasts! And for the injury of men, also, how many kinds of poisons, weapons, engines of destruction, have been invented, while for the preservation or restoration of health the appliances and remedies are infinite! To provoke appetite and please the palate, what a variety of seasonings have been concocted![143]

The last Roman philosopher was Boethius (c. AD 480–524), who unlike most of his contemporaries, knew Greek as well as and Latin. Though he lived in the first quarter of the sixth century, I include him on this period as the last philosopher of antiquity. He was an adviser to the Roman emperor Theodoric and later director of the mint. He was influenced by Plato, Aristotle, and Plotinus and became famous for his masterpiece, *Consolation of Philosophy*, which is a dialog between himself and a female personification of philosophy. It became one of the most popular schoolbooks of the Middle Ages.

Commenting on true nobility, Boethius wrote,

All men are of one kindred stock, though scattered far and wide;
For one is Father of us all—one doth for all provide.
He gave the sun his golden beams, the moon her silver horn;
He set mankind upon the earth, as stars the heavens adorn …
Our hopes and prayers also are not fixed on God in vain, and when they are rightly directed cannot fail of effect. Therefore, withstand

---

[143] St. Augustine, *City of God*, trans. M. Dods (New York: Modern Library, 1950), 852.

vice, practice virtue, lift your souls to right hopes, offer humble prayers to Heaven.[144]

Henry Osborn Taylor wrote, "He is first off all a translator from Greek to Latin, and, secondly, a helpful commentator on the works which he translates."[145] Cassiodorus, Theodoric's secretary of state, applauded the twenty-five-year-old Boethius.

> In your translations, Pythagoras the musician, Ptolemy the astronomer, Nichomachus the arithmetician, Euclid the geometer are read by Italians, while Plato the theologian and Aristotle the logician dispute in Roman voice; and you have given back the mechanician Archimedes in Latin to the Sicilians.[146]

Boethius had a major impact on the educational system prevailing in the West.

> Boethius invented the name quadrividium, which was the upper division of education in the liberal arts and included the mathematical disciplines of astronomy, arithmetic, geometry and music. Educationally, the trivium and the quadrivium comprised the curriculum of the seven liberal arts, imparted to the students of the Middle Ages from the Classical antiquity.[147]

According to Winks,

> Theodoric imprisoned Boethius on a charge of treason. After a year in jail, Boethius was executed, perhaps because he was sharply opposed to the Arian Christianity practiced by Theodoric and the Ostrogoths.[148]

Boethius is recognized as a martyr of the Catholic faith. With his death, philosophy and the arts with a few minor exceptions came to an end. The Roman West and East fell into an intellectual recession until the glory of the ancients was rediscovered and rekindled during the Renaissance.

In the meantime, some interesting events from environmental history were starting to take place and continued all the way through the Middle Ages.

---

[144] Boethius, *The Consolation of Philosophy*, 3, song 4, Gutenberg Book, Internet.
[145] Henry Osborn Taylor, *The Mediaeval Mind*, Internet.
[146] Ibid.
[147] D. Boorstin, *The Creators* (New York: Random House, 1992), 234.
[148] R. Winks, *A History of Civilization* (New Jersey: Prentice Hall, 1996), 108.

One of the early Church Fathers, Tertullian (c. A.D. 160 - 240), commented on the effects of human enterprise on the earth: "Farms have replaced wastelands, cultivated land has subdued the forests, cattle have put to flight the wild beast, barren lands have become fertile, rocks have become soil, swamps have been drained, and the number of cities exceeds the number of poor huts found in former times … Everywhere there are people, communities - everywhere there is human life!" To such a point that "the world is full. The elements scarcely suffice us. Our needs press … Pestilence, famine, wars, earthquakes, are intended, indeed, as remedies, as prunings, against the growth of the human race."[149]

In AD 410, the Visigoths led by Alaric sacked Rome. This was according to Ammianus Marcellinus, "the most disastrous defeat encountered by the Romans since Cannae." They pillaged and destroyed the city. The Vandals repeated this again in 455, and the Visigoth Odoacer deposed the last emperor, Romulus Augustulus, in 476. That was the end of the Roman Empire in the West.

Constantine the Great (c. AD 272–337), also known as Constantine I and St. Constantine, founded a new capital in the ancient Greek city of Byzantium, later named Constantinople in 324 and dedicated in 330 as the capital of the Eastern Roman Empire. The Eastern Roman Empire endured another 1,100 years till its capture by the Turks in 1453.

In the years that followed, besides the Goths, other tribes—Alans, Burgundians, Thuringinans, Huns, Frisians, Gepidae, Suevi, Alemanni, Angles, Saxons, Jutes, Lombards, Heruli, Quadi, and Magyars among them—settled all over Europe from the Don River all the way to the Atlantic Ocean. They ravaged settled lands, and civilization was practically gone.

About four hundred years later, a wave of Vikings descended on northern Europe, particularly in northern France and England, with the same results. Pillage and destruction were followed by famines, and eventually, the Black Death followed. As Gibbons stated, "The Roman world, was overwhelmed by a deluge of barbarians."

The Roman Empire was thus shattered into fragments, and all these barbarians with their conquests formed the British, Spanish, Portuguese, French, Dutch, German, and Italian Empires. All these new empires inherited the lasting influence of culture—the Latin and Greek languages, religion, philosophy, law, forms of government, arts, and inventions.

These nations were spread worldwide with farther conquests a thousand years later from Africa to North and South America and Australia and played a significant role in the development of the modern world.

The Roman Empire, which was among the most powerful economic, cultural,

---

[149] Ibid., 6.

political, and military forces in the world at its time, fell apart. At its peak under Emperor Trajan, it was the largest empire of the classical antiquity period and one of the largest empires in world history. Throughout the European medieval period, attempts were made to establish successors to the Roman Empire, but what came out of it were the modern European countries, which inherited ancient Greek and Roman culture.

MEDIEVAL PERIOD: 476—1320, DAWN OF THE RENAISSANCE

This period covers the time from the fall of the Western Roman Empire to the northern tribes to the dawn of the Renaissance.

The term *Middle Ages* was first used by Burckhardt in 1882 as an homage to antiquity; it means the middle period between antiquity and the Renaissance.[150]

In his famous *The History of the Decline and Fall of the Roman Empire*, Edward Gibbons (1737–1794) described medieval society as "the triumph of barbarism and religion" based on the time when numerous tribes were invading what had been Roman territory and the control of religion on its people.

Whitehead assessed the Western Empire in this period.

> The real failure consists in the fact that in the year AD 600, Western Europe was less civilized than in the year AD 100, and was further behind the Eastern Mediterranean during the third and fourth centuries before Christ. Pope Gregory the Great would have been poor company for Sophocles, Aristotle, Eratosthenes, or Archimedes. Gregory was the man of his time. But the delicacies of the civilization-in art, or in the thought, or in human behavior-were then at a discount.[151]

Thinkers of the European enlightenment looked back to this period and called this period the Dark Ages; however, historians in the past century looked at this period more kindly. Whitney stated,

> A misconception of the Middle Ages was that it was a time of no learning or creativity – a dark ages. However, over the past forty years, historians have increasingly recognized that technological development "took off" in the medieval and early modern West ... The "dry" compass, mechanical clock, firearms, all medieval inventions ... More mundane inventions including

---

[150] J. Burckhardt, *On History and Historians* (New York: Harper Torchbooks, 1958), 25.
[151] Whitehead, *Adventures of Ideas*, 100.

new agricultural methods, the wheelbarrow, the spinning wheel, the chimney, and eye glasses, had significant and long-lasting effects on European society. Medieval people also adapted older technologies, such as the watermill and windmill, the stirrup, and gunpowder, to new uses.[152]

Burckhardt remarked,

> After a dreadful period of decline, Romanism lives on partly as the Byzantine state, partly as the Western church; gradually it gathers all heathen and Arian Germani into its fold, and from night springs the new day of the Middle Ages which finds its spiritual unity in Rome.[153]

While the Roman Empire was coping with the newly arrived barbarian conquerors, St. Benedict (480–543) introduced the famous rules governing monastic life that are still in effect today. He wanted monasteries to be self-sufficient and the monks not be bored and be of high intellectual level. His mottoes were "Pray, Work and Read" and "Idleness is an enemy of the soul." The monasteries became the depositories of knowledge of antiquity and were famous for their *scriptoria* that copied and preserved ancient books.

The Eastern Roman Empire, the Byzantine Empire with its capital in Constantinople, flowered in the sixth century. Under Emperor Justinian, the Church of Saint Sophia was completed in 537; its dome and that of the Pantheon in Rome are the largest surviving from antiquity, and Saint Sophia contains the largest vaulted space of any building before modern times. No equivalent building with such dome was built until Santa Maria del Fiori in Florence and Saint Peter's in Rome in the sixteenth century. The Byzantines recovered Ravenna temporarily and built the Church of Saint Apollinaris with beautiful mosaics that have not been rivaled.

Another of Justinian's major accomplishments was the *Corpus Juris Civilis* (Body of Civil Law). It was translated into many languages and had no effective competition for the next 1,300 years. It had a major influence on public international law, and it is considered the foundation of the Western legal tradition. The Roman Empire of the West, as D. Boorstin said, survived in Justinian's Byzantine legal incarnation. Justinian's downside was the shutting down of Plato's academy in Athens in 529 after nine centuries of operation.

After Justinian's death, the empire started its long decline. The empire had to fight Avars, Arabs, and the Turks, an Altaic-Mongol tribe that appeared in Asia Minor in the eleventh century. During the seventh century, besides having to oppose

---

[152] Elspeth Whitney, *Medieval Science and Technology* (London: Greenwood Press, 2004), 111.
[153] Burckhardt, *On History and Historians*, 15.

external enemies, they had to put up with internal religious dissentions that sapped their energy and weakened their state.

Muhammad (c. 570–632) started the Muslim religion in Arabia in the first quarter of the seventh century. The Muslims had a religious split around the middle of the seventh century that continues to modern times. It has led to sectarian violence and has involved outside powers. The recent wars in the Middle East were fought primarily along religious lines and some ethnic lines as well. Once a split takes place along racial, ethnic, or religious lines, the curse of permanent animosity and hate descends on the minds of people and makes reconciliation impossible. All the ugly instincts of humanity surface like frozen seeds that sprout and create deleterious hate that is transmitted to their descendants for ages.

Within a hundred years of Muhammad's death, the Muslims captured the Middle East and Persia, moved West, captured all northern Africa, and crossed the straits of Gibraltar to capture the Iberian Peninsula. In the famous Battle of Poitiers near Tours, the Frankish ruler Charles Martel halted the Muslim advance into Europe, defeated them, and pushed them back to Spain in 732. The Muslim religion had spread from Spain to the borders of India and China.

Many historians, including Sir Edward Creasy, believe that had Charles Martel failed at Poitiers, Islam would probably have overrun Gaul and perhaps the rest of Western Europe. Gibbon made clear his belief that the Umayyad armies would have conquered from Japan to the Rhine and even England in spite of the English Channel. Creasy said,

> The great victory won by Charles Martel … gave a decisive check to the career of Arab conquest in Western Europe, rescued Christendom from Islam, and preserved the relics of ancient and the germs of modern civilization.[154]

The Arabs brought their cultural and scientific knowledge to Europe, which was valuable during medieval times.

Starting with the crowning of Charlemagne in 800 at St. Peter's and continuing to about 1000, a mini Renaissance was started in the great Holy Roman Empire that lasted about two centuries.

During the eighteenth and nineteenth centuries, the eastern Slavic European countries including Russia were Christianized by Byzantium's Greek Orthodox Church. The Eastern Empire got into a power struggle with the Western Catholic Church; they were entangled in minor religious dogmatic differences that culminated in the great schism of 1054. In Constantinople, Eastern and Western church officials excommunicated each other, and there has been no communion among them since. The schism had dramatic and catastrophic results for Christianity as a whole. D.

---

[154] Wikipedia

Geanakoplos, "One of the great tragedies of the medieval world some of which is still with us, was the increasing sharp division of Christendom into two disparate and ultimately hostile worlds, the Byzantine East and the Latin West."[155]

Though the separation was peaceful, in 1204, the Christian knights of the Fourth Crusade set off from Venice ostensibly to liberate the Holy Land, but they captured Constantinople, pillaged it, and kept it under their control until 1262. The city never recovered; it succumbed to the Turks in 1453. After more than a thousand years of civilization and Greek culture, the city of Constantine became the capital of the Turks.

During the medieval period, in terms of literature, the major works produced were rather insignificant in the Eastern and Western Empires.

In the East, Procopius of Caesarea (c. 500–c. 560) was a prominent scholar considered to be the last major historian of the ancient world. Accompanying the Byzantine general Belisarius in the wars of the Emperor Justinian, he became the principal historian of the sixth century with his *The Wars of Justinian*, the *Buildings of Justinian*, and his celebrated *Secret History* of Justinian's wife, Empress Theodora.

Peter Abelard (1079–1142) was a medieval French scholastic philosopher, theologian, logician, and composer. His affair with and love for Heloise is legendary.

Thomas Aquinas (1225–1274) was the dominant thinker of the Middle Ages. He reconciled the philosophy of Aristotle with the truth of Christian revelation or faith and reason. Through his writings, Aquinas provided a solid bridge between antiquity and Christianity. Aquinas considered Aristotle's works second only to the Bible and provided a detail explanation of the seven virtues. Platonism was hardly known in the West then; his books were not available until the fifteenth century.

Roger Bacon (c. 1214–1292) was an English philosopher and Franciscan friar who placed considerable emphasis on the study of nature through empirical methods.

In terms of major architectural monuments, except for Saint Sophia, Saint Apollinaris in Ravenna, and a copy of it built in Aachen, Germany, no other magnificent buildings were constructed until 1000.

During the so-called Romanesque period (1000–1140) as the art historians call it, the great Romanesque cathedrals were built including those in Mainz, Worms, Speyer, and Maria Laach in Germany. Among other monastery complexes are those of Cluny in France and the pilgrimage church in Santiago de Compostela in northwestern Spain. They are characterized by their large size, thick walls, small windows, and barrel domes.

From the year 1140 on and with the building of the first major Gothic cathedral of Saint Denis in a suburb of Paris, the Romanesque art period was succeeded by the Gothic period. Gothic architecture flourished in Western Europe for more than two centuries. The cathedrals were larger and higher and were characterized by spires, towers, and ornate facades. They included numerous large stained glass and luminous

---

[155] D. Geanakoplos, *Byzantine East and Latin West* (New York: Barnes and Noble, 1966), 1.

windows, rib vaults, and flying buttresses to support the weight of the roofs on the walls because of the walls' structural weakness due to the large windows.

Great Gothic-style cathedrals constituted an ornament and adornment for their cities, and many are still being used for service. Some of the most famous are Notre Dame in Paris, Reims, Laon, Amiens, Beauvais, Chartres, Bourges, Strasbourg, Seville, Milan, Cologne, Salisbury, Westminster Abbey, Canterbury, Saint Vitus in Prague, Saint Stephens in Vienna, and many others.

Besides the Romanesque and Gothic cathedrals, the major engineering achievements during this period were improved horse harnesses with padded horse collar for pulling plows and carts, improved metal plows, and improved water mills.[156]

The Chinese were also inventors, but because of their remoteness and their self-imposed control, they kept their creations secrets from the West but kept exporting the final products.

The Chinese developed certain science and engineering techniques independently; these include the kite, abacus, lacquer, hot-air balloons, archery, and seismographs. Among their large construction projects were irrigation systems and the Great Wall. In addition, they discovered acupuncture for anesthesia for operations and traditional plant and animal medicine.

A number of Chinese inventions had a great influence on the world. They discovered and cultivated tea, and discovered and developed the silk industry around the middle of the second millennium BC. The caravans on the Silk Road from China to Persia and on to Europe brought silk fabric around 106 BC. In the West, the Byzantines were the first to obtain silkworm eggs and develop sericulture in the sixth century AD. Sericulture was expanded in Italy on the eleventh century. While silk was invented in China, cotton was invented in India and linen was invented in Egypt.

The Chinese became very advanced in bronze casting as far back as the twelfth century BC and the Greeks in the fifth century BC. It was not until the Italian Renaissance that the ancient art of bronze casting was matched in Italy.

The Chinese invented papermaking from hemp and ramie (China grass), fibrous plants, and rags around the first century AD.

The Chinese developed porcelain starting in about the eighth century AD, but their best porcelain was made in the twelfth century. They developed great export businesses to the West especially after the great navigation routes opened. The Europeans did not invent hard porcelain until the Germans discovered the secret of doing so in Meissen in 1708 and thus broke the Chinese monopoly. Afterward, all major European countries developed porcelain industries.

Block printing was discovered in China in the ninth century AD. The Chinese

---

[156] Frances and Joseph Gies, *Cathedral, Forge, and Waterwheel* (New York: Harper Collins, 1994), 49.

discovered the compass in the eleventh century and gunpowder in the twelfth century.

With the Europeans living in the Middle Ages, where progress was stagnant, China was the most developed country in the world around AD 1200.

Derk Bodde (1909–2003) stated,

> How much poorer our Western civilization would be without the things that have just been described! Some, like playing cards, have afforded us untold amusement. Others, like porcelain, give us both efficient service and artistic pleasure. Still others have utterly changed our way of life and are basic to our whole modern civilization. Without paper and printing, for example, we should still be living in the Middle Ages. Without gunpowder, the world might have been spared much suffering … Nor would the building of the Panama Canal or of Boulder Dam have been possible! And finally, without the compass, the great age of discovery might never have come, with its quickening of European material and intellectual life, and its bringing to knowledge of worlds hitherto unknown, including our own country.[157]

Francis Bacon gave high marks to Chinese inventions.

> It is well to observe the force and virtue and consequence of discoveries … printing, gunpowder, and the magnet. For these three have changed the whole face and state of things throughout the world; the first in literature, the second in warfare, the third in navigation; whence have followed innumerable changes, insomuch that no empire, no sect, no star seems to have exerted greater power and influence in human affairs than these mechanical discoveries.[158]

Condorcet described medieval civilization.

> In the disastrous epoch at which we are now arrived, we shall see the human mind rapidly descending from the height to which it had raised itself, while Ignorance marches in triumph, carrying with her, in one place, barbarian ferocity; in another, a more refined and accomplished cruelty; everywhere, corruption and perfidy … Theological reveries, superstitious delusions, are

---

[157] Derk Bodde, *China's Gifts to the West* (Columbia University, 1942).
[158] Sir Francis Bacon, *Science Quotes*.

become the sole genius of man, religious intolerance his only morality; and Europe, crushed between sacerdotal tyranny and military despotism, awaits, in blood and in tears, the moment when the revival of light shall restore it to liberty, to humanity, and to virtue.[159]

Bertrand Russell wrote that there was an intellectual recession in the Middle Ages and that much knowledge possessed by the Greeks was forgotten.[160] Burckhardt had a kinder view of the medieval period.

It was possible to misjudge the Middle Ages, to be sure, but in the long run one could not despise the period. The realization prevailed that our existence had its roots in it, even though modern culture was derived predominantly from antiquity. Gradually the specific qualities of the Middle Ages were appreciated in innumerable ways ... There is an optical illusion with regard to so-called golden ages in which great spiritual capacities come together in a society, as though "happiness" had a definite address or domicile at some time or in some place ... in 1882, we have no business sitting in judgment on any past age—now when from every side there are complaints about, and threats against, our general situation as well as specific matters, and the nations are pitted one against the other, armed to the teeth.[161]

But let us close our eyes; experience teaches us that the human race has over the ages achieved very little of supreme excellence, and will do no better in the future; therefore, for the time being, we may well mourn when things of excellence are destroyed.

Our only consolation—and a very uncertain one—is this: the survival of the greatest works of antiquity, now lost, would have stood in the way of the newer literature and art and made their natural appearance or at least their independence impossible.[162]

The greatness of an epoch or a cause depends on the proportion of those capable of sacrifice, on whatever side it may be. In this

[159] M. de Condorcet, *Outlines of an Historical View*, 1796.
[160] Bertrand Russell, *The Expanding Mental Universe, Saturday Evening Post*, Adventures of the Mind (New York: Vintage Books, 1960), 296.
[161] Burckhardt, *On History and Historians*, 25.
[162] Ibid., 27–28.

respect, the Middle Ages pass muster rather well … Greatness is not dependent on mental superiority, for this can be paired with a wretched character. Greatness is the conjunction of a certain spirit with a certain will.[163]

Hobbes described medieval life as being

in such condition there is no place for industry, because the fruit thereof is uncertain, and consequently, not culture of the earth, no navigation, nor the use of commodities that may be imported by sea, no commodious building, no instruments of moving and removing such things as require much force, no knowledge of the face of the earth, no account of time, no arts, no letters, no society, and which is worst of all, continual fear and danger of violent death, and the life of man, solitary, poor, nasty, brutish, and short.[164]

Yet something great was about to take place: the Renaissance. No matter how we judge the level of the civilization of the Middle Ages, Whitehead stated,

At the close of the Dark Ages Europe started upon its second effort after civilization with three main advantages: its Christian ethics; its instinct for legal organization transcending local boundaries, derived from the church and the reminiscence of the Empire: and thirdly its wider inheritance of antecedent thought, gradually disclosing itself as Hebrew, Greek, and Roman literature. The total effect was the increased sense of man as man … This is the humanitarian spirit, gradually emerging in the slow of a thousand years.[165]

DAWN OF THE RENAISSANCE: 1320–1600, THE BEGINNING OF THE MODERN PERIOD

As discussed earlier, the first knowledge explosion took place in Greece between 600 and 323 BC. The second knowledge explosion started in Italy around 1320 and continues to this today. By the sixteenth century, it had spread to the rest

---

[163] Ibid., 33.
[164] Hobbes, *Leviathan*, XIII, 9.
[165] Whitehead, *Adventures of Ideas*, 103.

of Europe. The Renaissance was a cultural movement that profoundly affected European art, literature, philosophy, music, politics, science, religion, and other areas of intellectual inquiry. Renaissance scholars employed the humanistic method of study and searched for realism and human emotion in art. The invention of printing, the discovery of the New World, the rediscovery of the sun as being at the center of our solar system, and the Reformation shattered the established order and had great consequences for humanity.

The Renaissance signifies the rebirth of the classical period of the Greek and Roman ideas in all its intellectual activity. It started slowly but accelerated its progress; the accumulation of knowledge restarted, increased, and easily spread to the entire world with the exploration and discovery of new lands. People woke up from the lethargy of the Middle Ages, rediscovered their past, and built on it.

Art historians put the end of the Renaissance at around 1600, when modern times start and the Baroque period started for visual and performing arts.

The word *Renaissance* ("rebirth" in French) was first used by the French historian Jules Michelet (1798–1874) in his 1855 *History of France*. The consensus is that the Renaissance started in Florence and spread throughout Europe but not uniformly. The word *Renaissance* became widely used after Swiss historian Jacob Burckhardt (1818–1897) published *The Civilization of the Renaissance in Italy* in 1860. It was widely read, and it formed our modern view of the Renaissance.

The reasons for its origins were the political and social structures of Florence; the patronage of dominant, enlightened, and rich families; the fall of Constantinople in 1453 that generated a wave of immigration of Greek scholars bringing with them precious ancient Greek texts; and most important, the invention of printing, which brought the explosion of existing knowledge to a bigger section of the population.

In the revival of the Neoplatonist Renaissance, humanists did not reject Christianity; quite the contrary—many of the Renaissance's greatest works were devoted to it, and the church patronized many works of Renaissance art.

Historians of art and civilization cannot fix a date for the beginning of the Renaissance, but 1320 was the year that two major bursts of intellectual activity took place with Florence being the center of the Renaissance. Literary masterpieces were produced; a number of scholars instill the spirit of reawakening in their prominent works. Dante Alighieri (1265–1321) wrote the *Divine Comedy*, Giovanni Boccaccio (1313–1375) wrote the *Decameron*, and Petrarch (1304–1374) wrote a number of poems.

Second were the artistic and architectural triumphs starting with the paintings of Giotto (1267–1337) with his new style of painting that incorporated perspective in his creations including paintings in the Scroveni Chapel in Padua, the Maesta in the Florence Uffizi museum, and the bell tower of the Florence cathedral. Burckhardt set the date of the Renaissance from Giotto to Michelangelo.

The influence of Petrarch was profound; he was the acknowledged founder of the humanistic movement and the most prominent man of letters of the fourteenth century. As a theologian (he was a priest), he advanced the view held by many humanists who followed him that classical learning and Christian spirituality were mutually fulfilling as well as compatible. Petrarch helped reestablish the Socratic tradition in Europe by specifying self-knowledge as the primary goal of philosophy.

The history of the term *humanism* is complex but enlightening. It was first employed (as *humanismus*) by nineteenth-century German scholars to designate the Renaissance emphasis on classical studies in education.

Emmanuel Chrysoloras (1368–1415), a Byzantine teacher who lectured in Florence and Pavia, produced Latin translations of Plato and Aristotle that broke with medieval tradition by reproducing the sense of the Greek prose rather than following it word for word.

Besides the outstanding literature and art that set out the dawn of Renaissance, more artists, writers, scholars, philosophers, inventors, explorers, and theologians followed these forerunners in Italy but also throughout Europe. The list of these prominent artists, painters, sculptors, and architects is long: Fra Angelico, Masaccio, Fra Filippo Lippi, Botticelli, Ghirlandaio, Leonardo da Vinci, Michelangelo, Raphael, Andrea del Sarto, the Bellinis, Titian, Giorgione, Veronese, Donatello, Brunelleschi, Ghiberti, Alberti, and in the rest of Europe, the Van Eycks, Van Der Weyden, Memling, Brueghel, Rubens, Durer, Cranarch, and El Greco.

The list continues with philosophers, scholars, theologians, architects, inventors and explorers: Machiavelli, Marcilio Ficino, Pico Della Mirandola, Lorenzo Vala, Johannes Gutenberg, Erasmus, Martin Luther, Montaigne, Rabelais, Brunelleschi, Ghiberti, Copernicus, Columbus, Vasco da Gama, and Magellan.

During this period, poets and writers started using vernacular languages rather than the traditional Latin. Dante wrote the *Divine Comedy* in Italian, Geoffrey Chaucer (1340–1400) wrote the *Canterbury Tales* in English, Miguel de Cervantes (1647–1616) wrote *Don Quixote* in Spanish, and Francois Rabelais (1490–1553) wrote *Gargantua and Pantagruel* in French. Writing in the vernacular languages led to an increase of knowledge as few people could command Latin as well as they could their native languages.

The Flemish brothers Hubert and Jan van Eyck invented oil painting around 1420. Before that, paintings were done with tempera, which consisted of egg yolks as the carrier of the colors. Vasari said that this was "a most beautiful invention ... lit up the colors so powerfully that it gave a gloss of itself."[166] In addition, the use of oil-based paint was more convenient for painters, as oil dries slower than does egg yolk.

Falckenberg described the intellectual life of this period.

> Italy is the home of the Renaissance ... was nourished by the
> influx of Greek scholars, part of whom came in pursuance of an

---

[166] Giorgio Vasari, *Lives of the Artists*.

invitation to the Council of Ferrara and Florence 1438, called in behalf of the union of the Churches (among these were Pletho and his pupil Bessarion; Nicolas Cusanus was one of the legates invited), while part were fugitives from Constantinople after its capture by the Turks in 1453. The Platonic Academy, whose most celebrated member, Marsilius Ficinus, translated Plato and the Neoplatonists into Latin, was founded in 1440 on the suggestion of Georgios Gemistos Pletho … The writings of Pletho and of Ficinus show that the Platonism, which they favored, was colored by religious, mystical, and Neoplatonic elements.[167]

Before and after the fall of Constantinople in 1453, many Greeks, primarily men of letters from the Eastern Roman Empire, immigrated to northern Italy, where the Renaissance was flourishing. Constantinople's Greek traditions in language, art, and many other areas were imported by these scholars to Italy; they brought priceless copies of ancient Greek manuscripts including some by Plato, Aristotle, and others. Prior to that, *Timaeus* was the only work of Plato available in the West.

Interest in Greek literature was substantially increased by the availability in the West of the entire corpus of Plato brought by Giovanni Aurispa in the 1420s.[168] The works of Aristotle were available in the West during medieval times primarily from copies that were translated from the Greek to Arabic and back to Latin and Greek.

The transfer of these documents, the ancient depository of classical knowledge, was partially responsible for kindling the Renaissance. Schools were established to teach the classics in Italy, and the knowledge and the spirit of the ancients was revived. Thus, the West inherited the ancient classical heritage Byzantium had preserved for over eleven centuries.

Theodore Gaza (c. 1400–75) and Johannes Argyropoulos (1410–90) contributed major translations of Aristotle. John (originally Basil) Bessarion (1403–72), who became a cardinal in 1439, explored theology from a Platonic perspective and sought to resolve apparent conflicts between Platonic and Aristotelian philosophy; his large collection of Greek manuscripts, donated to the Venetian senate, became the core of the notable library of St. Mark.[169]

---

[167] Richard Falckenberg, *History of Modern Philosophy / From Nicolas of Cusa to the Present Time*, Internet.

[168] Encyclopedia.com, "Humanism in the Early Renaissance."

[169] *Encyclopedia Britannica*, "Humanism, 14th century."

Rousseau commented on the knowledge and thinking brought to Italy from Constantinople.

> The collapse of the throne of Constantine carried into Italy the debris of ancient Greece. France, in its turn, was enriched by these precious remnants. The sciences soon followed letters. To the art of writing was joined the art of thinking, a sequence which may seem strange but which is perhaps only too natural. And people began to feel the main advantage of busying themselves with the Muses, which is to make men more sociable.[170]

Printing

By pure coincidence, while the Renaissance was flourishing in southern Europe, a major invention took place in the north. Johannes Gutenberg (1395–1468), invented the moveable-type printing press in Mainz, Germany, in 1450. It is considered humanity's greatest invention of the last millennium and more likely of all times. It was to have a tremendous impact to the dissemination of knowledge. It reduced the costs of books while eliminating the errors and omissions caused by hand copying of texts. It remained as such with some minor improvements until 1990 and the invention of the Internet. Not to understate the value of books, the Internet made knowledge and the search for it much easier throughout the globe.

It took three inventions to make printing a success: block printing, page setting using multiple casts of the letters of the alphabet, and improvements in ink and paper. Woodblock printing is a technique for printing text, images, or patterns on textiles and later paper. "Movable type is the system of printing using movable pieces of metal type made by casting from matrices struck by letter punches. Movable type allowed for much more flexible processes than hand copying or block printing."[171] It was introduced in China around 1040, but the complexity and number of the language's characters made its implementation rather cumbersome.

The Arabs in Baghdad got the secret of paper making from the Chinese around AD 750. The West got the technology from the Arabs in Spain and set up the first paper mill in Italy in the twelfth century. Paper produced from rags was widely used in Europe after the first millennium. The Swedes discovered papermaking from wood pulp in the latter part of the nineteenth century. Before paper was invented, the media used for writing in the West were papyrus, invented in ancient Egypt; and parchment, invented in Pergamum in the second century BC.

Before the invention of printing, one person could copy about three pages a day; printing increased efficiency by more than a thousandfold. Alphabetic writing

---

[170] Jean-Jacques Rousseau, *Discourse on the Arts and Sciences*, Internet.
[171] https://en.wikipedia.org/wiki/Printing

proved again its ease of implementation for printing, and it was another key factor responsible for the knowledge explosion. The great dissemination of knowledge through the printed word was revolutionary. One wonders if the Reformation would have taken hold without printing.

And woodcut engraving added to the illustration of knowledge especially for the illiterate. Libraries were built with multiple copies of books as the cost of books was substantially reduced. The invention of printing had many implications for people's lives as well; literacy was substantially increased. As Condorcet stated,

> After the advent of printing … the transmission of written information became much more efficient. It was not only the craftsman outside universities who profited from the new opportunities to teach himself. Of equal importance was the chance extended to bright undergraduates to reach beyond their teachers' grasp. Gifted students no longer needed to sit at the feet of a given master to learn a language or academic skill.[172]

Eisenstein wrote on the implications of printing for humanity and the church.

> As communion with the Sunday paper has replaced church-going, there is a tendency to forget that sermons had at one time been coupled with news about local and foreign affairs, real estate transactions, and other mundane matters. After printing, however, news gathering and circulation were handled more efficiently under lay auspices … There is considerable irony about the enthusiastic reception accorded to printing by the church. Heralded on all sides as a "peaceful art," Gutenberg's invention probably contributed more to destroying Christian concord and inflaming religious warfare than the so-called arts of war ever did.[173]

Condorcet commented on the impact of printing.

> Had the art of printing been known, the sciences would have been able to preserve their ground; but the existing manuscripts of any particular book were few; and to procure works that might form the entire body of a science, required cares, and often journeys

---

[172] Marquis de Condorcet, *Sketch of a Historical Picture and the Progress of the Human Mind*, 1794, Internet.

[173] E. Eisenstein, *The Printing Press as an Agent of Change* (Cambridge: Cambridge University Press, 1979), 131, 176.

and an expense to which the rich only were competent. It was easy for the ruling party to suppress the appearance of books, which shocked its prejudices, or unmasked its impostures. An incursion of barbarians might, in one day, deprive forever a whole country of the means of knowledge. The destruction of a single manuscript was often an irreparable and universal loss.[174]

Printing provoked the worldwide dissemination of knowledge. No other invention has had more impact on history. Books were no longer in the hands of a few in monasteries and those who could afford them. In 1480, there were only three printing presses, but by 1500, there were more than 238.[175] In less than fifty years, all major European cities had printing presses, and knowledge spread rapidly.

The printing presses of Europe were on a roll. By the early sixteenth century, Venetian Aldus Manutius (1449–1515) had published all the Greek and Roman classics; after a thousand years, the West had rediscovered the wisdom of the ancients. This led to the writing of commentaries on the ancient manuscripts that dealt with history, philosophy, politics, law, and the whole ancient heritage. The Greek ideals of *paideia*, education and culture, and the Latin *humanitas*, first used by Cicero, inspired Renaissance scholars. This reawakening caused people to compare the scholasticism of the time to ancient ideals. They discovered the wisdom of the ancients, their virtues, and what they thought was the ideal life for humanity without dismissing the Bible.

The Renaissance prompted intellectual development; it and the Reformation, the Age of Enlightenment, and the scientific revolution laid the material basis for the modern, knowledge-based economy and the spread of learning to the masses.

Great universities were established all over Europe—from Aberdeen in Scotland and Uppsala in Sweden to Valencia in Spain, Frankfurt, and many other places in Europe.

Other Discoveries

In 1620, the English philosopher Francis Bacon wrote in his *Novum Organum*,

> Printing, gunpowder and the compass: These three have changed the whole face and state of things throughout the world; the first in literature, the second in warfare, the third in navigation; whence have followed innumerable changes, in so much that no

---

[174] M. de Condorcet, *Outlines of an Historical View*, 1796.
[175] D. Boorstin, *The Discoverers* (New York: Random House, 1983), 270.

empire, no sect, no star seems to have exerted greater power and influence in human affairs than these mechanical discoveries.[176]

The clock and the compass made navigation easier; that led to the discovery of previously unknown places and the pursuit of gold and glory.

During the later Renaissance and particularly in the sixteenth century, the arts had reached their zenith with the so-called High Renaissance. In addition to the invention of printing, three events were particularly earthshaking and had an unprecedented effect on humanity's understanding of the cosmos.

First, the age of exploration started; the earth was circumnavigated, the New World was discovered, and India was reached by mariners going around the Cape of Good Hope. Humanity's knowledge increased as new continents were discovered and first contact was made with more people and more plants and animals. Economic expansion started, and new places were settled.

Second, Nicholas Copernicus published his theory that Earth was not the center of our solar system; that had a major impact on knowledge, but it was not immediate. It was, however, the first step in understanding our planetary system that eventually led to space exploration.

Third, the Protestant Reformation took place and split the Catholic Church once more into the Protestant north and the Catholic south.

World Exploration

Christopher Columbus (1451–1506) discovered the New World in 1492 and opened the way to settling North and South America. The Spanish conquered and destroyed the Incan Empire in Peru and the Aztec Empire in Mexico and carried tons of gold back to Spain, making it the dominant nation in the sixteenth century. The Portuguese navigator Ferdinand Magellan (c. 1480–1520) set out to circumnavigate the globe from Spain in 1519 following a southern route; he sailed around Chile and reached the Philippines in 1521. Unfortunately, Magellan was killed in the Philippines in a fight with the natives, but one of his ships made it back to Portugal, the first to circumnavigate the world. It was followed by the circumnavigation of Africa and reaching India by the Portuguese explorers Bartolommeo Dias (c. 1450–1500) and Vasco da Gama (1462–1524). India was reached in 1497, and Australia was discovered in 1606. Thus, all the major earth's inhabited continents were discovered.

---

[176] Francis Bacon, *Quote, Novum Organum.*

High Renaissance

The Renaissance moved to its high point, called the High Renaissance, around the beginning of the sixteenth century with Leonardo da Vinci's, Michelangelo's, and Raphael's masterpieces that set new heights in painting, sculpture, and architecture. William Manchester stated, "Five centuries after Michelangelo, Raphael, Botticelli, and Titian, nothing matching their masterpieces can be found in contemporary galleries"[177]

No marble sculpture like Michelangelo's *David* and no bronze sculpture like Donatello's *David* had been produced since Greek antiquity. No dome like the one of the Santa Maria del Fiore in Florence was produced since those of the Pantheon in Rome in the first quarter of the second century AD and Saint Sophia in Constantinople. The Venetian painters Titian, Giorgione, Bellini(s), and Tiepolo produced excellent art along with others on the Italian peninsula.

The Renaissance spread to the rest of Europe, particularly the Low Countries, Germany, France, and Spain. Advanced trade and industry contributed much wealth to the city-states of Italy and subsequently to other cities in northern Europe. Cathedrals were built with icon paintings and statues for decoration and to promote belief.

Icon paintings were produced primarily for churches and affluent patrons. The majority of the themes of the painting were biblical, primarily those of the Virgin Mary and Christ on the cross, for the churches and from Greek and Roman mythology for other public buildings and palaces. In addition, many Christian works along with the Greek New Testament were brought to the West. The Protestant Reformation changed this in the northern countries as they stopped using icons in their churches.

The paintings produced in the Renaissance by artists such as Botticelli, Leonardo, Raphael, Michelangelo, Titian, and others remain unsurpassed five hundred years later. They are the rare masterpieces of today's museums and points of supreme admiration by the public.

Niccolò Machiavelli (1469–1527), a historian, politician, diplomat, philosopher, and humanist in Florence, published *Discourses* (c. 1514–19) followed by *The Prince* (1532); that was the first book on politics since Roman times. R. Falckenberg wrote, "Machiavelli was the first independent political philosopher of the modern period. Patriotism was the soul of his thinking, questions of practical politics its subject, and historical fact its basis."[178]

Baldassare Castiglione (1478–1529) of Urbino published *Courtier*, a book dealing with what constitutes a perfect courtier and a perfect lady in 1528.

---

[177] William Manchester, *A World Lit by Fire, The Medieval Mind and the Renaissance* (New York: Little, Brown), 87.

[178] Ibid.

Englishman Thomas More (1478–1535) wrote *Utopia* and lost his head due to the wrath of King Henry VIII because he did not approve his marriage to Anne Boleyn.

Erasmus of Rotterdam, one of the most famous Renaissance humanists, was a Catholic priest and a classical Platonist scholar. Erasmus's most important works are his *Enchiridion* or *Manual of the Christian Gentleman* and *The Praise of Folly*. In the *Manual*, he outlined the views of the normal Christian life and established himself as a Christian spokesman. Erasmus provided the best possible text of the New Testament translated from Greek to Latin. Both texts were widely circulated due to the use of printing. In his satirical *The Praise of Folly*, he mocked those who had an inflated sense of their importance, including merchants, philosophers, scientists, courtiers, clerics, and kings.

Erasmus believed that faith in God must always be combined with doing good works for others. According to H. Hyma,

> Erasmus said in many occasions that to imitate the life of Jesus was far more important than argue about dogma … Knowledge, or learning, fortifies the mind with salutary precepts and keeps virtue ever before us. These two are inseparable.[179]

We also see in Erasmus the fusing of the virtues of the ancients with Christianity. He admired Plato and quoted him extensively. He wrote,

> A sensible reading of the pagan poets and philosophers is a good preparation for the Christian life. We have the example of St. Basil who recommends the ancient poets for their natural goodness. Both St. Augustine and St. Jerome followed this method. St. Cyprian has worked wonders in adorning the Scriptures with the literary beauty of the ancients. … Of all philosophical writings, I would recommend the Platonists most highly. For not only their ideas but their very mode of expression approaches that of the Gospels.[180]

From his mouth came the ancient Greek maxim Know thyself. He wrote,

> The crown of wisdom is that you know yourself. … This then is the road to happiness: first, know yourself; do not let yourself to be led by the passions, but submit all things to the judgment of

---

[179] Erasmus, *The Essential Erasmus, The Handbook of the Militant Christian*, trans. J. Dolan (Mentor-Omega, 1964), 35.

[180] Ibid., 36.

the reason. Be sane and let reason be wise, that is, let it gaze upon decent things … Nothing is harder than for a man to conquer himself, but there is no greater reward or blessing … Assume a perfect life as your goal; having done so pursue it in a spirit of determination. The human mind has never strongly commanded itself to do anything it has failed to accomplish.[181]

People thought highly of their times as so many discoveries were happening compared to previous times. Erasmus, the most famous of all Christian humanists, wrote in 1517, "Immortal God, what a world I see dawning! Why can I not grow young again?"

[Erasmus] was surveying the European culture he knew so well and was full of hope for the future. By tragic irony, even as he wrote these words, a small storm was brewing in the remote university town of Wittenberg, which would in time obstruct and obscure everything Erasmus valued most. Even more confusingly, both Erasmus and Luther could be described as Christian humanists, sharing the excitement about the Bible.[182]

With the full swing of the Renaissance, people felt an optimism of their age. In 1472, the Florentine Benedetto Dei boasted of the prosperity, power, and riches of his city.

Our beautiful city Florence contains within the city two hundred seventy shops … We have … the trades of wool and silk … The number of banks amounts to thirty-three; the shops of cabinet-makers, whose business is carving and inlaid work, to eighty-four; and the workshops of the stone-cutters and marble workers in the city and its immediate neighborhood, to fifty-four. There are forty-four goldsmiths' and jewelers' shops, thirty gold-beaters, silver-wire-drawers, and a wax-figure maker … Another flourishing industry is the making of light and elegant gold and silver wreaths and garlands, which are worn by young maidens of high degree, and which have given their names to the artist family

---

[181] Ibid., 46–47.
[182] Lucy Wooding, *Christian Humanism from Renaissance to Reformation*, History Review 64 (September 2009).

of Ghirlandaio. Sixty-six is the number of the apothecaries' and grocer shops; seventy that of the butchers.[183]

In 1492, the Italian humanist Marsilio Ficino claimed the golden age after an age of darkness for his native city of Florence and exalted the times.

> What the poets once sung of the four ages, lead, iron, silver, and gold our Plato in the Republic transferred to the four talents of men ... If then we are to call any age to be golden, it is beyond doubt that age, which brings forth golden talents in different places ... For this century, like a golden age, has restored to light the liberal arts, which were almost extinct: grammar, poetry, rhetoric, painting, sculpture, architecture, music, ... and all this in Florence. Achieving what had been honored among the ancients, but almost forgotten since, the age has joined wisdom with eloquence, and prudence.[184]

In 1517, Erasmus wrote,

> I anticipate the near approach of a golden age, so clearly do we see the minds of princes, as if changed by inspiration, devoting all their energies to the pursuit of peace ... I am led to confident hope that not only morality and Christian piety, but also a genuine and purer literature, may come to renewed life or greater splendor ... I congratulate this our age, which bids fair to be an age of gold, if ever such there was![185]

In 1575, French humanist Loys le Roy wrote how the glory of the past had been recovered and people were living in a golden age.

> Now, just as the tartars, Turks, Mamelukes, and Persians have by their valor drawn to the East the glory of arms, so we have here in the West, have in the last two hundred years recovered

---

[183] *The Prosperity of Florence*, in *The Portable Renaissance Reader*, Ross–McLaughlin, ed. (New York: Viking Press, 1953), 166.

[184] M. Ficino, *The Golden Age of Florence*, in *The Portable Renaissance Reader*, Ross–McLaughlin, ed. (New York: Viking Press, 1953), 79.

[185] Erasmus, *Letter to Capito*, in *The Portable Renaissance Reader*, Ross–McLaughlin, ed. (New York: Viking Press, 1953) 81.

the excellence of good letters and brought back the study of the disciplines after they had long remained as if extinguished.[186]

Painter and art historian Giorgio Vasari wrote,

> For having seen in what way Art, from a small beginning, climbed to the greatest height, and how from a state so noble she fell into utter ruin, and that, in consequence, the nature of this art is similar to that of the others, which, like human bodies, have their birth, their growing old, and their death; they will now be able to recognize more easily the progress of her second birth and of that very perfection whereto she has risen again in our times.[187]

The Reformation

In 1517, an Augustinian Catholic priest and professor of theology, Martin Luther (1483–1546), unhappy with the abuses of the Roman Catholic Church, posted his Ninety-five Theses on the All Saints' Church in Wittenberg, Germany. The subject of indulgences of the church was his main dispute. The church was raising money by promising salvation to the givers. This started the Protestant Reformation, which led to his excommunication and produced a major split in Christianity and the rest of Western Europe.

The printing press helped spread his theses widely. The turmoil eventually spread to England and King Henry's dispute with the pope over the king's marriage. With this coincidence of history, England became Protestant as Henry VIII broke off from the Vatican. The church split caused hundreds of thousands of deaths, horrendous destruction, and a permanent division of the church between a Protestant north and a Catholic south.

Luther translated the Bible from Greek into German, making it more accessible; that had a tremendous impact on the church and German culture as it further fostered the development of a standard version of the German language. His hymns influenced the development of singing in churches.

The Reformation created an intellectual climate that made it possible to question the Roman Catholic Church's authority. This was a prelude to what was to follow—people started questioning any and all authority using their own reason to think and investigate.

---

[186] Le Roy, *The Excellence of this Age*, in *The Portable Renaissance Reader*, Ross–McLaughlin, ed. (New York: Viking Press, 1953), 91.
[187] Giorgio Vasari, *The Lives of the Most Excellent Painters, Sculptors, and Architects*, trans. Gaston du C. de Vere (Modern Library, 2006), 22.

The Heliocentric Solar System

In 1543, Nicholas Copernicus revived the heliocentric system first proposed by Aristarchus of Samos in the second century BC, and his famous *De Revolutionibus* was published after his death. He was concerned about publishing it before as the church considered this subject to be under its domain and control. The heliocentric system was ultimately accepted despite objections from the church and had a major influence on scientific thought. Galileo wrote about *De Revolutionibus*,

> Philosophy is written in this grand book, the universe, which stands continually open to our gaze. But the book cannot be understood unless one first learns to comprehend the language and read the letters in which it is composed. It is written in the language of mathematics, and its characters are triangles, circles, and other geometric figures without which it is humanly impossible to understand a single word of it; without these, one wanders about in a dark labyrinth.[188]

Continuing the steps of Copernicus, Giordano Bruno (1548–1600)

> completes the picture of the world by doing away with the motionless circle of fixed stars with which Copernicus, and even Kepler, had thought our solar system surrounded, and by opening up the view into the immeasurability of the world. [189]

For introducing all these revolutionary astronomical beliefs opposed by the Catholic Church, Bruno suffered the consequences; he was burned at the stake.

The heliocentric system was simplified in the following century by Brahe, Kepler, and Galileo. Johannes Kepler examined the observations made by Brahe and established that the orbits of the planets were not circular but elliptical. He described the planetary elliptical motions with greater accuracy with the so-called Kepler's laws. Galileo provided the observational proofs using a self-made telescope for the first time. Isaac Newton provided the theoretical explanation based on laws of gravitational attraction and dynamics in 1687.

But there were still unbelievers. The political thinker of the sixteenth century, Jean Bodin (1520–1596), expressed Aristotle's theory that supported the geocentric system.

---

[188] Galileo, *The Assayer, Discoveries and Opinions of Galileo*, trans. S. Drake (New York: Doubleday, 1957), 237–38.
[189] Ibid.

No one in his sense, or imbued with the slightest knowledge of physics, will ever think that the earth, heavy and unwieldy from its own weight and mass, staggers up and down around its own center and that of the sun; for at the slightest jar of the earth, we would see cities and fortresses, towns and mountains thrown down … For if the earth were to be moved, neither an arrow shot straight up, nor a stone dropped from the top of a tower would fall perpendicularly,[190]

Michel Eyquem de Montaigne (1533–1592) was one of the early and most influential writers of the French Renaissance known for popularizing the essay as a literary genre. His massive volume, *Essays* (1580), contains some of the most influential essays ever written. Montaigne had a direct influence on writers all over the world including Rene Descartes, Blaise Pascal, Jean-Jacques Rousseau, Friedrich Nietzsche, and possibly on the later works of William Shakespeare.

Falckenberg wrote of Montaigne,

The earliest and the most ingenious among the representatives of this philosophy of doubt was Michel de Montaigne, who in his Essays—which were the first of their kind and soon found an imitator in Bacon; they appeared in 1580 in two volumes, with an additional volume in 1588—combined delicate observation and keen thinking, boldness and prudence, elegance and solidity. The French honor him as one of their foremost writers. The most important among these treatises or essays is the "Apology for Raymond of Sabunde" with valuable excursuses on faith and knowledge. Montaigne bases his doubt on the diversity of individual views, each man's opinion differing from his fellow's, while truth must be one.[191]

By the end of this period, there were no more menacing external barbarian invasions in Europe, but there would be civil and religious wars and wars of liberations that continue to the present.

MODERN PERIOD: 1600–1900, MODERN TIMES

The three-hundred-year "modern" period is notable for the continuation of Renaissance ideas and progress, an increase of knowledge in all fields of philosophy,

---

[190] Falckenberg, *History of Modern Philosophy*.
[191] Ibid.

science, and the arts, and completion of the exploration of the earth. Technological achievements reached unprecedented heights in multiple areas. The two main achievements of this period were intellectual and technical—the Enlightenment, and the Scientific and Industrial Revolutions.

This period witnessed the acceptance of heliocentric theory, the identification of all the planets of our solar system, the Enlightenment, steam engines, the use of fossil fuels, thermodynamics, the automobile, electricity, indoor plumbing, definition of chemical elements, telescopes, and microscopes, Morse code, telephones, baroque music and architecture, drama, neoclassical architecture, classical music, impressionism, photography and sound recording, discovery of the electron, and many other advances.

According to Butterfield, the impetus that changed the natural sciences was the creation and use of scientific instruments.

> The telescope, the microscope, the thermometer and barometer, as well as the pendulum-clock made momentous discoveries the possibility of every experimental practitioner. No longer were scientists tied to the knowledge placed in their hands by the ancients. Scientists could now discover and demonstrate advances based on experimentation. In a comparison of Francis Bacon and Descartes, Butterfield examines the scientific methodologies that came to the forefront due to increased experimentation. Bacon advanced and glorified the inductive method, while Descartes came to be associated with the deductive method.[192]

Giants of philosophy, sciences, and the arts made enormous contributions to this unprecedented progress. The list includes many famous people such as Descartes, Spinoza, Kant, Hegel, Goethe, Shakespeare, Cervantes, Bacon, Locke, Berkeley, Hume, Bach, Beethoven, Mozart, Voltaire, Rousseau, Kepler, Galileo, Newton, Watt, Pascal, Pasteur, Lavoisier, Faraday, Maxwell, Bell, Thomson, Darwin, Dalton, Mendeleev, Victor Hugo, Dostoyevsky, Tolstoy, and Nietzsche.

Wars, revolutions, and wars of liberation caused great devastation due to the progress that had been made in weapons technology. Along with that came additional negatives: the exploitation of the earth's resources and misuse of science.

Falckenberg stated,

> In this speculative intercourse of nations, however, the French, the English, and the Germans are most involved, both as producers and consumers. France gives the initiative (in Descartes), and then

---

[192] Butterfield,   http://courses.unt.edu/rdecarvalho/h5040/StudentPapers/ Butterfield0,Herbert.htm.

England assumes the leadership (in Locke), with Leibnitz and Kant the hegemony passes over to Germany. Besides these powers, Italy takes an eager part in the production of philosophical ideas in the period of ferment before Descartes … the Socratic maxim, "I know that I am ignorant," should not lead to despairing resignation but to courageous further inquiry. The duty of speculation is to penetrate deeper and deeper into the secrets of the divine, even though the ultimate revelation will not be given us until the hereafter.[193]

Descartes (1596–1650) is considered the father of modern philosophy; he expressed his distrust of sensory experience and trusted reason for his existence and that of God. He obtained a clear and certain knowledge of mathematics and invented analytic geometry. The Cartesian coordinate system bears his name.

Descartes asserted that reason was the supreme human intellectual quality. He drew many followers in the modern era to his concept of rationalism.

J. B. Bury stated that Cartesianism

affirmed the two positive axioms of the supremacy of reason, and the invariability of the laws of nature; and its instrument was a new rigorous analytical method, which was applicable to history as well as to physical knowledge. The axioms had destructive corollaries. The immutability of the processes of nature collided with the theory of an active Providence. The supremacy of reason shook the thrones from which authority and tradition had tyrannized over the brains of men. Cartesianism was equivalent to a declaration of the Independence of Man. It was in the atmosphere of the Cartesian spirit that a theory of Progress was to take shape.[194]

Descartes helped prolong the Renaissance into modern times. The torch of knowledge was passed on to the many gifted intellectuals and geniuses who followed and expanded knowledge to our days.

Descartes separated sensory knowledge from mental capabilities.

Accordingly, six grades of mental function are to be distinguished: 1) The external senses, 2) The natural appetites, 3) The passions, 4)

---

[193] Falckenberg, *History of Modern Philosophy*.
[194] J. B. Bury, *The Idea of Progress: An inquiry into its origin and growth* (Echo Library, 2006), 36.

The imagination with its two divisions, passive memory and active phantasy, 5) The intellect or reason, 6) The will.[195]

Descartes was a real believer in God.

The idea of God as infinite, independent, omnipotent, omniscient, and creative substance, has not come to me through the senses, nor have I formed it myself. The power to conceive a being more perfect than myself, can have only come from someone who is more perfect in reality than I.[196]

Baruch Spinoza (1632–1677) was a Dutch philosopher and contemporary of Descartes. He was concerned about ethics; Falckenberg wrote,

Spinoza's ethics is intellectualistic—virtue is based on knowledge. [1] It is, moreover, naturalistic—morality is a necessary sequence from human nature; it is a physical product, not a product of freedom; for the acts of the will are determined by ideas, which in their turn are the effects of earlier causes. The foundation of virtue is the effort after self-preservation: How can a man desire to act rightly unless he desires to be (IV. prop. 21, 22)? Since reason never enjoins that which is contrary to nature, it of necessity requires every man to love himself, to seek that which is truly useful to him, and to desire all that makes him more perfect ... That virtue which springs from knowledge is alone genuine. The painful, hence inactive, emotions of pity and repentance may impel to actions whose accomplishment is better than their omission ... Whence the evil in the world? Vice is as truly an outcome of "nature" as virtue. Virtue is power, vice is weakness; the former is knowledge, the latter ignorance. Whence the powerless natures? Whence defective knowledge? Whence imperfection in general?[197]

On reason and God, Spinoza advised,

It is most profitable to us in life, to make perfect the intelligence or reason as far as possible ... and to perfect the intelligence is

---

[195] Falckenberg, *History of Modern Philosophy*, 105.
[196] Ibid.
[197] Ibid.

nothing but to understand God together with the attributes and actions of God, which follow from the necessity of his nature.[198]

Blaise Pascal (1623–1662) was a French polymath—a mathematician, physicist, inventor, Christian philosopher, and writer. He became famous for his mechanical calculator. Pascal's major work was in the fields of hydrodynamics and hydrostatics. His famous writings included *The Provincial Letters* and *Pensées* (Thoughts).

Pascal commented on science and ethics: "The vanity of the sciences- Physical science, will not console me for the ignorance of morality in the time of affliction. But the science of ethics will always console me for the ignorance of the physical sciences."[199]

In the modern era, science was about to make major steps. As Falckenberg stated,

> In no field has the modern period so completely broken with tradition as in physics. The correctness of the Copernican theory is proved by Kepler's laws of planetary movement, and Galileo's telescope observations; the scientific theory of motion is created by Galileo's laws of projectiles, falling bodies, and the pendulum; astronomy and mechanics form the entrance to exact physics— Descartes ventures an attempt at a comprehensive mechanical explanation of nature. And thus, an entirely new movement is at hand. Forerunners, it is true, had not been lacking. Roger Bacon had already sought to obtain an empirical knowledge of nature based upon mathematics; and the great painter Leonardo da Vinci had discovered the principles of mechanics, though without gaining much influence over the work of his contemporaries.[200]

John Kepler (1571–1630) first published his chief work, *The New Astronomy or Celestial Physics, in Commentaries on the Motions of Mars* in 1609 detailing the elliptical motions of the planets. Galileo put modern thinking into action—theory and experimental proof, a move from sense perception to memory, then to thinking, experimenting, and perceiving, and repeat the cycle. Galileo built the first telescope with which he proved the theories of Kepler, Copernicus, and ancient Aristarchus of Samos.

In 1642, the year Galileo died, Isaac Newton, the greatest scientist of all times, was born on Christmas Day. He was considered the greatest man of influence of the past millennium in the year 2000. He became famous for his magnum opus

---

[198] Spinoza, IV App. 4, 187.
[199] Blaise Pascal, *Pensées*, ebooks.
[200] Ibid., 169.

published in 1787, *Mathematical Principles of Natural Philosophy*, which laid the foundations for classical mechanics that includes the laws of motion and gravity.

Newton also made seminal contributions to optics with his publication in 1692 on the topic; he shares credit with Gottfried Leibnitz for the invention of calculus. Newton built the first reflecting telescope, and from his observations of a prism splitting white light into many colors of the visible spectrum, he developed a theory of color. His discovery and formulation of the fundamental force of gravity explained the harmony of the planets' orbits and the cosmos and removed the last doubts about the validity of the heliocentric system.

Newton's monument inscription in Westminster Abbey exalts his contributions.

> Here is buried Isaac Newton, Knight, who by a strength of mind almost divine, and mathematical principles peculiarly his own, explored the course and figures of the planets, the paths of comets, the tides of the sea, the dissimilarities in rays of light, and, what no other scholar has previously imagined, the properties of the colors thus produced. Diligent, sagacious and faithful, in his expositions of nature, antiquity and the holy Scriptures, he vindicated by his philosophy the majesty of God mighty and good, and expressed the simplicity of the Gospel in his manners. Mortals rejoice that there has existed such and so great an ornament of the human race! He was born on 25 December 1642, and died on 20 March 1726/7.[201]

We cannot say enough about Newton; better let the famous people exalt him. The French mathematician Joseph-Louis Lagrange often said that Newton was the "greatest genius who ever lived," and English poet Alexander Pope was moved by Newton's accomplishments to write the famous epitaph: "Nature and nature's laws lay hid in night; God said, 'Let Newton be' and all was light."

Though Newton worked alone, he built his discoveries on the work of earlier scientists. He had been rather more modest of his own achievements famously writing in a letter to Robert Hooke in February 1676, "If I have seen further than others, it is because I have stood on the shoulders of giants."

This was Newton's humble acknowledgement to those who preceded him in the study of astronomy from antiquity to his time: Thales, Archimedes, Hipparchus, Aristarchus, Ptolemy, Copernicus, Brahe, Kepler, and Galileo.

Newton's descriptions of fundamental laws of physics were essential for the Industrial Revolution that was about to start.

Francis Bacon, a contemporary of Shakespeare, was the founder of the empirical philosophy of modern times; with the philosophers of the Enlightenment that

---

[201] Trans. G. L. Smyth, 1826, Wiki.

followed, he believed the systematic application of science to the service of humanity would bring prosperity and happiness.[202]

Until the time of Bacon, Aristotle's established theories about matter and the solar system were still widely held; the heliocentric theory was not yet accepted. Bacon stated,

> The sciences we possess have been principally derived from the Greeks; for the addition of the Roman, Arabic, or more modern writers, are but few and of small importance, and such as they are, are founded on the basis of Greek invention. But the wisdom of the Greeks was professional and disputatious, and thus most adverse to the investigation of truth.[203]

But the dawn of a new era in science was to take place. In *Novum Organum*, Bacon wrote,

> Knowledge and human power are synonymous, since the ignorance of the cause frustrates the effect; for nature is only subdued by submission, and that which in contemplative philosophy corresponds with the cause in practical science becomes the rule.[204]

According to Falckenberg, Bacon declared three things indispensable for the attainment of this power-giving knowledge.

> The mind must understand the instruments of knowledge; it must turn to experience, deriving the materials of knowledge from perception; and it must not rise from particular principles to the higher axioms too rapidly, but steadily and gradually through middle axioms. The mind can accomplish nothing when left to itself; but undirected experience alone is also insufficient (experimentation without a plan is groping in the dark), and the senses, moreover, are deceptive and not acute enough for the subtlety of nature—therefore, methodical experimentation alone, not chance observation, is worthy of confidence.[205]

[202] R. Dubos, *Reason Awake: Science for Man* (New York: Columbia University Press, 1970), 47.
[203] R. Bacon, *Novum Organum*, *Encyclopedia Britannica*, Great Books, vol. 30 (Chicago, 1952), 117.
[204] Ibid., 107.
[205] Falckenberg, *History of Modern Philosophy*.

Locke and the Empiricists

John Locke (1632–1704), a major English philosopher, made a major contribution to political philosophy and the acquisition of knowledge. He stated,

> Perception is the first step toward knowledge. After perception, the most indispensable faculty is retention, the prolonged consciousness of present ideas and the revival of those which have disappeared, or, as it were, have been put aside. For an idea to be "in the memory" means that the mind has the capacity to reproduce it at will, whereupon it recognizes it as previously experienced … This antithesis remained decisive in the development of philosophy down to Kant, so that it has long been customary to distinguish two lines or schools, the Empirical and the Rationalistic.[206]

A real dispute was ranging between two groups of philosophers in the seventeenth and eighteenth centuries on how knowledge was acquired—the continental Rationalists and the British Empiricists. The first group, the so-called Rationalists, consisted of among others Rene Descartes, Baruch Spinoza, and Gottfried Wilhelm von Leibnitz (1614–1716), who invented calculus independently of Isaac Newton. The second group, the so-called Empiricists, consisted of British philosophers including John Locke (1632–1704), Berkeley (1685–1753), and David Hume (1711–1776); they influenced society by publishing widely read works and having many discussions with the monarchs. The Empiricists believed we learned only through experience derived from the five senses. The Rationalists emphasized reason as the primary source of knowledge. We can gain knowledge by using reason only and without relying on our senses (experience), which they regarded as unreliable.

Diderot stated the difference.

> There are three principal means of acquiring knowledge available to us: observation of nature, reflection, and experimentation. Observation collects facts; reflection combines them; experimentation verifies the result of that combination. Our observation of nature must be diligent, our reflection profound, and our experiments exact. We rarely see these three-means combined; and for this reason, creative geniuses are not common.[207]

The Enlightenment was a European intellectual movement of the late seventeenth and eighteenth centuries that emphasized rationalism and faith in progress, toleration,

---

[206] Ibid.
[207] Denis Diderot, quote, Wiki.

analysis, science, skepticism, and individualism rather than tradition. It has not been eclipsed; we are still affected by its tenets. It challenged the authority of deeply rooted institutions such as the church.

Late sixteenth- and seventeenth-century philosophers and writers such as Bacon, Descartes, Spinoza, Newton, and Locke heavily influenced it. Its prominent exponents included Kant, Goethe, Voltaire, Rousseau, and Adam Smith. The Age of Enlightenment coincided with the scientific revolution.

> The cosmopolitan qualities of the century were expressed in the Enlightenment. Yet the Age of Reason also marked the high point of French cultural leadership, when, as Thomas Jefferson put it, every man had two homelands, his own and France.

> By the eighteenth-century French was the accepted international language. Louis XIV had made it supreme in diplomacy; the writers of his age, like Boileau, La Rochefoucaud, Racine, and Molière, had made it preeminent in literature. There was much justice in the claim that, "a dangerous work written in French is a declaration of war on the whole of Europe."[208]

One of the major inventions of this age was the *Encyclopedia*, one of the greatest tools to store and disseminate knowledge.

> The great organ of the philosophes was the Encyclopedie, begun in 1751 and completed a century later. Its contributors included Voltaire, Montesquieu, Rousseau, Condorcet, Quesnay, and Turgot. Its editor –in-chief, Denis Diderot did not intend to compile an objective compendium of information; he and his encyclopedists sought to assemble knowledge and experience, in order that the labors of past centuries should not prove useless for succeeding centuries; that our descendants, by becoming better informed, will at the same time become happier and more virtuous … The purposes of the Encyclopedie were didactic, the effect subversive: to expose and thereby ultimately to destroy what its contributors saw as the superstition, the intolerance, and the gross political and religious inequalities of the Old Regime and to instruct the public in the virtues of natural law and the wonders of science.

---

[208] R. Winks, *A History of Civilization* (New Jersey: Prentice Hall, 1996), 359.

It accomplished its purposes, antagonizing many defenders of the Old Regime while gaining enough subscribers to prove a profitable business venture. Louis XV tried to prevent its being printed or circulated, the church condemned it for its materialism and skepticism, and even the publishers, without consulting Diderot, ordered the printers to cut out passages likely to cause offense—to no avail. The Encyclopedic reached a substantial reading public.[209]

Falckenberg described the English, French, and German national characteristics.

The English philosopher resembles a geographer who, with conscientious care, outlines a map of the region through which he journeys; the Frenchman, an anatomist who, with steady stroke, lays bare the nerves and muscles of the organism; the German, a mountaineer who loses in clear vision of particular objects as much as he gains in loftiness of position and extent of view. The Englishman describes the given reality, the Frenchman analyses it, and the German transfigures it.[210]

In the Enlightenment, two French philosophers stood out—Voltaire (1694–1778) and Rousseau (1712–1778). R. Winks wrote, "It is said Voltaire was able to write verses almost as soon as he could write his name. His earliest education was provided by a dissolute priest whose behavior taught him skepticism even as he learned his prayers from him."[211]

In his *The Age of Louis the XIV*, Voltaire wrote,

Of those who have commanded battalions and squadrons, only the names remain. The human race has nothing to show for hundred battles that have been waged. But the great men I speak to you about have prepared pure and lasting pleasures for men yet to be born. A canal lock uniting two seas, a painting by Poussin, a beautiful tragedy, a newly-discovered truth – these are things a thousand times more precious than all the annals of the court or all the accounts of military campaigns. You know that, with me, great men come first and heroes last.

---

[209] Ibid.
[210] Falckenberg, *History of Modern Philosophy*.
[211] Winks, *A History of Civilization*, 362.

I call great men all those who have excelled in creating what is useful or agreeable. The plunderers of the provinces are merely heroes.[212]

Candide, Voltaire's most famous work, demonstrated the imperfections of the world even under the best circumstances.

Rousseau wrote *The Social Contract* in 1732; it became a sacred text for the French Revolution of 1789. He wrote *Emile* in 1762, it was a revolutionary book on the philosophy of education. His other writings included *Confessions, Perpetual Peace,* and *Discourse on Inequality.*

The *Social Contract* starts out with a bold statement.

Man is born free; and everywhere he is in chains. One thinks himself the master of others, and still remains a greater slave than they. How did this change come about? I do not know. What can make it legitimate? That question I think I can answer.

Rousseau was a worshipper of virtue: "A country cannot subsist well without liberty, nor liberty without virtue ... Virtue is a state of war, and to live in it means one always has some battle to wage against oneself."[213]

In his *Discourse on Inequality*, he wrote,

Always asking others what we are, and never daring to ask ourselves, in the midst of so much philosophy, humanity, and civilization, and of such sublime codes of morality, we have nothing to show for ourselves but a frivolous and deceitful appearance, humor without virtue, reason without wisdom, and pleasure without happiness.[214]

In the spirit of enlightenment, Rousseau was an ardent supporter of freedom and independent thinking.

Adopt only those of my sentiments which you believe are true, and reject all the others; and whatever religion you may ultimately embrace, remember that its real duties are independent of human institutions—that no religion upon earth can dispense with the sacred obligations of morality—that an upright heart is the temple

---

[212] D. Boorstin, *Seekers* (New York: Vintage Books, 1999), 192.
[213] Tryon Edwards, *A Dictionary of Thoughts: Being a Cyclopedia of Laconic Quotations from the Best Authors of the World, Both Ancient and Modern* (1908), 301.
[214] *Discourse on the origin and foundations of inequality among men*, 1755.

of the Divinity—and that, in every country and in every sect, to love God above all things, and thy neighbor as thyself, is the substance and summary of the law—the end and aim of religious duty.[215]

Immanuel Kant (1724–1804) ranks as the greatest modern philosopher due to his profound and influential writings on ethics, epistemology, metaphysics, and aesthetics. H. J. Puton, who translated and analyzed Kant's ethics, wrote,

Kant's Groundwork of the Metaphysics of Morals, is one of the small books which are truly great: it has exercised on human thought an influence almost ludicrously disproportionate to its size. In moral philosophy, it ranks with the *Republic of Plato* and the *Ethics of Aristotle*; and perhaps-partly no doubt through the spread of Christian ideals and through the long experience of humanity during the last two thousand years-it shows in some respects a deeper insight even than these. Its main topic-the supreme principle of morality-is of the utmost importance to all who are not indifferent to the struggle of good against evil … but its message was never more needed than it is at present, when a somewhat arid empiricism is the prevailing fashion in philosophy.[216]

The centerpiece of Kant's most famous proposition, the categorical imperative, states, "Act as if the maxim of our action were to become by our will a universal law of nature." This is often equated with the golden rule; it argues for a more universal set of moral actions.

Kant defined the influence of the enlightenment on the individual.

Enlightenment is man's emergence from his self-incurred immaturity. Immaturity is the inability to use one's own understanding without the guidance of another. This immaturity is self-incurred if its cause is not lack of understanding, but lack of resolution and courage to use it without the guidance of another. The motto of enlightenment is therefore: Sapere aude! Have courage to use your own understanding!

Kant made major progress in philosophy and epistemology. He settled the

---

[215] Jean Rousseau, *Profession of Faith of a Savoyard Vicar* (Harvard Classics, 1909–14).
[216] H. J. Puton, *Preface to Kant's Groundwork of the Metaphysics of Morals.*

burning question of the time on how knowledge was acquired, which had divided philosophers into the British Empiricists and the continental Rationalists. He stated,

> Our knowledge springs from two fundamental sources of the mind; the first is the capacity of receiving representations (receptivity for impressions), the second is the power of knowing an object through these representations (spontaneity [in the production] of concepts).[217]

Kant, himself a scientist and later a philosopher, stated, "Science is organized knowledge. Wisdom is organized life."

About two hundred years before Kant's writing in 1509, during the High Renaissance (c. 1490–1530), the twenty-five-year-old painter Raffaello Sanzio, better known as Raphael, painted his famous fresco *The School of Athens* at the Vatican in the Stanza della Segnatura; it is regarded as one of the greatest Renaissance paintings. The School of Athens, representing Philosophy, Plato, and Aristotle, is pictured at the center of a group of other philosophers in a scene set in ancient Greece that symbolizes the wisdom of classical antiquity and represents the seeking of truth through reason. Plato is pointing to the sky holding his masterpiece, *Timaeus*, a dialogue concerning speculation on the nature of the physical world, the universe, and its creation, properties, and purpose. Aristotle is pointing to earth holding his book of ethics, symbolizing humanity's search for happiness through ethics here on earth. Kant's wondering about the starry heavens and the human soul was prompted by Plato's and Aristotle's concepts of the universe and ethics respectively.

We got to an age where, as Kant said, "people woke up from the slumber of ignorance" with inquires and availability of books they gained knowledge and felt free to question authority.

Goethe (1749–1832), a famous German writer and statesman, was not as optimistic as the French idealists were especially in his *Condorcet in his Outlines of a Historical View of the Progress of the Human Mind* on the perfection of man. According to J. B. Bury,

> Towards the end of his life, in conversation with Eckermann, he made some remarks which indicate his attitude. "The world will not reach its goal so quickly as we think and wish. The retarding demons are always there, intervening and resisting at every point, so that, though there is an advance on the whole, it is very slow. Live longer and you will find that I am right ... The development of humanity," said Eckermann, "appears to be a matter of thousands of years ..." "Who knows?" Goethe replied,

---

[217] Immanuel Kant, *Critique of Pure Reason*, trans. Norman Kemp Smith (1929), 92.

"perhaps of millions. But let humanity last as long as it will, there will always be hindrances in its way, and all kinds of distress, to make it develop its powers. Men will become more clever and discerning, but not better nor happier nor more energetic, at least except for limited periods."[218]

Adam Smith (1723–1790), a Scottish moral philosopher and political theorist, published his two classic works *The Theory of Moral Sentiments* and *An Inquiry into the Nature and Causes of the Wealth of Nations*. *Wealth of Nations* is considered his magnum opus; it is as current today as it was when he published it; it was the first modern work of economics, and he is considered the father of modern economics.

John Dalton (1766–1844), an English chemist, physicist, and meteorologist, revived Democritus's work on the atom with his pioneering work in the development of modern atomic theory. The main points of Dalton's atomic theory were these.

Elements are made of extremely small particles called atoms.

Atoms of a given element are identical in size, mass, and other properties; atoms of different elements differ in size, mass, and other properties.

Atoms cannot be subdivided, created, or destroyed.

Atoms of different elements combine in simple whole-number ratios to form chemical compounds in which atoms are combined, separated, or rearranged.

He first published the table of relative atomic weights.[219]

Then one by one, the elements as we know them today were isolated and their properties defined. Mendeleev (1834–1907) classified the chemical elements into a periodic table organized on the basis of the elements' atomic numbers, which is the number of proto Pythagoras ns and neutrons in the nucleus, electron configurations, and chemical properties.

Around 1775, James Watt invented the steam engine, which ushered in the Industrial Revolution. The steam engine gave humanity a source of energy much greater than what windmills, water mills, and draft animal provided—enough to power trains, ships, and other modes of transportation.

---

[218] Ibid., 140.
[219] Wiki.

The use of coal has had a detrimental effect on the environment. As Jean Gimpel stated,

> The building of thousands of furnaces in hundreds of medieval forests to he very beginning, the fuel used was charcoal, the black porous residue of burned wood ... The extent of the damage caused by iron smelters to forests can be appreciated when one realizes that to obtain 50 kilograms (110 pounds) of iron it was necessary at that time to reduce approximately 200 kilograms (440 pounds) of iron ore with as much as 25 steres (25 cubic meters) (883 cubic feet) of wood. It has been estimated that in forty days, one furnace could level the forest for a radius of 1 kilometer (over a square mile.)[220]

In the early 1830s, Michael Faraday (1791–1867) discovered that varying magnetic fields could induce electric currents and vice versa. Until then, electricity and magnetism had been thought of as unrelated phenomena.

In 1865, James Maxwell (1831–1879) published his famous classical unified field theory of electromagnetism. That was followed by its application to electric motors, electric energy, electric transport, and the electric lightbulb. The publication of *A Dynamic Theory of Electromagnetism* was the second great unification in physics after the first one realized by Isaac Newton in mechanics and optics.

Oil was discovered in the second part of the nineteenth century and became the prime fuel for the upcoming internal combustion engine. Other major inventions made in the last part of the nineteenth century were the vulcanization of rubber, Portland cement, the telegraph, milk pasteurization, dynamite, Darwin's theory of evolution, the Gatling gun, photography, motion pictures, X-rays, incandescent bulbs, radio, aspirin, artificial dyes, and antiseptics.

MODERN TIMES: 1900—TODAY

The twentieth century's most notable events were

- two world wars
- the greatest scientific discoveries in all fields including antibiotics, DNA, and landing man on the moon
- a social experiment that divided the world into two camps, the Communist revolutions in Russia, in China, and others

---

[220] Jean Gimpel, *The Medieval Machine: The Industrial Revolution of the Middle Ages* (New York: Penguin, 1975), 79.

- the Great Depression
- the invention of nuclear and thermonuclear weapons and atomic energy
- the invention of the transistor, computer, and the Internet
- European economic unification

Most of these events outstripped similar events in the past by far.

World Wars I and II

The First World War started on 1914 and lasted until 1918. It killed about 16 million as a result of trench warfare, chemical warfare, machine guns, tanks, and other modes of destruction. It ended with exhaustion of the participants and precipitated World War II.

World War II lasted from 1939 to 1945 and caused about 60 to 84 million deaths. Tanks and aircraft were introduced on a large scale, and brutality, including genocide, reached new highs. The war in the Pacific ended with the dropping of two nuclear bombs for the first time in history. More than thirty counties and over 100 million people were involved in this, the deadliest conflict in human history.

At its conclusion, Europe was divided along ideological lines in two blocks—East and West—from 1945 to 1989. During the Cold War, the world lived under the threat of nuclear holocaust. It ended with the collapse of the Eastern Bloc, and some normalcy returned to Europe compared to the pre-Berlin unification.

The Cold War has subsided, but the total number of countries with nuclear capabilities has grown to nine. After 1989 and the fall of communism, some countries split apart, some peacefully, others violently with open wounds remaining. I will discuss war further in chapter 6.

Scientific Discoveries

In the twentieth century, humanity made great leaps in understanding nature; very sophisticated instruments were able to define the smallest particles, quarks, and electrons that make up all matter and observe the immense number of stars and galaxies.

The greatest discoveries of the twentieth century were the structure of the atom and its tiniest constituents, a credible theory of the creation of the universe, and the discovery of DNA along with drugs and advances in surgery. I will discuss these in following sections.

Atoms and Matter

According to Democritus's theory in the fifth century BC, all matter was made of indivisible and immutable atoms. Starting in 1896 with the discovery of the electron by J. Thompson, the discovery of quantum mechanics by Max Planck in 1900, the Bohr model of the atom, and the discovery of the neutron in 1932, the model was completed. All matter is made of atoms with their neutrons and protons being in the nucleus and the electrons rotating around them. The atom was split in Germany in 1938.

Almost simultaneously with the development of the atomic theory, Einstein discovered the famous equation $E = mc^2$ in 1905. This simple equation was one of the greatest inventions in human history. This finding has and will have an immense influence on our lives and destiny. This equation means that matter can be converted into energy and vice versa. By splitting (fission) of the atom, part of the mass is converted into energy.

About four hundred nuclear plants around the world use controlled fission to create electricity. Fission has been used to produce nuclear bombs such as those that destroyed Hiroshima and Nagasaki. We can see that that the proper use of an invention can have beneficial results and its misuse can have detrimental results. This general rule may be applicable to other inventions as well.

The hydrogen bomb relies on the fusion rather than the fission of atoms. Many countries are doing cooperative research for the use of a controlled method of fusion to produce electricity. This could produce an inexhaustible supply of clean energy with no residual radioactive material, whose disposal is problematic. The exploration is ongoing, but predictions are that this may not happen in the near future.

Further research determined that the constituents of the atomic nucleus, protons and neutrons, are quarks. Thus, all living and nonliving matter is made of combinations of ninety-two naturally occurring substances known as elements, and these elements are made of atoms, which are made of electrons and the nucleus. The nucleus is made up of protons and neutrons. Both protons and neutrons are made of quarks.

Understanding the Universe

With the construction of larger telescopes and other sensitive instruments, scientists have determined that the universe is expanding. The fusion theory explains how the energy of the sun and other stars is created. Each star is a thermonuclear reactor continually fusing hydrogen into helium and other elements and sending a continuous stream of energy in the form of light (photons) to the universe.

All the living stars are nothing more than live infernos with continuous fusion taking place that light up the universe, not unlike our sun, which illuminates the earth and the other planets in our planetary system. By understanding the smallest particles and the equation of interchangeability of matter and energy, the big bang theory as the genesis of the universe was developed. During the big bang, all the energy that exists was produced, and it will always exist as either matter or energy.

The big bang theory, formulated in the second half of the twentieth century, determined that the big explosion took place about 13.7 billion years ago and created only energy. And from that dense and hot energy, 10 billion trillion trillion degrees C, quarks and electrons were created, which formed protons and neutrons. Clusters of neutrons and protons made up the nucleus of atoms with electrons, protons, and neutrons and stars with their planets and galaxies. Afterward, larger atoms with a higher numbers of electrons, protons, and neutrons were formed when large stars exploded into supernovae creating interstellar debris, which also condensed and produced more planets.

The earth was created around 4.5 billion years ago, and life in its most primitive form of cells and multicells started around 3.7 billion years ago.

Semiconductors

John Bardeen, Walter Brattain, and William Shockley invented the transistor in 1947. It is a semiconductor device used to amplify and switch electronic signals and power. The transistor is the fundamental building block of modern electronics, and it revolutionized the electronics industry. The transistor is smaller, and it consumes less power than does the vacuum tube it replaced. Transistors can be integrated in many numbers to create integrated circuits.

Today, some transistors are packaged individually, but by far, the majority of them are in integrated circuits. The level of integration of transistors into integrated circuits has been phenomenal. Now, more than 500 billion of them are integrated into a single chip without a fundamental limit in sight.

The integrated circuit has been responsible for the immense power of our electronics such as personal devices, computers, smartphones, tablets, communications, industrial controls, and a myriad of other applications.

Integrated circuits, diode lasers, fiber optics, and telecommunication satellites are the key elements for superfast global communications.

Computers

The first computers were produced in the 1940s using vacuum-tube technology for switching signals. With the advent of the transistor and integrated circuits, computers have had an astronomical growth in speed, low power, size, and weight. Today's laptop far surpasses the capabilities of the fastest supercomputer of the 1980s.

Internet

Progress in computers and telecommunications led to the Internet explosion in the early 1990s. This progress continuous with unprecedented growth. The world became wired and entered the age of information age. It has had many changes in people's lives, but its full potential has not been comprehended yet.

Properly used, the Internet could become the best educational tool ever. People can exchange all information instantly anywhere in the globe. We can download and read almost all the books out of copyright from it and have access to any book or record in print for a fee.

Space Travel and Communications

With progress in electronics and rocket propulsion, man orbited the Earth in 1957 and landed on the Moon in 1969. Now, orbiting the Earth has become a tourist phenomenon.

Space probes have reached other planets in our solar system, and some are on the way out to the vast universe. The sky is full of synchronous satellites broadcasting TV at about 25,000 miles from Earth, while global positioning system (GPS) satellites orbit at about 12,000 miles; spying and weather satellites do the same at around 200 miles. One can look and admire satellite pictures of almost any place on the globe. New, bigger telescopes and other instruments will enable us to look further into the universe. Who can predict what we will observe with the twenty-seven-meter, multimirror telescope being manufactured now that will go operational in 2020?

Medicine

Parallel with technological inventions have been major medical inventions such as penicillin and other antibiotics to fight infections, the discovery of DNA, organ transplants, and other major advancements. We can expect immunizations and new biotechnology drugs to keep people healthy for much longer periods. Life expectancy has been increased and keeps increasing.

Man's Predictions

History shows that humanity has not always made accurate predictions and has at times greatly underestimated its powers of invention.

In the July 1899 edition of *Scientific American* was a discussion of the probable effects that the motor car would exert on urban life once mass production had lowered its price. The internal combustion engine revolutionized this form of transport, and it did not take long before the utopia was conceived. The article stated,

The improvement in city conditions by the general adoption of the motorcar can hardly be overestimated. Streets clean, dustless and odorless, with light rubber tired vehicles moving swiftly and noiselessly over the smooth expanse would eliminate a greater part of the nervousness, distraction, and strain of modern metropolitan life.[221]

In 1898, Charles Holland Duell, the US commissioner of patents, became famous for saying, "Everything that can be invented has been invented."

Martin Rees, former president of the British Association for the Advancement of Science, referred to a 1937 study by the US National Academy of Sciences aimed at predicting coming breakthroughs.

It came up with some wise assessments about agriculture, about synthetic gasoline and synthetic rubber. But what is remarkable is the things it missed. No nuclear energy, no antibiotics (though this was eight years after Alexander Fleming had discovered penicillin), no jet aircraft, no rocketry nor any use of space, no computers; certainly, no transistors. The committee overlooked the technologies that actually dominated the second half of the twentieth century. Still less could they predict the social and political transformations that occurred during that time.[222]

Author Charles Eisenstein stated some of the undesirable effects of the Industrial Revolution.

Meanwhile, the horrors of the industrial revolution seemed to be in retreat—its hellish slums, child labor, disease epidemics, 16-hour workdays, and starvation wages. The blossoming new sciences of economics, psychology, and sociology promised to bring the same wonders to the social universe that the hard sciences had brought to the physical universe. The goal of a rational society, engineered for maximum happiness just as a machine is engineered for maximum efficiency, was just around the corner.[223]

Kenneth Olsen (1926–2011), the founder of Digital Equipment, a major computer manufacturer, said in 1987, "There is no reason for any individual to have

---

[221] R. Dubos, *Reason Awake: Science for Man* (New York: Columbia University Press, 1970), 9.
[222] Martin Rees, *Our Final Hour* (Basic Books, 2003), 13.
[223] C. Eisenstein, *The Ascent of Humanity* (Harrisburg, PA), 15.

a computer in his home."[224] He could not envision computers running a house, opening doors, and controlling voice-activated faucets, etc.

In summary, the main inventions of the twentieth century as Harold Varmus, director of the National Institute of Health, observed, "There are three great themes in science in the twentieth century: the atom, the computer, and the gene."[225]

However, up until around 1950, most people's lives were hardly different from those of the lives of the ancient Greeks and Romans; they were not touched by the technologies discovered since the Renaissance and up to modern times. They were tilling the earth with horses and mules and using horse-drawn carriages; their houses were hardly different from those of the ancients.

We live in a world of stunning scientific and technological progress. We have made more progress in the last 150 years than all the years before. This progress will continue at an accelerating rate. There are more scientists and engineers today at work than at any other time searching to find better, smaller, faster devices for communication, computers, and instruments that will enhance progress and contribute to more knowledge, cure diseases, and clean up the environment.

---

[224] https://en.wikiquote.org/wiki/Ken_Olsen
[225] M. Kaku, *Visions: How Science Will Revolutionize the 21ˢᵗ Century* (Random House, 1998).

HAPPINESS, VIRTUE, AND KNOWLEDGE

All the political, social, and economic improvements, all the technical progress cannot have any regenerating significance, so long as our inner life remains as it is at present. The more the intelligence unveils and violates the secrets of nature, the more the danger increases and the heart shrinks.[226]
—Nikos Kazantzakis

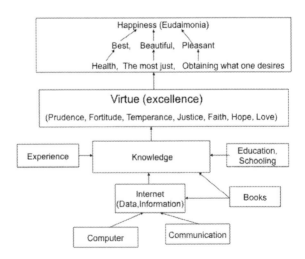

Diagram 1. Happiness comes from virtue, which comes from knowledge, which comes from experience, education schooling, book reading, and now the Internet.

---

[226] Quoted in *Nikos Kazantzakis* by Helen Kazantzakis, 529.

In Diagram 1, at the peak of the pyramid stands happiness, *eudaimonia*—the highest good. Happiness is the universal good, the ultimate aim and destination for humanity's self-perfection. Human perfection and thus happiness is achieved through moral and intellectual virtue.

The great German poet Friedrich Schiller stated the synergy of truth, virtue, and happiness in this way.

> The intellectual man has the ideal of virtue, of truth, and of happiness; but the active man will only practice virtues, will only grasp truths, and enjoy happy days. The business of physical and moral education is to bring back this multiplicity to unity, to put morality in the place of manners, science in the place of knowledge; the business of aesthetic education is to make out of beauties the beautiful.[227]

We can grasp truth through knowledge. We will examine the route to happiness later in this chapter. Happiness is humanity's ideal state, its goal. The strife apparent in our lives reflects our continuous effort to reach virtuous perfection, from which happiness springs. Virtue springs from knowledge, and anything that impedes human progress is resolved only by knowledge; it has provided humanity the impetus to create the civilization we have today. Knowledge comes from experience and education. Education comes from schooling, learning from all sources of information (books, Internet) and practice.

The chart shows how humanity started to understand happiness as coming from virtue and knowledge since about the sixth century BC; the concept flourished in the fifth and fourth centuries BC and continues today.

John Lord described the Socratic trinity of happiness, virtue, and knowledge.

> Virtue became the foundation of happiness, and almost a synonym for knowledge. He discoursed on knowledge in its connection with virtue ... Happiness, Virtue, and Knowledge: this was the Socratic Trinity, the three indissolubly connected together, and forming the life of the soul, — the only precious thing a man has, since it is immortal, and therefore to be guarded beyond all bodily and mundane interests. But human nature is frail.[228]

---

[227] Friedrich Schiller, *Aesthetical Essays*, Internet.
[228] Lord, *Beacon Lights of History*, vol. 1, ebook.

WHAT IS HAPPINESS?

From time immemorial, the ultimate aim of every human activity has been to achieve the Highest Human Good, or Happiness. It will continue to be an objective of mankind to eternity. Happiness (Eudaimonia: literally meaning "having a good demon," demon: literally meaning "destiny, good sense, divine") signifies more than mere sentiment or feeling, perfection in respect of virtue, success in life, an ability which suffices for living well, more than the pleasure of the moment or even of series of satisfied desires. Encompasses the excellence specific to human beings as human beings.[229]

The pursuit of happiness played an important role in ancient moral theory. It means an overall flourishing of one's life, reaching an overall completeness, perfection, knowledge, and responsibility; it is a state in which virtue and reason are in harmony.

Plato and Aristotle considered the analysis of knowledge, virtue, and happiness as the greatest single occupation of the Greek philosophical mind.

About twenty-two centuries later, Immanuel Kant, the greatest philosopher of modern times and since ancient times, stated,

The whole interest of reason is centered in the three fundamental questions on knowledge, morality or virtue and happiness.

What can I know? **Knowledge, Epistemology,**

What ought I to do? **Morality**

What may I hope for? **Happiness.**[230]

These are question we should ask about any subject or project we are about to undertake in everyday life or to address metaphysical questions. We need to ask these questions all through life and answer them in ways that are consistent with human reason.

The first of Kant's question is a question of epistemology—how one acquires knowledge. Knowledge is essential before we deliberate on actions and take them. Knowledge is one of the prerequisites for any undertaking. The second is to act

---

[229] Aristotle, *Nicomachean Ethics*, trans. R. C. Bartlett and S. D. Collins (Chicago: University of Chicago Press, 2012), x.

[230] I. Kant, *The Critique of Pure Reason*, *Encyclopedia Britannica*, Great Books, vol. 42 (Chicago, 1952), 236 (emphasis added).

rightly based on reason, virtue, and knowledge. The third has to do with reaching happiness, self-perpetuating peace, prosperity, equality, justice, and harmony. This may sound idealistic, but we need to set goals as idealistic and ambitious as they may be. We may able to reach higher than we have and let the generations to come reach higher yet. The attempt is worth it as well as is the journey that requires knowledge and virtue in our minds and hearts.

As the ancients said, knowledge does not bring wisdom; we need virtue to accompany us as well. The journey will become our knowledge. We must study the past, acquire knowledge and universal virtue, and act on it with virtue and reason if we want to achieve eternal peace and happiness. Never stop! Always pursue!

Aristotle's philosophical masterpiece *Nicomachean Ethics* is considered one of the greatest and the most influential books on ethics. It details how a person achieves happiness through virtue. Homer, Hesiod, the pre-Socratic philosophers, Socrates, and Plato discussed virtue, but Aristotle absorbed all the virtue, ethics, and knowledge up to his time and produced a monumental work that remains unsurpassed. *Nicomachean Ethics* precedes Aristotle's *Politics*; he was trying to define a political system for a state whose citizens needed to behave virtuously to promote happiness and prosperity for all.

Aristotle wrote,

> Every art and every inquiry, and similarly every action as well as choice is held to aim at some good. Hence people have nobly declared that the good is that at which all things aim … Now since there are many actions, art, and sciences, the ends too are many: of medicine, the end is health; of shipbuilding, is ship; of generalship, victory; of house, wealth management.[231]

Of the numerous definitions of happiness, I prefer Aristotle's; he quoted an inscription from the island of Delos.

> Happiness, therefore, is the best, noblest and the most pleasant thing; and these are not separated. Noblest is what is most just, but best is to be healthy: And most pleasant by nature is for someone to attain what he passionately desires … For all these features are present in the best activities; and we assert that happiness is these activities-or the best one among them. Yet evidently, as we said, it needs external goods as well; for it is impossible or not easy, for someone to do noble acts if he lacks the proper resources … happiness seems to require some such external prosperity in

---

[231] Aristotle, *Nicomachean Ethics*, 1094a1-a7, 1.

addition. This is why some make good fortune equivalent to happiness, and others, virtue.[232]

The reason for stating justice on the definition of happiness can be explained by the following maxim by the Pythagorean Polos, who lived before Aristotle, and which explains the role of the importance of justice versus the other virtues.

I think, we can call justice the mother and the nurse of men and of the other virtues; as without justice, one can be neither temperate, neither courageous, and neither prudent. As justice brings harmony and peace to the whole soul with gracefulness … and for people wisdom comes from knowledge and justice.[233]

In his *Rhetoric*, Aristotle detailed prosperity and other qualities of happiness.

We may define happiness as prosperity combined with virtue; or as independence of life; or as the secure enjoyment of the maximum of pleasure; or as a good condition of property and body, together with the power of guarding one's property and body and making use of them. That happiness is one or more of these things, pretty well everybody agrees.[234]

John Lord wrote,

Socrates, again, divorced happiness from pleasure … Happiness is the peace and harmony of the soul; pleasure comes from animal sensations, or the gratification of worldly and ambitious desires, and therefore is often demoralizing. Happiness is an elevated joy, —a beatitude, existing with pain and disease, when the soul is triumphant over the body; while pleasure is transient, and comes from what is perishable.[235]

From these definitions of happiness, it follows that its constituent parts are: Good birth, plenty of friends, good friends, wealth, good children, plenty of children, a happy old age, also such bodily excellences as health, beauty, strength, large stature,

[232] Ibid., 1099a25-b9, 16–17.
[233] Stobaeus, *Anthology*, 8, 51.
[234] Aristotle, *Rhetoric*, 1360b13-17, in *The Complete Works of Aristotle*, ed. J. Barnes (Princeton University Press, 1995), 2163.
[235] Lord, *Beacon Lights of History*, vol. 1.

athletic powers, together with fame, honor, good luck, and virtue. A man cannot fail to be completely independent if he possesses these internal and these external goods; for besides these there are no others to have. (Goods of the soul and of the body are internal. Good birth, friends, money, and honor are external). Further, we think that he should possess resources and luck, in order to make his life really secure.[236]

In his *Rhetoric*, Aristotle detailed the constituents of happiness being a virtue.

The following is a more detailed list of things that must be good: Happiness, as being desirable in itself and sufficient by itself, and as being that for whose sake we choose many other things. Also, justice, courage, temperance, magnanimity, magnificence, and all such qualities, as being excellences of the soul. Further, health, beauty, and the like, as being bodily excellences and productive of many other good things: for instance, health is productive both of pleasure and of life, and therefore is thought the greatest of goods, since these two things which it causes, pleasure and life, are two of the things most highly prized by ordinary people. Wealth, again: for it is the excellence of possession, and also productive of many other good things. Friends and friendship: for a friend is desirable in himself and also productive of many other good things. So, too, honor and reputation, as being pleasant, and productive of many other good things, and usually accompanied by the presence of the good things that cause them to be bestowed. The faculty of speech and action; since all such qualities are productive of what is good. Further-good parts, strong memory, receptiveness, quickness of intuition, and the like, for all such faculties are productive of what is good; Similarly, all the sciences and arts. And life: since, even if no other good were the result of life, it is desirable in itself. And justice, as the cause of good to the community.[237]

Aristotle said that virtue had to be cultivated.

This is an activity of soul and actions accompanied by reason, the work of a serious man being to do these things well and nobly, and each thing is brought to completion well in accord with virtue, … and if there are several virtues, then in accord which the best and

---

[236] Aristotle, *Rhetoric*, 1360b18-30, 2163.
[237] Ibid., 1362b10-b27, 2166.

most complete one. But, in addition, must be done in a complete life. For one swallow does not make a spring, nor does one day. And in this way, one day or a short time does not make someone blessed and happy either.[238]

Plato separated the human soul into three parts: intellect or logical, the spirit, and the appetites. With that in mind, Metopos wrote,

> Of the intellect part of the soul, virtue is prudence; as it has critical and theoretical capabilities. Of the spirited part, virtue is courage; as it is the ability to withstand and endure sufferings. Of the appetitive (desiring) part, virtue is temperance; as it is the moderation and self-control of the bodily pleasures. And of the whole soul, virtue is justice.[239]

Happiness and the opportunities and means to achieve it must be open and possible for the greatest number of people. Humanity will achieve long-lasting peace and prosperity only when happiness is widespread. Happiness, peace, and some level of prosperity are interconnected; one cannot exist without the others. Humans need to have knowledge and free will to interpret all these concepts.

According to Aristotle, happiness is justice, health, and achieving goals. If someone is not just and has attained wealth without merit or committed other crimes, his conscience and maybe the law will make him unhappy by denying him peace of mind. People cannot be happy if they cannot attain their goals. And enjoyment of life is obviously difficult with physical or mental pain.

While virtue is not the only constituent of happiness, it is the indispensable means of attaining happiness.

In the *Republic*, Plato mentioned the need for the state to achieve happiness.

> But that our aim in founding the State was not the disproportionate happiness of any one class, but the greatest happiness of the whole; we thought that in a State which is ordered with a view to the good of the whole we should be most likely to find justice, and in the ill-ordered State injustice … And can there be anything better for the interests of the State than that the men and women of a State should be as good as possible?[240]

In his *Politics*, Aristotle described how ethics was of paramount importance for

---

[238] Aristotle, *Nicomachean Ethics*, 10948a14-17, 13.
[239] Metopos, *Stobaeus Anthology*, A, 64.
[240] Plato, *Republic*, trans. Benjamin Jowett, book 4, 420b5, book 5, 456e6.

the state and provided happiness, internal goods—virtues—and external goods. He wrote,

> Assuming that enough has been already said in discussions outside the school concerning the best life, we will now only repeat what is contained in them. Certainly no one will dispute the propriety of that partition of goods which separates them into three classes, viz., external goods, goods of the body, and goods of the soul, or deny that the happy man must have all three. For no one would maintain that he is happy who has not in him a particle of courage or temperance or justice or prudence, who is afraid of every insect which flutters past him, and will commit any crime, however great, in order to gratify his lust of meat or drink, who will sacrifice his dearest friend for the sake of half-a-farthing, and is as feeble and false in mind as a child or a madman … Thus, the courage, justice, and wisdom of a state have the same form and nature as the qualities which give the individual who possesses them the name of just, wise, or temperate.[241]

Aristotle concluded with his brilliant statement on the importance of virtue to the state.

> Let us assume then that the best life, both for individuals and states, is the life of virtue, when virtue has external goods enough for the performance of good actions. If there are any who controvert our assertion, we will in this treatise pass them over, and consider their objections hereafter … Now it is evident that the form of government is best in which every man, whoever he is, can act best and live happily.[242]

Seneca followed Aristotle on his definition of happiness.

> There is not anything in this world, perhaps, that is more talked of, and less understood, than the business of a happy life. It is every man's wish and design; and yet not one of a thousand that knows wherein that happiness consists. We live, however, in a blind and

---

[241] Aristotle, *Politics, Complete Works of Aristotle*, J. Barnes, ed. (Princeton, 1984), trans. Jowett, J. Barnes, vol. 2, book 7, 1323a24-1323b35, 2100.
[242] Ibid., 1323b39-1324a22, 2101.

eager pursuit of it; and the more haste we make in a wrong way, the further we are from our journey's end.[243]

Seneca continued on the topics of happiness, wisdom, and virtue.

Human happiness is founded upon wisdom and virtue; Taking for granted that human happiness is founded upon wisdom and virtue we shall treat of these two points in order as they lie: and, first, of wisdom; not in the latitude of its various operations but as it has only a regard to good life, and the happiness of mankind.

Wisdom is a right understanding, a faculty of discerning good from evil; what is to be chosen, and what rejected; a judgment grounded upon the value of things, and not the common opinion of them; an equality of force, and a strength of resolution. It sets a watch over our words and deeds, it takes us up with the contemplation of the works of nature, and makes us invincible by either good or evil fortune ... To be wise is the use of wisdom.[244]

They that ascribe the invention of tillage, architecture, navigation, etc., to wise men, may perchance be in the right, that they were invented by wise men, as wise men; for wisdom does not teach our fingers, but our minds: fiddling And dancing, arms and fortifications, were the works of luxury and discord; but wisdom instructs us in the way of nature, and in the arts of unity and concord, not in the instruments, but in the government of life; not to make us live only, but to live happily. She teaches us what things are good, what evil, and what only appear so; and to distinguish betwixt true greatness and tumor. She clears our minds of dross and vanity; she raises up our thoughts to heaven, and carries them down to hell: she discourses of the nature of the soul, the powers and faculties of it.[245]

Seneca declared there could be no happiness without virtue.

Virtue is that perfect good which is the complement of a happy life; the only immortal thing that belongs to mortality—it is the knowledge both of others and itself—it is an invincible greatness

---

[243] Seneca, *Seneca's Morals of a Happy Life, Benefits, Anger and Clemency*, Internet, 184.
[244] Ibid., 191.
[245] Ibid., 193–94.

of mind, not to be elevated or dejected with good or ill fortune. It is sociable and gentle, free, steady, and fearless, content within itself, full of inexhaustible delights, and it is valued for itself. One may be a good physician, a good governor, a good grammarian, without being a good man, so that all things from without are only accessories, for the seat of it is a pure and holy mind.[246]

Thomas Aquinas, the great theologian of the Middle Ages, stated, "The prize of reward of virtue is happiness" as Aristotle clearly states in Ethics I, 9 (1099b16).[247] In his book *The Perfectibility of Man*, John Pasmore wrote,

Here, perhaps, Aristotle stands most at odds with the general tendency of post-Renaissance thought, which tends to value the journey more than the arrival, the process of finding out more than the truth arrived at, the doing rather than the having.[248]

Leibnitz wrote in 1718,

Our happiness will never consist and ought not to consist, in a full enjoyment, in which there is nothing more to desire, and which would make our mind dull, but in a perpetual progress to new pleasures and new perfections.[249]

Pythagoras, the mystic of the pre-Socratic philosophers, stated,

Which is the wisest thing? The number, and secondly that which gave a name to things. Which is the most beautiful thing? Harmony. The most powerful thing? Intelligence. The best thing? Happiness. What is said with most truth? That men are evil.[250]

According to John Lord,

Socrates, again, divorced happiness from pleasure, -identical things, with most pagans. Happiness is the peace and harmony

[246] Ibid., 199, 204.
[247] Thomas Aquinas, *Summa Theologica*, *Encyclopedia Britannica*, Great Books, vol. 19 (Chicago, 1952), 629.
[248] John Passmore, *The Perfectibility of Man* (New York: Charles Scribner's Sons, 1970), 48.
[249] Leibnitz, *Principles of Nature and of Grace*, trans. from *Philosophische Schriften*, ed. Gerhardt, VI, 606, in A. O. Lovejoy: *The Great Chain of Being* (Cambridge, MA, 1948), 248.
[250] Hyamblicus, *De vita Pythagorica*, 82.

of the soul; pleasure comes from animal sensations, or the gratification of worldly and ambitious desires, and therefore is often demoralizing. Happiness is an elevated joy, a beatitude, existing with pain and disease, when the soul is triumphant over the body; while pleasure is transient, and comes from what is perishable.[251]

In addition, Hegel stated,

> Aristotle hence also looks on political philosophy as the sum total of practical philosophy, the end of the state as general happiness. First of all, then, we must see that every science and art has an end, and that too a good one ... that the end of the best art, will be the best good. But statecraft is the best art, so that the end of this will be the good (happiness).[252]

In his *Ethics*, Aristotle realized that the supreme good—the perfection that led to happiness—applied not only to individuals but also to the state. He wrote, "Man is a political animal with reason," and people must engage in politics to perfect society since happy people make happy and harmonious societies. He stated,

> A social instinct is implanted in all men by nature, and yet he who founded the state is the greatest of benefactors. For man, when perfected, is the best of animals, but, when he is separated from law and justice, he is the worst of all.[253]

Modern man was not the first to discover that good, honest people made honest politics and that the perfection of people led to perfection of the state. Aristotle has the highest respect for politics.

> Now it would seem that this supreme End must be the object of the most authoritative of the sciences—some science which is pre-eminently a master-craft. But such is manifestly the science of politics ... This then being its aim, our investigation is in a sense the study of Politics.[254]

[251] Lord, *Beacon Lights of History*, vol. 1, Internet.

[252] Aristotle, *Magna Moralia*, 1182a34-1182b1, Ross translation, Internet.

[253] Aristotle, *Politics*, 1253a30.

[254] Aristotle, *Nicomachean Ethics*.

In more-modern times, intellectuals stressed the moral aspects required for a harmonious state. In his *Representative Government* (1861), John Stuart Mill wrote,

> The first element of good government, therefore, being the virtue and intelligence of the human beings composing the community, the most important point of excellence which any form of government can possess is to promote the virtue and intelligence of the people themselves.[255]

The famous philosopher William Turner wrote on the subject of happiness.

> The supreme good of man is happiness ... Of this no Greek had the least doubt ... But how is this well-being to be attained? What is it that constitutes happiness? Happiness is determined by the end for which man was made, and the end of human existence is that form of good which is peculiar to man, the good which is proper to a rational being. Now, reason is the prerogative of man. It should, therefore, be the aim of man's existence to live conformably to reason, to live a life of virtue.[256]

There have been numerous other definitions of happiness; I present some of them in the following pages, but I believe Aristotle's definition of happiness on the Delos epigram is the best as it is complete and includes all elements of happiness.

In his *Improvement of the Understanding*, Baruch Spinoza defined the *summum bonum* and provided some principles in attaining it.

> We must understand as much of nature as is necessary in order to bring about the highest possible nature in man.

> We must establish the kind of society that is necessary if many men are to attain this end as easily and surely as possible.

> We must find an ethical philosophy and a doctrine of education leading in this direction.

> We must promote medicine for the sake of men's health, which is far from negligible as a means to our end.

---

[255] John Stuart Mill, *Representative Government* (1861).
[256] W. Turner, *History of Philosophy* (Boston: Ginn & Co.), 154.

We must improve mechanics to make difficult things easy, so saving much time and trouble …

Thus, all the science should be oriented toward a single aim, which is the highest human perfection.[257]

Spinoza continued,

It is … most profitable to us in life to make perfect the intellect or reason as far as possible, and in this one thing consists the highest happiness or blessedness of man; for blessedness is nothing but the peace of mind which springs from the intuitive knowledge of God … The final aim, therefore, of a man who is guided by reason, that is to say, the chief desire by which he strives to govern all his other desires, is that by which he is led adequately to conceive himself and all things which can be conceived by his intelligence.[258]

The US Declaration of Independence states the following on happiness: "We hold these truths to be self-evident, that all men are created equal, that they are endowed by their Creator with certain unalienable Rights, that among these are Life, Liberty and the pursuit of Happiness." The words *life, liberty and the pursuit of happiness* are attributed to Thomas Jefferson.

Kant equated happiness with virtue and morality.

Now in as much as virtue and happiness together constitute the possession of the highest good in a person, and the distribution of happiness in exact proportion to morality (which is the worth of the person, and his worthiness to be happy) constitutes the highest good of a possible world; hence this highest good expresses the whole, the perfect good, in which, however, virtue as the condition is always the supreme good, since it has no condition above it; whereas happiness, while it is pleasant to the possessor of it, is not of itself absolutely and in all respects good, but always presupposes morally right behavior as its condition.[259]

---

[257] Karl Jaspers, *The Great Philosophers*, vol. 2, *Spinoza* (New York: Harcourt Brace Jovanovich), 8.

[258] Project Gutenberg's, "The Philosophy of Spinoza," by Baruch de Spinoza, Ethics, appendix, Life of Virtue, IV.

[259] Kant, *Critique of Practical Reason*, part 1, chapter 2, 339 GB.

In *War and Peace,* Leo Tolstoy asked, "How can one be well, when one suffers morally?"

In *Morals,* Plutarch wrote, "Happiness comes from within, not from without. The true seat of happiness is the mind."

In the New Testament, Christ spoke to crowds about his eight famous beatitudes in Matthew 5:3–12.

> Happy/Blessed are the poor in spirit, for theirs is the kingdom of heaven.

> Blessed are they who mourn, for they shall be comforted.

> Blessed are the meek, for they shall inherit the earth.

> Blessed are they who hunger and thirst for righteousness, for they shall be satisfied.

> Blessed are the merciful, for they shall obtain mercy.

> Blessed are the pure of heart, for they shall see God.

> Blessed are the peacemakers, for they shall be called children of God.

> Blessed are they who are persecuted for the sake of righteousness, for theirs is the kingdom of heaven.

Luke 6:20–22 mentions four beatitudes.

> Blessed are you who are poor, for yours is the kingdom of God.

> Blessed are you who hunger now, for you will be satisfied. Blessed are you who weep now, for you will laugh.

> Blessed are you when people hate you, when they exclude you and insult you and reject your name as evil, because of the Son of Man.

> Rejoice in that day and leap for joy, because great is your reward in heaven.

Schopenhauer stated that over time, happiness was changed to salvation for believers: "It is Kant's great service to moral science that he purified it of all Eudaemonism. With the ancients, Ethics was a doctrine of Eudaemonism; with the moderns, for the most part it has been a doctrine of salvation."[260]

VIRTUE

The ancient Greek word for virtue is *aretê*, ἀρετή, and it has many meanings: excellence of character of any kind, goodness, righteousness, perfection, merit, fitness, bravery, valor, capability to excel, or excellence of any kind. The most common translations are excellence, moral excellence, or moral virtue. It has been used interchangeably as virtue or excellence. Virtue comes from the Latin *virtus*, meaning strength or courage; it comes from *vir*, man.

According to P. Angeles, the philosophic meaning of virtue has to do with "the functioning excellence of a thing … A human's virtue consists of his development and use of his reason to his outmost functioning excellence."[261] I believe the best modern translation of arête is "excellence" of any kind or "moral virtue" or plain virtue.[262]

Throughout this book, the word *virtue* will be used for *aretê* and interchangeably with *excellence*; it contains all the above meanings, not just moral virtue. More specifically, virtue is the knowledge and skill to perform and excel in various activities as well as moral virtue. An artist who paints a beautiful picture possesses the virtue of a great painter, and as Plato says, the horse has the virtue of speed.

Ethical or moral character comes from the word *ethos* (Greek for "custom" or "habit"), as does the word *ethics*. Ethics and morality are synonyms. Thus, all activities include ethics, the idea of good and bad, and the backbone of ethics is the idea of virtue.

Edith Hamilton stated,

> "Virtue or Excellence" is the nearest equivalent we have to the word they commonly used for it, but it meant more than that. It was the utmost perfection possible, the very best and highest a man could attain to, which when perceived always has a compelling authority. A man must strive to attain it. Aristotle summed up the search and struggle: "Excellence much labored for by the race of men." The long and steep and rough road to it was the road Greek religion took.[263]

---

[260] Arthur Schopenhauer, *The Basis of Morality*, 72, part 2, chapter 1, Internet.

[261] P. Angeles, *A Dictionary of Philosophy* (London: Harper and Row), 17.

[262] H. G. Liddell and R. Scott, *A Greek–English Lexicon*, 9th ed. (Oxford, 1940).

[263] E. Hamilton, *The Greek Way* (Book of the Month Club, 1942), 287.

According to Werner Jaeger,

> The root of the word arête is the same as "aristos," the word which shows superlative ability and superiority, and "aristos" was constantly used in the plural to denote the nobility … the Greeks felt that arête was above everything else a power, an ability to do something. Strength and health are the arête of the body, cleverness and insight are the arête of the mind … An essential commitment to arête is honor.[264]

Virtues constitute the core, the main tenet of ethics and morality, and our obligations as well. Virtues are the highest ideals and constitute the core moral rules of conduct for a given culture. Therefore, those possessing virtue achieve excellence, perfection, happiness, and well-being. Aristotle considered virtues as a system of values, the moral virtues that lift the character and the intellectual virtues and cultivate the intellect of an individual.

Without virtue, societies and nations can become human jungles of the worst kind. In today's world, almost everyone agrees that virtue is the greatest good, but most think everyone but themselves and their societies lack it.

One may define virtue as an activity of the soul we need to engage in to achieve moral and intellectual self-perfection along with material goods for ourselves and our society. Various philosophies and religions include various virtues; some are common among them while others are unique to them.

The prerequisites for the acquisition of virtue are two: rationalism and knowledge of the good. This is what Socrates meant by saying knowledge was virtue and virtue was knowledge. Socrates believed that knowledge was virtue and would be sufficient to produce the perfect man.

About two thousand years later, Montaigne repeated the relationship of knowledge and the essence of the good: "Every other knowledge is harmful to him who does not have knowledge of goodness."[265] That is valid more than ever today.

In *Menexenus*, Plato had Socrates describe virtue as the highest good: "Remember our words, then, and whatever is your aim let virtue be the condition of the attainment of your aim, and know that without this all possessions and pursuits are dishonorable and evil."[266]

The highest achievement for humanity is virtue, excellence. Virtue leads to happiness, and there can be no happiness without virtue. Virtues must be the

---

[264] Jaeger, *Paideia*, vol. 1, 5.
[265] Montaigne, *Essays*, trans. E. J. Trechmann (New York: Oxford University Press), 139.
[266] Plato, *Menexenus*, 246e1, trans. B. Jowett, *Plato the Collected Dialogues*, Hamilton and Cairns eds. (Pantheon Books), 196.

universal guiding principle in all human activities, as humanity's ultimate goal is happiness.

The history of the development of virtues and their evolution started around the sixth century BC with the pre-Socratics. These so-called main or cardinal virtues were further identified and refined by Socrates, Plato, and Aristotle, among the most remarkable intellects in history in the fifth century BC, and they were accepted totally or partially by subsequent philosophers. These cardinal virtues are prudence, temperance or moderation, courage or fortitude, and justice. Homer, Hesiod, and the pre-Socratics believed this, but Socrates reinforced the virtues. As Rackham stated,

> It is my view, and it is universally agreed, that Socrates was the first person who summoned philosophy away from mysteries veiled in concealment by nature herself, upon which all philosophers before him had been engaged, and led it to the subject of ordinary life, in order to investigate the virtues and vices, and good and evil generally, and to realize that heavenly matters are either remote from our knowledge or else, however fully known, have nothing to do with the good life.[267]

St. Paul established in the New Testament the three theological virtues: "Three things will last forever—**faith, hope, and love**—and the greatest of these is love." The same chapter further defined love as "patient, kind, not envious, boastful, arrogant, or rude" (Corinthians 1:13). Christianity adopted the four ancient cardinal virtues, and thus the main virtues became seven. These three virtues constitute the pillars of Christianity. The three theological virtues were mentioned in various ancient Greek texts, but they were singled out by St. Paul as the trinity of theological virtues. The Christian virtue of love is sometimes called charity. Pope Gregory I (c. 540–604), commonly known as St. Gregory the Great, formally adopted all seven of them into Christian dogma.[268]

Throughout history, many illustrious people composed sets of ethics, rules, or aphorisms for people to live ethical lives that led to happiness. The list is long and started with the Code of Hammurabi (c. 1750 BC), king of Babylonia. The code dealt with punishments and emphasized retribution, but one can infer from the punishment what not to do. The Ten Commandments (Exodus 20:1–17) constitute such a code.

The disciples of Confucius (551–479 BC), the classical Chinese philosopher, collected his thoughts in the *Analects*, a collection of maxims and aphorisms.

---

[267] *History of Philosophy*, vol. 1, *From the Beginning to Plato*, I. 5. 15, trans. Rackham, ed. C. C. W. Taylor (Routledge, 1997).
[268] Manchester, *A World Lit by Fire*, 8.

Confucianism is not a religion but a code of ethics. Confucius believed that humanity could be improved by education.

Religions—Hinduism, Buddhism, Taoism, Christianity, Islam, and others—have codes of ethics written by their adherents; some were believed to have been passed down from God through their prophets. There are numerous other virtues that various religious and philosophies developed.

In Western culture, the main seven virtues—the four cardinal virtues and the three theological virtues—were adopted and discussed extensively in literature. All other virtues are secondary and are included in the main ones. The word *cardinal* comes from the Latin word *cardo*, which refers to a door hinge. All other virtues are in the periphery hinged on them. Plato and Aristotle had introduced a crucial point of the unity of virtues, meaning that one cannot possess one virtue but not the others.

Our first philosophical records date from about 600 BC, when the seven sages of Greece and the pre-Socratic philosophers first asked the following: How best can humans live? What is the ideal human existence? How should they be governed? They tried to infuse ethics into politics and left us with great texts on these subjects. They are as current today as at the time they were written twenty-five hundred years ago.

Trying to determine how best to live was one of the major topics discussed in antiquity, and it led to numerous philosophies and writings starting from the pre-Socratics in the sixth century BC to Boethius in the sixth century AD. The search continued during the Renaissance and still goes on today.

The seven main virtues were meant to constitute the backbone of Christianity in the practical and intellectual sense. These virtues have a history for about 2,000–2,600 years. They are the distilled extracts of wisdom that came from the best human intellects from the pre-Socratics to today. Starting with Homer, Hesiod, and the pre-Socratics, who invented them in the sixth century BC, they were debated by Socrates and Plato and expanded by Aristotle in *Nicomachean Ethics*. They were adopted by the Stoics and partly by the Epicureans. They were discussed by Jesus and his followers; St. Paul introduced and summarized the three theological virtues in the New Testament.

For the past two millennia, they were analyzed, praised, justified, exalted, and sometimes preached by all the major philosophers, humanists, and saints from Plutarch, Epictetus, the emperor Marcus Aurelius, St. Augustine, the three hierarchs (Chrysostom, Gregory Nazianzus, Basil the Great), St. Athanasius, Pope St. Gregory the Great, St. Thomas Aquinas, Erasmus, and many more philosophers up to our modern times.

Numerous other philosophers pointed out the purpose of virtues and came up with the same rules quite independently. Pittacus of Mytilene (640–568 BC) stated one of the earliest versions of the golden rule: "Do not do yourself what you resent to your neighbor."[269]

---

[269] http://politicalquotes.org/node/55546#sthash.3PNvlutF.dpuf. D.L.I. 77, 79.

Confucius independently introduced the golden rule. Zi Gong, a disciple, asked, "Is there any one word that could guide a person throughout life?" The master replied, "How about 'reciprocity'! Never impose on others what you would not choose for yourself."[270]

As stated in Wikipedia,

> Often overlooked in Confucian ethics are the virtues to the self: sincerity and the cultivation of knowledge. Virtuous action towards others begins with virtuous and sincere thought, which begins with knowledge. A virtuous disposition without knowledge is susceptible to corruption and virtuous action without sincerity is not true righteousness. Cultivating knowledge and sincerity is also important for one's own sake; the superior person loves learning for the sake of learning and righteousness for the sake of righteousness.[271]

The golden rule was explicitly stated in Matthew 7:12: "So whatever you wish that others would do to you, do also to them, for this is the Law and the Prophets."[272]

Besides the cardinal virtues, in more modern times, Kant introduced the so-called categorical imperative. This is like a command or obligation, one of the virtuous acts of human beings; it was a major addition to ethical principles since the establishment of virtues. The categorical imperative stated, "Act only according to that maxim whereby you can at the same time will that it should become a universal law without contradiction."[273]

After reviewing other religions' beliefs about virtues or commandments, I believe these seven virtues are universal. All humans can find them to their benefit but not to the exclusion of other virtues their beliefs may hold. All people can use them to achieve moral perfection.

Almost all the philosophers mentioned above, preachers, and theologians of all religions came up with many theories, transparent and confusing, contradicting and clear statements, and short and much longer discourses on them. However, they left others confused about how to live good, moral lives and thus achieve happiness.

The virtues provide a simple, memorable code that further religious explanation and dogmatic clarifications simply confuses. Simply put, virtue leads to salvation. Various religions have their own rules and requirements for achieving salvation. It

---

[270] *Analects* XV.24, trans. David Hinton.

[271] Wiki.

[272] http://biblehub.com/matthew/7-12.htm

[273] Immanuel Kant, *Fundamental Principles of the Metaphysic of Morals*, trans. H. J. Patton (Harper Torchbooks, 1964), 88.

is a common belief that in Western cultures, there is no happiness or morality and thus salvation without virtue.

Humanity must set aside all religions and ideologies and ask, What can one tell me to do now or tomorrow in a few words or sentences to become better ethically for myself and society? This does not mean abandonment of one's religious or philosophical beliefs. Following these universal, eternal, and immutable virtues, we cannot go wrong.

Ethics is a continuous activity throughout our lives. We agonize over many decisions while striving for perfection. This activity is nothing more than trying to be virtuous always. It is an obligation and duty, as Kant said, of every human to act with virtue.

Arnold Toynbee, one of the great historians of the twentieth century, wrote, "As human beings, we are endowed with freedom of choice, and we cannot shuffle off our responsibility upon the shoulders of God or nature. We must shoulder it ourselves. It is our responsibility."[274]

Moral states have a great impact on individuals living in them. Toynbee had a pessimistic comment about the United States around the second quarter of the twentieth century: "Of the twenty-two civilizations that have appeared in history, nineteen of them collapsed when they reached the moral state the United States is in now."[275]

The ancient Greeks had defined the four main virtues we discussed previously: wisdom or prudence, courage or fortitude, moderation or temperance, and justice. Aristotle defined the individual virtues in detail.

> The Noble is that which is both desirable for its own sake and also worthy of praise; or that which is both good and also pleasant because good. If this is a true definition of the Noble, it follows that virtue must be noble, since it is both a good thing and also praiseworthy.

> Virtue is, according to the usual view, a faculty of providing and preserving good things; or a faculty of conferring many great benefits, and benefits of all kinds on all occasions.

> The forms of Virtue are justice, courage, temperance, magnificence, magnanimity, liberality, gentleness, prudence, and wisdom. If virtue is a faculty of beneficence, the highest kinds of it must be

---

[274] http://www.brainyquote.com/quotes/quotes/a/arnoldjto101735.html#ZoFRPYxxCV tyJtby.99.
[275] http://www.brainyquote.com/quotes/authors/a/arnold_j_toynbee.html#tGA QTJjhIjZ3y tfI.99.

those which are most useful to others, and for this reason men honor most the just and the courageous, since courage is useful to others in war, justice both in war and in peace.

Next comes liberality; liberal people let their money go instead of fighting for it, whereas other people care more for money than for anything else. Justice is the virtue through which everybody enjoys his own possessions in accordance with the law; its opposite is injustice, through which men enjoy the possessions of others in defiance of the law.

Courage is the virtue that disposes men to do noble deeds in situations of danger, in accordance with the law and in obedience to its commands; cowardice is the opposite.

Temperance is the virtue that disposes us to obey the law where physical pleasures are concerned; incontinence is the opposite. Liberality disposes us to spend money for others' good; illiberality is the opposite.

Magnanimity is the virtue that disposes us to do good to others on a large scale; [its opposite is meanness of spirit].

Magnificence is a virtue productive of greatness in matters involving the spending of money. The opposites of these two are smallness of spirit and meanness respectively.

Prudence is that virtue of the understanding, which enables men to come to wise decisions about the relation to happiness of the goods and evils that have been previously mentioned.

… And those qualities are noble which give more pleasure to other people than to their possessors; hence the nobleness of justice and just actions.[276]

Philippians 4:8 reads, "Finally, brethren, whatever is true, whatever is honorable, whatever is just, whatever is pure, whatever is lovely, whatever is gracious, if there is any excellence (areté), if there is anything worthy of praise, think about these things."[277]

---

[276] Aristotle *Rhetoric*, 1366a-33, 1367a18, 2174.
[277] http://biblehub.com/philippians/4-8.htm

Additional listings of virtues besides the traditional Christian virtues appear in the Christian Bible. Such is the fruit of the spirit mentioned in Paul's epistle to the Galatians (5:22, 22–24): "But the fruit of the Spirit is love, joy, peace, forbearance, kindness, goodness, faithfulness, gentleness and self-control. Against such things there is no law."[278]

St. Augustine defined virtue as "Ars bene recteque vivendi," "The art of good and right living."[279]

Boethius was one of the last ancient philosophers. In his closing statements in his famous *Consolation of Philosophy*, he wrote,

> Therefore, all of you: Avoid vices, cherish virtues; raise up your minds to blameless hopes; extend your humble prayers into the lofty heights. Unless you want to hide the truth, there is a great necessity upon-you the necessity of righteousness, since you act before the eyes of a judge who beholds all things.[280]

The seven virtues are or can be the highest ideals or forms of conduct in a culture and lead to the perfection of humanity. They have been analyzed, challenged, and accepted through the ages from ancient days to today by the world's greatest minds, and they have been recognized as universal, rational, immutable, all encompassing, and eternal.

Virtues are personal qualities and characteristics valued for promoting collective and individual greatness or moral perfection. Kant stated, "Moral laws have to hold for every rational being as such."[281]

The seven contrary virtues, which are opposites of the seven deadly sins or vices are humility rather than pride, kindness rather than envy, abstinence rather than gluttony, chastity rather than lust, patience rather than anger, liberality rather than greed, and diligence rather than sloth.

Starting with Homer's *Iliad* and *Odyssey*, the virtue of epic heroes referred to valor, strength, nobility, wit, and striving for effectiveness and immortal glory. In an adversarial world, people can succeed by excelling, that is, being virtuous.

In the fifth century BC, Plato described in his *Protagoras* dialogue the four cardinal virtues—wisdom, courage, temperance, and justice. In addition, the virtue of piety was also introduced. In the same dialogue, virtue and knowledge were

---

[278] https://www.pinterest.com/pin/158540849357650872

[279] Turner, *History of Philosophy*, 233.

[280] Boethius, *Consolation of Philosophy*, trans. J. C. Relihan (Indianapolis: Hackett, 2001), 150.

[281] Kant, I., *Foundation for the Metaphysics of Morals*, Modern Philosophy, trans by W. Kaufman, vol. 3 (Prentice Hall) 614.

discussed. "In this familiar Platonic doctrine, it is brought out that no man does evil voluntarily. … and that wickedness has its roots in ignorance."[282]

In his *Gorgias* dialogue, Plato stated,

> So that it is absolutely necessary, Callicles, that the temperate man, as we have described him, being just, brave, and pious, should be a perfectly good man, and that a good man should do whatever he does well and honorably, and that he who does well should be blessed and happy, but that the wicked, who does ill, should be wretched.[283]

In the *Republic*, Plato discussed the virtues except piety. In his three books on ethics—*Eudaemian Ethics*, *Ethics*, and the towering *Nicomachean Ethics*, the doctrine of virtue found its fullest flowering. Aristotle replaced wisdom by prudence, which he called "practical wisdom."

The following connects virtue with knowledge.

> Accordingly Socrates the senior thought that the End is to get to know virtue, and he pursued an inquiry into the nature of justice and courage and each of the divisions of virtue. And this was a reasonable procedure, since he thought that all the virtues are forms of knowledge, so that knowing justice and being just must go together, for as soon as we have learnt geometry and architecture, we are architects and geometricians; owing to which he used to inquire what virtue is, but not how and from what sources it is produced.[284]

There are many other definitions of virtue. The founders of the American constitution placed virtue over all.

> There is no truth more thoroughly established, than that there exists … an indissoluble union between virtue and happiness … Human rights can only be assured among a virtuous people. The general government … can never be in danger of degenerating into a monarchy, an oligarchy, an aristocracy, or any despotic or

---

[282] Plato, *Protagoras*, 330b3, 308.

[283] Plato, *Gorgias*, 507c, trans. W. Woodhead, *Plato the Collected Dialogues*, Hamilton and Cairns, eds. (Pantheon 1961), 289.

[284] Aristotle, *Eudaemian Ethics*, *Complete Works of Aristotle*, trans. J. Solomon, ed. J. Barnes (Princeton, 1984), 1216b1, 1925.

oppressive form so long as there is any virtue in the body of the people. —George Washington

Only a virtuous people are capable of freedom. As nations become more corrupt and vicious, they have more need of masters ... Laws without morals are in vain. —Benjamin Franklin.

When virtue is banished, ambition invades the minds of those who are disposed to receive it, and avarice possesses the whole community. —Thomas Jefferson.

In *Nicomachean Ethics*, Aristotle divided virtues into two kinds: intellectual (perfections of the human intellect) and moral (excellences of the character). The intellectual virtues are art (knowledge of how to do things), science, prudence (practical wisdom), philosophic wisdom, and intuitive reason (understanding). Of the five intellectual virtues, only prudence was selected as one of the cardinal virtues; the rest were considered of lesser significance. Intellectual virtues result from teaching; moral virtues result from habit. Prudence includes the science of political government and organization as well as the general questions of moral science.[285]

Of these, intellect, science, and wisdom are perfections of scientific reasoning, the capability to think, investigate, search for, and demonstrate the highest causes. It takes science, intellectual development, to acquire a broad knowledge of sciences and humanities. Art is the perfection of the practical reason providing the ability to make things. Prudence (practical wisdom) refers to actions of excellence in making the correct decisions.

Aristotle stated that prudence was concerned with all things human and individuals themselves. Intellectual virtues result from teaching while moral virtues result from habit. Bertrand Russell wrote,

It is the business of the state to teach citizens to acquire all the arts and other intellectual virtues and make them good by forming good habits. We become just by performing just acts, and similarly as regards other virtues. By being compelled to acquire good habits, we shall in time, Aristotle thinks, come to find pleasure in performing good actions.[286]

According to Turner "The most characteristic of Aristotle's ethical teachings is the superiority, which he assigns to intellectual over moral virtue, and the most

---

[285] Aristotle, *Nicomachean Ethics, Complete Works of Aristotle*, trans. J. Solomon, ed. J. Barnes (Princeton, 1984),, 1139b-15.
[286] Bertrand Russell, *Western Philosophy*, Internet Books.

serious defect in his ethical system is his failure to refer human action to future reward and punishment." [287]

St. Augustine (354–430) stated,

> No one can be happy unless he possesses wisdom; for all men desire wisdom, and no one is happy unless he attains that which he desires. To deny that wisdom is possible of attainment is, therefore, to deny that happiness is possible.[288]

Plotinus (AD 204/5–270), regarded as the founder of Neoplatonism, commented on virtues.

> Indeed, as the ancient oracle declares, temperance and fortitude, prudence and every virtue, are certain purgatives of the soul; and hence the sacred mysteries prophesy obscurely, yet with truth, that the soul not purified lies in Tartarus, immersed in filth. Since the impure is, from his depravity, the friend of filth, as swine, from their sordid body, delight in mire alone.
>
> For what else is true temperance than not to indulge in corporeal delights, but to fly from their connection, as things which are neither pure, nor the offspring of purity? And true fortitude is not to fear death; for death is nothing more than a certain separation of soul from body, and this he will not fear, who desires to be alone.[289]

In *Summa Theologica*, Thomas Aquinas asserted the following correspondences between the seven cardinal virtues and the seven gifts of the Holy Spirit.

The gift of wisdom corresponds to the virtue of charity.

The gifts of understanding and knowledge correspond to the virtue of faith.

The gift of counsel (right judgment) corresponds to the virtue of prudence.

The gift of fortitude corresponds to the virtue of courage.

---

[287] Turner, *History of Philosophy*.
[288] Ibid., 226.
[289] Plotinus, *An Essay on the Beautiful / From the Greek of Plotinus*, Internet.

The gift of fear of the Lord corresponds to the virtue of hope.

The gift of Reverence corresponds to the virtue of justice.

To the virtue of temperance, no Gift is directly assigned; but the gift of fear can be taken as such, since fear drives somebody to restrict himself from forbidden pleasures.[290]

I shall describe the four cardinal virtues in more detail.

PRUDENCE OR PRACTICAL WISDOM

Plato defined prudence as "the ability which by itself is productive of human happiness; the knowledge of what is good and bad; the knowledge that produces happiness, the disposition by which we judge what is to be done and what is not to be done."[291]

A major component of prudence is reasoning; in his oration to Demonicus, Isocrates exalted reasoning and wisdom.

Take thought for everything that concerns your life, but especially cultivate your own reasoning power; for a sound mind in a man's body is the greatest thing in the smallest compass. Try to be in your body a lover of toil, and in your soul a lover of wisdom, that with the one you may be able to execute your resolves, and with the other may know how to foresee what is expedient.[292]

Seneca, the Roman Stoic said that, "perfect prudence is indistinguishable from perfect virtue. His point was that if you take the longest view and consider all the consequences, in the end, a perfectly prudent person would act in the same way as a perfectly virtuous person." [293]

"Plato in Meno, expressed the same rationale, when he wrote that people only act in ways that they perceive will bring them maximum good. It is the lack of wisdom that results in the making of a bad choice instead of a prudent one. In this way, wisdom

---

[290] *Summa Theologia: Secunda Secundae Partis*, NewAdvent.org, 2010, webpage: NA3.

[291] Plato's Definitions, *Complete Works*, J. M. Cooper, D. S. Hutchison, eds. (Indianapolis: Hackett 1997), 1679.

[292] Isocrates, *Demonicus*, trans. J. A. Freese, Internet.

[293] http://encyclopedia.kids.net.au/page/fi/Five_cardinal_virtues?title=Unforgiveness.

is the central part of virtue. Plato realized that because virtue was synonymous with wisdom it could be taught, a possibility he had earlier discounted." [294]

COURAGE OR FORTITUDE

There are two types of courage. First is physical courage when one is in danger or in battle. The second is moral courage before responsibility; to act through knowledge and use the right prudence to achieve the best possible outcome.

Courage is the mean between fear and overconfidence. Plato defined courage as

the state of the soul which is unmoved by fear; military confidence; knowledge of the facts of warfare; self-restraint in the soul about what is fearful and terrible; boldness in obedience to wisdom; being intrepid in the face of death; the state which stands on guard over correct thinking in dangerous situations; force which counterbalances danger; force of fortitude in respect of virtue; calm in the soul about what correct thinking takes to be frightening or encouraging things; the preservation of fearless beliefs about the terrors and experience of warfare; the state which cleaves to the law.[295]

TEMPERANCE

Plato defined temperance or self-control.

Moderation of the soul concerning the desires and pleasures that normally occur in it; harmony and good discipline in the soul in respect of normal pleasures and pains; concord of the soul in respect of ruling and being ruled; normal personal independence; good discipline in the soul; rational agreement within the soul about what is admirable and contemptible; the state by which its possessor chooses and is cautious about what he should.[296]

Temperance is a habitual moderation in the indulgence of the appetites, thoughts, or passions. Jean Jacques Rousseau wrote,

---

[294] https://studymoose.com/virtue-plato-2-essay
[295] Plato's Definitions, *Complete Works*, 1679.
[296] Ibid.

Temperance and labor are the two real physicians of man ... labor sharpens his appetite and temperance prevents him from abusing it. It teaches him to control it ... but health can only be bought by temperance, and as there is no real pleasure without health, I should be temperate from sensual motives.[297]

JUSTICE

Aristotle stated that justice was the greatest of virtues.

This form of justice then is complete excellence-not absolutely, but in relation to others. And therefore, justice is often thought to be the greatest of excellences and "neither evening nor morning star" is so wonderful; and proverbially "in justice is every excellence comprehended." And it is complete excellence in its fullest sense, because it is his actual exercise of complete excellence.[298]

The virtues discussed are universal and have withstood the test of time. At different times, humanity has come up with various explanations for natural phenomena, some more complete than others. The physical laws we have unlocked provide a good explanation as progress has been immense since the first explosion of knowledge. But when it comes to the nonphysical world, moral principles are applied. In this area, humanity is somewhat confused, and not all people have adopted universal principles due to the variety of religious, social, and political backgrounds and states of development. Not all knowledge of the nonphysical world is cumulative.

There is very little dispute about the universal applicability of physical laws, but there is plenty of doubt about moral principles. The key to bridging the gap between the physical and moral laws and making moral principles more acceptable is knowledge. Knowledge is the key for physical laws and moral principles alike. Knowledge of the good must be the essential undertaking for all.

KNOWLEDGE

Knowledge defines an individual and a society as it drives thoughts, actions, behaviors, beliefs, and creativity. Our level of civilization is reflected by our level of

---

[297] Rousseau, *Émile.*
[298] Aristotle, *Nicomachean Ethics*, 1129b27, 1783.

knowledge. As James Burke wrote, "We are what we know. And when the body of knowledge changes, so do we."[299]

Throughout history, knowledge has been the most important and powerful tool for survival and understanding of oneself. A thorough understanding of ourselves and our natural surroundings allows us to become better morally, physically, and intellectually. As Plato said, "knowledge is virtue" and knowledge is "justified, true, belief." Knowledge is the very key to understanding what is known and the unfathomable. Through cumulative knowledge, step by step, humanity reached its present level of civilization.

Knowledge is being preserved in man's memory; as Aeschylus said, "Memory is the mother of wisdom."

Reason is the fountainhead of knowledge and understanding; without it, knowledge is nothing but simple awareness. Reason is the internal driver of any inquiry.

As quoted in the *Analects* (16:9), Confucius put a high value on knowledge.

> Those who are born with the possession of knowledge are the highest class of men. Those who learn, and so, readily, get possession of knowledge, are the next. Those who are dull and stupid, and yet compass the learning, are another class next to these. As to those who are dull and stupid and yet do not learn; they are the lowest of the people.

In his *Preliminary Discourse to the Encyclopedia*, D'Alembert gave the way of learning and acquiring knowledge.

> Memory, reason and imagination are the three different manners in which our soul operates on the objects of its thoughts ... these three faculties form at the outset the three general divisions of our system of human knowledge: History, which is related to memory; Philosophy, which is the fruit of reason; and the Fine Arts, which are born of imagination. Placing reason ahead of imagination appears to us to be a well-founded arrangement and one that is in conformity with the natural progress of the operations of the mind. Imagination is a creative faculty, and the mind, before it considers creating, begins by reasoning upon what it sees and knows. Another motive, which should decide us, to place reason

---

[299] James Burke, *The Day the Universe Changed* (Little, Brown, 1984), 11.

ahead of imagination, is that in the latter faculty the other two are to some extent brought together.[300]

Lewis XVI recognized the power of knowledge when he stated that Voltaire and Rousseau provided the intellectual powder for the French Revolution. Voltaire said, "Books rule the world or at least those nations in it which have a written language; the others do not count." And he proceeded to enfranchise France. "When once a nation begins to think, it is impossible to stop it."[301]

Napoleon was very aware of the power of the press: "The Bourbons might have preserved themselves if they had controlled writing materials. The advent of cannon killed the feudal system; ink will kill the modern social organization."[302]

Knowledge is transferred through symbols, imitation, narrative exchange, and writing. Writing has proven to be one of the most significant and universal tools; it was one of the important inventions triggering the Greek knowledge explosion, while printing was important for the marvelous expansion of the Renaissance in word, deed, and area. Modern communication can be used to transfer information in audio, video, or document form instantly and anywhere. However, it takes more for information to become knowledge. In following Plato's statement, it has to be evaluated by gained experience, must be true, and must be believed.

Socrates believed in knowledge; he felt great humility for what he did and did not know. The two mottos written at Apollo's temple at Delphi—Know thyself and Nothing to excess—constitute the crown of philosophy. Self-knowledge is the very essence of prudence, temperance. It urges individuals to assess their self-knowledge so they can make the right decisions and take the right actions. Nothing to excess means to use temperance and act in moderation.

In his *Protagoras* dialogue, Plato extolled knowledge.

And what, Socrates, is the food of the soul? Surely, I said, knowledge is the food of the soul; Knowledge is a fine thing quite capable of ruling a man, and if he can distinguish good from evil, nothing will force him to act otherwise than as knowledge dictates, since wisdom is all the reinforcement he needs … I agree with you Socrates, said Protagoras; and not only so, but I, above all other men, am bound to say that wisdom and knowledge are the most powerful elements of human life.[303]

---

[300] Jean Le Rond d'Alembert, *Preliminary Discourse to the Encyclopedia of Diderot*, in Simonyi Karoly, *A Cultural History of Physics* (CRC Press, 2010), 216.
[301] J. Casperson, *The Butterfly Effect, Flutters of Wisdom and Kindness* (New York: Page Publishing, 2017).
[302] http://catholicism.org/enlightenment-not-over.html.
[303] Plato, *Protagoras*, 313c7, 352c2, 344.

In *Charmides*, Plato stated, "The life according to knowledge is not that which makes men act rightly and be happy, not even if knowledge include all the sciences, but one science only, that of good and evil."[304]

Throughout his *Metaphysics*, Aristotle wrote, "All men by nature desire to know." People wish to acquire knowledge, which is worthy of being called wisdom. The desire to know, he pointed out, was innate in human beings and it led to excellence. Aristotle continues in his *Parts of Animals*,

> Every study and investigation, the humblest and the noblest alike, seems to admit of two kinds of proficiency; one of which may be properly called educated knowledge of the subject, while the other is a kind of acquaintance with it. For an educated man should be able to form a fair judgment as to the goodness or badness of an exposition. To be educated is in fact to be able to do this; and the man of general education we take to be such. It will, however, of course, be understood that we only ascribe universal education to one who in his own individual person is thus able to judge nearly all branches of knowledge, and not to one who has a like ability merely in some special subject. For it is possible for a man to have this competence in some one branch of knowledge.[305]

According to Diogenes Laertius, Socrates said there was only one good—knowledge—and only one evil—ignorance; wealth and good birth brought their possessors no dignity but on the contrary, evil.[306]

One who strives for virtue or excellence must have knowledge. Knowledge provides not only the technical capability to learn how to do things but also the dialectic knowledge of understanding behavioral rules, moral actions, etc. Each generation builds on the knowledge and abilities of its predecessors. This leads to a continuous improvement of the human race as far as technical knowledge is concerned. Knowledge produces more knowledge, progress, civilization, and culture. Only knowledge will elevate people to perfection in the technical fields and in the humanities where truth, good government, and mutual assistance are just some human activities.

Socrates believed the people lacked knowledge of virtue when they were not virtuous and were ignorant of the source of evil. In Plato's *Crito*, Socrates was asked why when other people were accusing him of crimes that were going to cost him his

---

[304] Plato, *Charmides*, 174c1, trans. B. Jowett, in *Plato the Collected Dialogues*, Hamilton and Cairns, eds. (Pantheon Books, 1961), 120.
[305] Aristotle, *Parts of Animals*, in *The Complete Works of Aristotle*, trans. W. Ogle, ed. J. Barnes (Princeton University Press), book 1, 639a1, 994.
[306] Diogenes Laertius, vol. 1, Perseus.

life, he accepted the judgment with humility. He said, "They are doing what they are doing because they do not know any better ... Then we ought not to retaliate or render evil for evil to anyone, whatever evil we may have suffered from them." Four hundred years later, not unlike Socrates, Christ on the cross prayed, "Father, forgive them as they know not what they do"[307] (Luke: 23:34).

Knowledge is acquired through learning, which is modified by experience. Only knowledge of good behavior can be modified for the good. Education is the process of imparting knowledge, values, skills, and attitudes that can benefit the individual.

In *Menexenus*, Plato warned that knowledge must be accompanied by virtue.

> All knowledge, when separated from justice and virtue, is seen to be cunning and not wisdom; wherefore make this your first and last and constant and all-absorbing aim, to exceed, if possible, not only us but all your ancestors in virtue; and know that to excel you in virtue only brings us shame, but that to be excelled by you is a source of happiness to us.[308]

When not accompanied by virtue, knowledge can be a source of mischief and grief.

In his *Basic Writings*, Bertrand Russell (1872–1970) connected ethics, knowledge, and happiness in a way similar to Aristotle's.

> The conclusion on ethics may be summed up in a single phrase: "The good life is the one inspired by love and guided by knowledge ... the knowledge of science, history, literature and art, ought to be attainable by all who desire it ... a good life is a virtuous life ... To live a good life in the fullest sense a man must have a good education, friends, love, children (if he desires them), a sufficient income to keep him from want and grave anxiety, good health, and work which is not uninteresting."[309]

A. E. Housman stated the interdependence of knowledge, virtue, and happiness.

> Let a man acquire knowledge not for this or that external and incidental good which may chance to result from it, but for itself; not because it is useful or ornamental, but because it is knowledge, and therefore good for man to acquire.[310]

---

[307] http://www.jesuswalk.com/7-last-words/1_forgive.htm
[308] Plato, *Menexenus*, 247a1-b4, 196.
[309] B. Russell, *Outline of Philosophy*, in *The Basic Writings of Bertrand Russell*, 382.
[310] A. E. Housman (London: University College, 1892).

The ancient Greeks put much emphasis on knowledge and the concept of *paideia*, translated best by Jaeger as "education and culture."

The ideals of knowledge and culture and the transmission of knowledge were stated by Isocrates (436–338 BC), one of the most influential Greek rhetoricians of his time. He made many contributions to rhetoric and education through his teaching and written works. In his speech to Demonicus, Isocrates said,

> If you love learning, you will attain to much learning. What you know, preserve by exercise, and what you have not learnt, add to your knowledge … Spend the leisure time of your life in cultivating a ready ear for conversation; for thus you will be able to learn easily what others have acquired with difficulty … Consider that there are many precepts which are better than much wealth; for wealth speedily fails, but precepts abide with a man forever; wisdom is the only possession which is immortal.[311]

In his Panegyricus speech, Isocrates stated what separated Greeks from non-Greeks was not blood but intellect—culture and education.

> So far has Athens left the rest of mankind behind in thought and expression that her pupils have become the teachers of the world, and she has made the name of Hellas distinctive no longer of race but of intellect, and the title of Hellene a badge of education rather than of common descent … For just as we see the bee settling on all blossoms and sipping what is best from each, so ought those who strive after education to have some knowledge of everything, and to collect what is profitable from every side. For it is only with difficulty even by this diligence that a man will overcome the defects of nature.[312]

Knowledge is acquired through experience or education by perceiving, discovering, or learning. Having knowledge means having awareness and understanding of facts and information that provide the skills to perform technical functions or to make decisions. Knowledge can be theoretical or practical.

Humanity's ascent from its primitive state to modern times involved a series of accomplishments and innovations through the gain of knowledge. Knowledge and reason are our two most important faculties; we know what we can accomplish with knowledge and where we stand today.

Some people and some nations have grown powerful, but the use of power can

---

[311] Isocrates to *Demonicus*, trans. J. A. Freese, Internet.
[312] Isocrates, *Panegyricus*, no. 50, trans. J. A. Freese, Internet.

have catastrophic effects on the quality of life and even our planet. Prudent use of knowledge can bring happiness and prosperity, but imprudent use of power can have calamitous results. Governments have enacted laws to limit the power of people in and out of government, but that has not always worked out successfully. Ambitious and corrupt leaders have been abusing power.

Socrates stated that knowledge was virtue, and the highest knowledge is the knowledge of good and evil; those who know what is good will do no evil. Such knowledge is the wisdom of life.

Plato said, "According to Anaxagoras it is the mind, that brings order and is the originator of all things."[313]

In his Theaetetus dialogue, Plato inquired about the definition of knowledge. It became the founding document of what ended up being the epistemological branch of philosophy—*episteme* means knowledge in ancient Greek; it is the branch of philosophy that studies the nature and possibility of knowledge and asks, What is knowledge?

> Where does knowledge come from? How is it formulated, expressed, and communicated? Is sense experience necessary for all types of knowledge? What part does reason play in knowledge and is knowledge derived from reason only? Is knowledge possible?[314]

Crane Brinton raised questions about how some types of knowledge were used and why knowledge became the problem, not the solution, to our progress.

> Now this noncumulative knowledge, whether philosophy, theology, practical wisdom, or plain horse sense, has never yet been sufficient to preserve peace in earth, let alone to banish all kinds of evil in human relations. Unless we get another kind of knowledge of human behavior, say the alarmists, cumulative knowledge of the sort of the physicists or biologists has, we shall get affairs in such a mess that our civilization, and possibly even the human race, will be destroyed.[315]

Tcnities is our only hope of improvement; we must be prudent and eliminate extreme desires.

The ancients exalted knowledge that men with knowledge are more inclined to be virtues and not inclined to commit vices as the following statement by Euripides states,

---

[313] Plato, *Phaedo*, 97c.

[314] P. Angeles, *A Dictionary of Philosophy* (London: Harper and Row), 78.

[315] C. Brinton, *Ideas of Man: The Story of Western Thought* (Prentice Hall, 1950), 18.

Happy is the man who has gained knowledge through inquiry, not aiming to trouble his fellow citizens, nor to act unjustly, but observing eternal nature's ageless order, the way it was formed, and whence and how. Such men are never inclined to practice shameful deeds.[316]

For many years before even the outstanding achievements of the twentieth century, people voiced concerns about the impact of new technologies and its effects on humanity; they thought technical knowledge did not necessarily bring happiness.

People act based on partial knowledge and do so inconsistently and hypocritically. Nations must stop using double standards at home and abroad, and those who drive huge SUVs and waste energy should not call themselves environmentalists.

In a wall of a Munich palace were written the words, "Humilitas Lumen Intelligentiae," "Humility Lights Intelligence." This maxim expresses the relation of the virtue of humility and knowledge.

The Sophist Antiphon, a contemporary of Socrates, stated that knowledge was a product of education.

The first thing, I believe, for mankind is education. For whenever anyone does the beginning of anything correctly, it is likely that the end also will be right. As one sows, so can one expect to reap. And if in a young body one sows a noble education, this lives and flourishes through the whole of his life, and neither rain nor drought destroys it.[317]

Another Sophist, Protagoras, a teacher of ethics, stated the relationship between education and knowledge.

Toil and work and instruction and education and wisdom are the garland of fame which is woven from the flowers of an eloquent tongue and set on the head of those who love it. Eloquence however is difficult, yet its flowers are rich and ever new, and the audience and those who applaud and the teachers rejoice, and the scholars make progress and fools are vexed—or perhaps they are not even vexed, because they have not sufficient insight … Education does not take root in the soul unless one goes deep.[318]

Francis Bacon equated knowledge with power.

[316] Loeb Series, *Clement of Alexandria, Miscellanies*, 4.25, fragment 910 N.
[317] *Antiphon the Sophist, Ancilla to the Pre-Socratic Philosophers*, 223.
[318] Protagoras of Abdera, *Ancilla to the Pre-Socratic Philosophers*, 1.

Knowledge and human power are synonymous, since the ignorance of the cause frustrates the effect; for nature is only subdued by submission, and that which in contemplative philosophy corresponds with the cause in practical science becomes the rule.[319]

The literature is full of letters from fathers to sons on what to do and how to become happy. Priests and preachers bombard people daily in person or through the media with various conflicting and in time inconsistent ideas. "St. Bonaventura long ago wrote that 'to Aristotle was granted the spirit of knowledge, to Plato that of wisdom.'"[320]

Professor G. C. Field said,

No philosophic writer of past ages has such permanent interest and value as Plato. We ought to read him primarily for the help that he can give to our own philosophical thinking. That is certainly what he himself would have wished.

And Professor A. E. Taylor wrote,

To few men does the world owe a heavier debt than to Plato. He has taught us that philosophy, loving and single-minded devotion to truth, is the great gift of God to man and the rightful guide of man's life, and that the few to whom the intimate vision of truth has been granted are false to their calling unless they bear fruit in unwearied and humble service to their fellows. All worthy civilization is fed by those ideas, and whenever, after a time of confusion and forgetfulness, our Western world has recaptured the sense of noble living, it has sought them afresh in the Platonic writings.[321]

Plutarch (AD 46–120), a Greek biographer and moralist, wrote that to achieve happiness, people had to acquire education, virtues, values, reason, and knowledge, the last of which he considered divine.

In brief therefore I say, that the one chief thing in this matter which comprises the beginning, middle, and end of all is good education and regular instruction; and that these two afford great help and assistance towards the attainment of virtue and happiness. For

---

[319] Francis Bacon, *Novum Organum*, Internet.
[320] H. Gauss, *Plato's Conception of Philosophy*, Internet.
[321] Ibid.

all other good things are but human and of small value, such as
will hardly recompense the industry required to the getting of
them. It is, indeed, a desirable thing to be well descended; but the
glory belongs to our ancestors. Riches are valuable; but they are
the goods of Fortune, who frequently takes them from those that
have them, and carries them to those that never so much as hoped
for them … But the weightiest consideration of all is, that riches
may be enjoyed by the worst as well as the best of men. Glory is a
thing deserving respect, but unstable; beauty is a prize that men
fight to obtain, but, when obtained, it is of little continuance;
health is a precious enjoyment, but easily impaired; strength is
a thing desirable, but apt to be the prey of diseases and old age.
And, in general, let any man who values himself upon strength
of body know that he makes a great mistake; for what indeed is
any proportion of human strength, if compared to that of other
animals, such as elephants and bulls and lions? But learning?
alone, of all things in our possession, is immortal and divine …
Stilpo, a philosopher of Megara, gave to Demetrius, who, when he
leveled that city to the ground and made all the citizens bondmen,
asked Stilpo whether he had lost anything. Nothing, said he,
for war cannot plunder virtue. To this saying that of Socrates
also is very agreeable; who, when Gorgias asked him what his
opinion was of the king of Persia, and whether he judged him
happy, returned answer, that he could not tell what to think
of him, because he knew not how he was furnished with virtue
and learning, — as judging human happiness to consist in those
endowments, and not in those which are subject to fortune …
Moreover, as it is my advice to parents that they make the breeding
up of their children to learning the most important of their care,
so I here add, that the learning they ought to train them up unto
should be sound and wholesome, and such as is most remote from
those trifles which suit the popular humor.[322]

In *The Descent of Man*, Charles Darwin wrote, "Ignorance more frequently
begets confidence than does knowledge: it is those who know little, not those who
know much, who so positively assert that this or that problem will never be solved
by science."[323]

Within a century of Socrates, all the other branches of knowledge and philosophy
were introduced—logic, aesthetics, metaphysics, politics, and epistemology. Ethics

---

[322] Excerpt from Plutarch, *Plutarch's Morals*, vol. 1, Internet.
[323] Charles Darwin, *The Descent of man*

became the main branch of philosophy. Other philosophies on ethics occupied the minds of many philosophers since and became the center. These included Epicureans, Stoics, and Neoplatonists, Romans such as Cicero and Seneca, and Christian and other religious theologians from Anselm to Thomas Aquinas, Nicholas of Souza, and moderns including Descartes, Kant, and Hegel.

ETHICS AND RELIGION

If ethics is the guide to what we need to do and how to act, why should we act ethically? If we establish that the seven virtues and their subordinates are enough, what if people do not have knowledge of the good and the virtuous and instead obey their worst instincts? Can virtue tame vicious human passions? What about religion and the immortality of the soul? Many giants of philosophy, science, art, and literature have discussed the question of faith and religion., and the majority of them were religious.

Besides the discourses of the church fathers from Augustine, Anselm, and Thomas Aquinas, who wrote on the existence of God, other nonclerics but notable philosophers, scientists, and writers such as Descartes, Pascal, Dostoyevsky, and Tolstoy wrote extensive discourses on the existence of God.

The ten greatest minds of all time—philosophers and scientists—were all believers. The list includes Socrates, Plato, Aristotle, St. Thomas Aquinas, William of Ockham, Descartes, Kant, Hegel, and scientists Newton and Einstein. Aristotle, Descartes, Newton, and Kant were notable philosophers as well as scientists.

Fyodor Dostoyevsky, considered one of the greatest explorers of the human soul, stated in *The Brothers Karamazov,*

> The whole natural law lies in that faith, and that if you were to destroy in mankind the belief in immortality, not only love but every living force maintaining the life of the world would at once be dried up. Moreover, nothing then would be immoral, everything would be lawful, even cannibalism … I asked him, without God and immortal life? All things are lawful then, they can do what they like … if there's no immortality of the soul, then there's no virtue, and everything is lawful.[324]

Dostoyevsky's brief answer best answers the great dilemma of God, immortality, and virtue. If there is no God, all is permitted, and there is no individual ethics or rules of behavior other than state laws. The state will always be chaotic when it comes

[324] Fyodor Dostoyevsky, *The Brothers Karamazov*, trans. C. Garnett (New York: Modern Library, 1950), 717.

to enforcing the law in a fully amoral society; there can be no moral state with amoral people. Faith frees us from despair, gives us hope, and makes us strive for a virtuous life and a harmonious society.

Can morality survive without religion? In his essay "Religion and Morality" (1894), Leo Tolstoy wrote,

> The attempts to found a morality apart from religion are like the attempts of children who, wishing to transplant a flower that pleases them, pluck it from the roots that seem to them unpleasing and superfluous, and stick it rootless into the ground. Without religion, there can be no real, sincere morality, just as without roots there can be no real flower.[325]

Glenn C. Graber called this the "cut-flower" thesis: "Morality cannot survive, in the long run, if its ties to religion are cut." Ethics must be rooted in a morally perfect being—God.[326]

The bond between religion and morality is strong as shown by the theological virtues of faith, hope, and love in conjunction with the four cardinal virtues as stated by Plato and Aristotle. Tolstoy acknowledged the fundamental morality of all world religions, a universal principle: Do unto others as would be done unto thy self. He had this principle in mind when he stated, in his Last Message to Mankind, "You shall not kill under any circumstances."[327] Yet societies still have the death penalty; throughout the centuries, people fought, killed, and were killed and not a few times in the name of God. Religious killing goes on today, and colossal nuclear weapons are in silos ready to cause Armageddon. Humanity needs to reach a higher level of virtue and perfection to prevent this.

Voltaire had no doubts about the usefulness of religion for the masses. "Man," he stated, "has always needed a break … If God did not exist, he would have to be invented."[328] Without God or the fear of him, we would be hopeless, fearful, and without virtue.

Plato and Aristotle primarily defined the ideal culture in ancient Greece. Since that time, the world got bigger, and the men of the Enlightenment best defined the ideal culture of Western civilization practically unchanged to today. These were Voltaire, Rousseau, Locke, Hume, Kant, Hegel, and Jefferson. Ideal culture systems depend on humanity's excellence as defined by the ancients and Christianity. The human mind has found no better.

---

[325] Leo Tolstoy, *Religion and Morality, Selected Essays*, trans. Aylmer Maude (Random House), 31.

[326] http://ourhappyschool.com/philosophy/theistic-ethics-and-cut-flower-thesis

[327] http://www.peacehost.net/PacifistNation/Tolstoy.htm

[328] Winks, *History of Civilization*, 362.

WORLD ISSUES

This is why the salvation of the Universe is also our salvation, why
solidarity among men is no longer a tenderhearted luxury but a
deep necessity and self-preservation, as much a necessity as, in an
army under fire, the salvation of your comrade-in arms.[329]
—Nikos Kazantzakis

THE GOAL

Despite brilliant discoveries and engineering achievements, the twentieth
century proved that science per se cannot solve all society's problems; sometimes, it
makes them worse. Examples are the two world wars and their consequences, the
threatening nuclear arsenals, and the severe deterioration of the environment.

In his article "The Uses of Knowledge" (1960), Lyman Bryson raised the concern
of the misuse of scientific knowledge.

> Our own time is not the first period in history in which the luck
> of knowledge made self-governing people a danger to themselves
> and to their country. Ours is a time when the accumulations
> of knowledge are so huge and so complicated that the average
> citizen has to work much harder to play his part in intelligent
> democracy … Knowledge, freely available to a people who have
> the right and the will to use it wisely is the only real safety this
> world provides. Freedom of the mind is the foundation of all other

---

[329] Nikos Kazantzakis, *The Saviors of God: Spiritual Exercises*, trans. Kimon Friar (1960).

freedoms and if it is lost the others are soon found not worth keeping.[330]

We need more than science to address these problems. We will find solutions to them if we apply reason, knowledge, and virtue to these issues. Belief is hunted by doubt, but the knowledgeable mind can conquer doubt, produce a high standard of living, a healthy environment, and a future rather than extinction.

Before we discuss the problems we face today, let's establish the goal—achieving intellectual and moral perfection for all people and sustaining prosperity not only for ourselves but also for our environment and planet. Our intellectual capabilities can allow us to progress and address issues as they arise. In parallel to this pursuit of morality, we should take action that assures human cooperation, harmony, and happiness.

The goal should be to abolish nuclear weapons and the threat presented by global warming if we do not want a lifeless earth. These issues were selected as the most critical as they may end human life on earth. Energy, overpopulation, the lack of resources such as water and food, climate, poverty, and pollution affect global warming directly or indirectly with energy being the main driver of them all. When it comes to war, even small, regional conflicts can escalate into all-out nuclear war.

Before the industrial age, people were going to war over resources or to satisfy their leaders' egos. This has not changed. In recent years, countries have gone to war over energy, specifically oil. In 1931, the Japanese invaded China. Consequently, the United States put an oil embargo on the Japanese. The Japanese retaliated and attacked Pearl Harbor resulting in the United States entering the war.

Oil played a major role on the US-Iraq war. No one would have been concerned if Iraq was in Africa with no oil resources. The case of Idi Amin in Uganda did not cause the world to take actions for his abhorrent treatment of Ugandans; it was estimated that three hundred thousand civilians were massacred.

These issues are so interdependent and so interconnected that one can easily get lost in the details. As Martin Luther King Jr. (1929–1969) stated, "All of life is interrelated. We are all caught in an inescapable network of mutuality, tied to a single garment of destiny. Whatever affects one directly affects all indirectly."

In the previous chapters, I discussed virtue, the intellectual and moral excellence humanity needs to act with reason. In this and subsequent chapters, I will discuss intellectual excellence, the knowledge and technology required to address the issues discussed above. It is a monumental task to address them especially on a global basis. I shall discuss each issue separately, their interdependences, and the overall technology drivers that affects them. The moral virtues are self-evident of their functions and were discussed in the previous chapter.

[330] L. Bryson, *An Outline of Man's Knowledge of the Modern World* (New York: McGraw Hill, 1960), 15.

Despite all the world's problems, people are living longer than ever. They are fed better compared to the past, and more can be done in this area. However, the world looks very fragile; great empires are drowning in debt, unemployment is very high, and the banking system periodically proves to be hanging by a thread. People feel very uncertain and concerned being in economies that are not producing the essentials of life: food and shelter for all.

The gap between rich and poor is increasing constantly. The world population keeps increasing especially in the poorer southern hemisphere, and many people emigrate from there to the richer northern hemisphere. In the United States, 1 percent of the people own as much as do the 40 percent in the lowest economic bracket. Capital is moving electronically to tax-haven countries with the full awareness of governments whose politicians are unwilling to set up legal impediments. The world economic crisis of 2008 could be repeated just as quickly, with just as little warning, and with just as many adverse results worldwide. So much uncertainty, primarily economic and political, has the world in turmoil.

Earth's resources are stretched to the breaking point, especially clean water in poor areas of the globe. Defense spending, particularly the United States, breaks new records as do the deficits with no major war in sight, and terrorism shows no signs of abating.

The Middle East is afire and is the most unstable area along with some parts of sub-Saharan Africa. Besides war and terrorism, nuclear-weapons proliferation is on the increase. North Korea's nuclear capabilities and its associated long-range missiles threaten world peace.

GLOBAL WARMING AND WAR

Global warming is caused by the overuse of fossil fuels; its affects are rising temperatures, climate change, melting of polar ice, and rising ocean levels. This could lead to extinction of the earth's species. Our environment is a complex system with many variables such as human activity, atmosphere, vegetation, chemical compounds, weather, and interactions. Overpopulation and pollution are the two items we control and affect all others. Developing green and renewable sources of energy will reduce global warming

There is controversy as to whether there is global warming. The editors of *Scientific American* wrote in a June 2001 editorial,

> Scientists are often lampooned as living in an ivory tower, but lately it seems that it is the scientists who are grounded in reality and the U.S. political establishment that is floating among the clouds ... Ample research indicates that human activity is the

main cause of global warming. Estimates of the economic damage by mid-century range in the hundreds of billions of dollars per year-uncertain, to be sure, but if you've been smoking in bed, it makes sense to take out some fire insurance. Kyoto is far from perfect; its emissions targets represent a diplomatic agreement rather than any careful weighing of cost and benefit. But it is a start.[331]

This statement pertains to many other countries in the world that damage the environment.

The United Nations Climate Change Conference held in Paris in December 2015 was very decisive in establishing beyond a doubt that the world recognizes the global warming threat and will take action to address it. Based on the actions being taken and investments being made in renewable energy, it is very encouraging that we finally are turning the tide, and the development of renewable energy looks promising.

What is causing global warming or greenhouse effect? The Industrial Revolution created a need for energy that humanity found in fossil fuels—coal, oil, and natural gas that had been underground for millions of years. Their use released immense amounts of carbon dioxide along with other pollutants into the atmosphere. The sun's rays pass through the atmosphere and heat the earth; the earth radiates the infrared part of the spectrum. This part of energy is reflected back on the earth as carbon dioxide does not let it pass through at that wavelength. Energy gets trapped on the surface of the earth beneath a layer of carbon dioxide, and earth's temperature rises. This phenomenon, called the greenhouse effect, is very beneficial to life on earth as it keeps the environment temperate and comfortable for living. However, the continuous and increasing burning of fossil fuels increases carbon dioxide in the atmosphere, which increases the temperature.

Over the last fifty years, the amount of carbon dioxide in the atmosphere has been rising rapidly with dangerous consequences. It has turned some areas into uninhabitable deserts, melted arctic ice, caused a rise of the ocean waters resulting in flooding, created problems for people, and caused gigantic, unpredictable climatic changes. Though there are disputes in the scientific community about the rising temperature and its effects, do we want to take a chance? Technology is causing global warming, and technology can turn global warming around. The solution is to start using renewable energy resources and to reduce and eventually eliminate the use of fossil fuels.

The technological progress made in the last ten years in wind and solar energy, batteries, and information systems make it feasible to move massively and globally and address the global warming issue now. Increased mass production of further

---

[331] The Editors, editors@sciam.com, *Scientific American*, June 2001.

technological developments in renewable energy can do this on an unprecedented scale. And that can create jobs worldwide. Private enterprise can lead the effort; governments can assist by coordinating with private industry and eliminate red tape.

The major industrial countries are on their way to doing this, but more coordination will be helpful. The issue of overpopulation cannot be solved overnight, but an information global program can be helpful and should start now.

Of all the issues—energy, water, food, overpopulation, pollution, climate change, and war—energy is the most important as it provides sustenance to all others. Electricity improves people's life the most; nonetheless, almost a quarter of earth's population does not have it, and that means they do not have modern medicine or communication capabilities.

I shall concentrate on energy, provide costs, and point out its effect on the other issues mentioned. The other issues are not underestimated, but one great step forward in one area will lead all humanity to more understanding and cooperation. Simply put, the availability of renewable energy will remove the causes of many conflicts from regional battles to those that involve whole countries and provoke mass migrations.

Global issues require global participation by the major countries and major powers primarily; smaller countries have a limited effect on this because of their smaller sizes and resources. If the major countries participate and cooperate, we can be optimistic that the imitation effect (virtue learned by imitation) will take place and will prompt more participation and benefit the whole globe. Plenty of clean and renewable energy addresses all the issues to a certain degree and improves the quality of life the most. In addition, it solves the issue of the finite fossil-fuel sources.

Water scarcity is increasing. The US Southwest is a good example where due to increase of population, the Colorado River runs dry. Having an adequate supply of energy can provide an adequate supply of clean water through desalination; with water, more food can be grown to feed a growing world population. Renewable energy has no negative impacts on people and the environment; it does not pollute, so it has no effect on global warming. Plenty of energy reduces conflicts. Information and family planning can help the overpopulation problem.

In the following sections is a short history of how humanity got to the state it is in now.

Primitive man first discovered speech and fire around 8000 BC, during the Neolithic period. People learned the value of increasing their ability to work through the use of large animals, sails, windmills, and water mills. Oxen, horses, camels, mules, donkeys, and llamas pulled or carried heavy loads; this occurred during the Neolithic period.

At about the end of the second millennium BC, sails replaced oars on boats. We know from Homer that sail-bearing ships were used in the Trojan War around 1200 BC.

During the first millennium BC, man started using windmills, and around the third century BC, water mills. Even though the original sails, windmills and water mills were improved, they remained as the main energy engines until the Industrial Revolution. The primary use of the windmills and water mills was to grind grains into flour and to raise water for irrigation. Later, water mills were used to pump air into mines and used in forging factories.

The Industrial Revolution was driven by steam engines in the last quarter of the eighteenth century; the engines were fueled with wood, coal, and other fossil fuels. With the invention of the internal combustion engine and of electricity and motors, production became more distributed, cleaner, and quieter. In the twentieth century, the invention of the assembly line reduced costs and further accelerated the production of goods.

Other technologies such as radio, TV, telecommunication, private cars, airplanes, nuclear energy, computers, and the Internet led to a consumer society. With today's computers and the Internet, we are now in the information age.

Technology is the daughter of science. With so much science performed during the early parts of the last century and especially during the last century, many inventions were developed to produce a wide variety of goods. Computers extended the human mind, and robots extended the human reach. Even agriculture became highly mechanized and automated. With advanced GPS technology, the day is not far away when tractors and other farm implements will be managed robotically. US farmers, making up less than 2 percent of the population, produce more food today than ever thanks to higher levels of automation, better seeds, and fertilizer; they can feed the entire population and export their harvests, while 15 percent of the US workforce transports, processes, and sells the food.

Knowledge and technology combined extended automation to a very high level in industry, highly mechanized agriculture, and displaced labor and capital. Knowledge and technology have become the key drivers of the world's economy. The possessors of knowledge and technology are the key drivers of the world economy in the present information age.

Investments in robotics and in the automation and globalization of production have had a devastating effect on jobs and wages in industrialized countries. Jobs were lost not only to automation but also to cheaper labor overseas. Attention to quality, the inherent quality of the robotic production, reduced or eliminated the last vestiges of home production in high-cost industrialized countries. Improved engineering and technology, onsite inspection, and air transportation logistics made it easier to move production to low-cost labor countries. Improved manufacturing materials made products lighter, smaller, and better. Production knowledge was transferred and extended overseas, and that created greater competition.

Societies became very efficient in producing goods with automation, but along with the displacement of labor came lower wages. Knowledge and technology—the primary economic drivers—and capital invested in automation leaves labor in a disadvantageous position. This is responsible for the distribution of wealth. Capital invested in capital-intensive production produces more capital and drives wages down. This wealth disparity is constantly increasing with alarming social consequences. Economies have had their ups and downs, but as we see the economies recovering from the 2008 recession, wages remain stagnant in the United States and Europe.

The world has not figured this one out yet, but there is one undisputable truth: we cannot go back to pre-industrialization days.

TECHNOLOGY CHANGES

In the tragedy *Hippolytus*, Euripides stated another myth to demonstrate another human folly in meddling with forces beyond their control. Theseus said, "O futile humans! Why does your folly teach skills innumerable, and search out manifold inventions still? But there is one knowledge you do not gain and have never sought it: to implant a right mind where no wisdom dwells."[332] The myths of Prometheus, Pandora, Daedalus, and Icarus are similar. Twenty-five centuries later, we continue on the same path to marvelous inventions that are good or bad, that prompt glory and defeat.

Rousseau, Tolstoy, and Wells saw technology's effects on people in the nineteenth century and made predictions for the twentieth century.

In his *Discourse on the Arts and Sciences*, Rousseau questioned the use of sciences and arts on human life.

> But if the progress of the sciences and the arts has added nothing to our true happiness, if it has corrupted our morality, and if that moral corruption has damaged purity of taste, what will we think of that crowd of simple writers who have removed from the temple of the Muses the difficulties which safeguarded access to it and which nature had set up there as a test of strength for those who would be tempted to learn? ... A man who all his life will be a bad versifier or a minor geometer could perhaps have become a great manufacturer of textiles. Those whom nature destined to make her disciples have no need of teachers.[333]

In *What is Art?* Tolstoy assessed civilization at the end of the nineteenth century.

---

[332] Theseus, Euripides, Hippolytus, line 919.
[333] Jean-Jacques Rousseau, *Discourse on the Arts and Sciences*.

People of today's world cannot take enough delight in the brilliant, unprecedented and colossal achievements of nineteenth century technology. There is no doubt that never before in history has such material success, i.e. in conquering the forces of human nature, been achieved as in the nineteenth century. But there is also no doubt that never in history has there been such a display of immoral living, free of any force restraining man's animal desires, as that which exists now in our Christian humanity … The material progress achieved in the nineteenth century is truly enormous, but it was, and still is being, purchased at a cost of neglect for the most elementary demands of morality, such as humanity has never witnessed before, not even under Genghis Khan, Attila, or Nero.

No one would argue that iron ships, railroads, printing presses, tunnels, phonographs, Roentgen rays and so forth are very fine things … So long as people do not consider all men as their brothers and do not consider human life as the most sacred thing … will always ruin one another's lives for the sake of personal gain.[334]

In *The Discovery of the Future* (1914), H. G. Wells (1866–1946) agreed with Tolstoy on the immense technical progress of the eighteenth century.

The conditions under which men live are changing with an ever-increasing rapidity, and, so far as our knowledge goes, no sort of creatures have ever lived under changing conditions without undergoing the pro-fondest changes themselves. In the past century, there was more change in the conditions of human life than there had been in the previous thousand years. A hundred years ago inventors and investigators were rare scattered men, and now invention and inquiry are the work of an unorganized army. This century will see changes that will dwarf those of the nineteenth century, as those of the nineteenth dwarf those of the eighteenth.[335]

One must admit that it is impossible to show why certain things should not utterly destroy and end the entire human race and story, why night should not presently come down and make all our

[334] Leo Tolstoy, *What is Art? What is Religion?*
[335] H. G. Wells, *The Discovery of the Future / A Discourse Delivered at the Royal Institution* (1914), Internet.

dreams and efforts vain ... Human society never has been quite static, and it will presently cease to attempt to be static ... We are in the beginning of the greatest change that humanity has ever undergone. There is no shock, no epoch-making incident—but then there is no shock at a cloudy daybreak.

This century will see changes that will dwarf those of the nineteenth century, as those of the nineteenth dwarf those of the eighteenth ... Human society never has been quite static, and it will presently cease to attempt to be static ... We are in the beginning of the greatest change that humanity has ever undergone.[336]

The same can be said about today and our unfolding twenty-first century. Every generation thinks its time has been the best; Tolstoy's statement speaks for the nineteenth century and Wells's for the twentieth century. Since their time, more marvelous technical achievements have been accomplished, but humanity remains the same—good and bad, compassionate and dangerous, to others and nature. We have had two world wars, nuclear weapons abound, and global pollution and terrorism have become our heritage. Numerous gadgets are available, people live longer, but I sense we have to address the big issues, a heritage from the past on a grand scale.

Tolstoy and Wells were not aware of the two most dangerous threats realized at the second half of the twentieth century: global warming and nuclear weapons. Either one can wipe life off the planet—the first one gradually but the second almost overnight.

At times, humanity's destructive behavior seems to have reached its climax especially in the last century. The deaths from war set new records and at times reached unprecedented barbarity.

Sir Martin Rees, the distinguished cosmologist, astrophysicist, and president of the Royal Society, stated,

I think the odds are no better than fifty-fifty that our present civilization on Earth will survive to the end of our present century. Our choices and actions could ensure the perpetual future of life ... or in contrast, through malign intent, or through misadventure twenty-first century technology could jeopardize life's potential, foreclosing its human and post human future. What happens here on Earth, in this century, could conceivably make the difference

---

[336] Ibid.

between a near eternity filled with ever more complex and subtle forms and one filled with nothing but base matter.[337]

Sir Rees raised many issues that lurk in the new technologies and may have detrimental effects on human life. He talked of

lethal airborne viruses engineered to wipe out populations ... human characters changed by drugs ... rogue Nano machines that replicate catastrophically ... experiments that crash atoms together with immense force that starts a chain reaction that erodes everything on Earth ... and engulfs the entire universe.[338]

All these doomsday effects are beyond human capacity now, but history teaches us that there can be surprises. However, we must face the issues of global warming and nuclear war. The first has many scientists concerned; the weather has been rather unstable and at times intense. The ice caps are melting, and summers are getting hotter. Not everyone agrees about the danger, but the December 2015 Paris Conference on global warming has established that practically every major country agrees on the dangers of global warming and signed onto ways to control emissions and lessen the long-term effect. The question we can ask doubters is, Why take a chance and wait until the process is irreversible? Addressing global warming now makes economic sense, it will result in clean air, and it will take care of the long-range problem of running out of nonrenewable energy resources.

The nuclear bomb has already proved its destructiveness; the bombs we have now are on orders of magnitude more destructive than those used in World War II. No one doubts their destructive capacity, and they have been stockpiled.

During the twentieth century, we gained great understanding of the smallest subatomic particles and the universe as a whole. Medicine, drugs, and improvement in diet has increased the average human life at least twenty-five years. During the twenty-first century, genetic engineering and biotechnology seem to be on their way to taking giant steps similar to those taken by atomic physics in the last century.

Progress in understanding the atom created the nuclear energy industry, which was heralded as a great blessing at the time. It also created the nuclear weapon age. Similarly, genetic engineering is at its dawn. It can create the genes of a superman who never catches a cold or other horrible diseases, or it can create a super master that rules with unprecedented power, benevolence or malignance, intended or unintended.

[337] Rees, *Our Final Hour*, 8.
[338] Ibid., 1.

OUR WONDERFUL PLANET EARTH

For all practical purposes, we cannot go anywhere from earth, not now or in the foreseeable future. People fantasize about sending people to other planets if overpopulation becomes a greater threat, but let's look at some of the facts.

What a marvelous and wonderful our planet is! Earth is in an ideal location in our solar system. Its distance from the sun has made it a place that sustains rich and diverse life. Its axis of rotation prompts the seasons and all the beauty that it brings that make our lives more interesting and pleasant. The earth receives an immense amount of free, continuous, and constant solar energy that we can capture and use rather than fossil fuels that pollute the atmosphere. Our earth's atmosphere sustains life for breathing and protects us by reducing the sun's UV and X-rays and provides partial protection from small meteorites.

In addition, the earth's size provides us with the appropriate gravity for our human size to be what it is now. If the earth was twice as large in radius, its mass and gravity would triple and our weight would triple. A different type of human would be walking around. The rotation of the earth every twenty-four hours makes it ideal for humans, plants, and animals. The earth sustains such a rich, beautiful, and diverse ecosystem for our enjoyment. If the earth did not rotate around its axis, nights and days would be six months long with very cold nights and very hot days. Man, animals, and plants would be quite different if they existed at all.

One has to contrast this to the moon, which has no atmosphere due to its small size and thus its small gravity pull. The moon is about the same distance from the sun as is the earth and rotates around the earth every twenty-nine days. Because of its lack of atmosphere, its surface temperature during its fourteen-day-long days averages +101 degrees C and during its fourteen-day-long nights, its temperature averages -153 degrees C. The lack of atmosphere and water, the extreme hot and cold temperatures, exposure to UV and X-rays from the sun, and the bombardment of the moon's surface with meteorites make the moon unable to support life. The moon is not rotating around its axis, so it always presents the same hemisphere to earth.

Let us examine what extraterrestrial travel and migration would involve: the two planets closest to the Sun, Mercury and Venus, are too hot to sustain life. The five planets and their satellites in our planetary system that are the farthest from the sun are too cold, and some of them are gaseous masses. This leaves Mars as the only possible planet in our solar system as a potential place for colonizing. Mars is about half the size of the earth; it rotates as Earth does every 24.6 hours, and its rotation around the Sun takes 687 earth days; it is six months away with today's spacecraft. It is a frozen planet with an average temperature of -81 F (-63 C), and an atmosphere with about 96 percent carbon dioxide, 1.93 percent argon, and 1.89 percent nitrogen along with traces of oxygen and water, all of which make it not very hospitable.

We can see the Milky Way from remote areas here on Earth; it comprises 400 billion stars. We can marvel at it and dream about visiting and discovering richer worlds or lands. Beyond our galaxy are about 200 billion more galaxies that make up our known universe. The earth occupies a space in the universe that compares to the space a speck of sand occupies on all earth.

The closest sun outside our solar system in the Milky Way is Alpha Centauri, 4.4 light-years away. The Andromeda galaxy, the closest to ours, is approximately 2.5 million light-years away. We cannot determine easily which of the closest suns have planets suitable for us. We cannot see such planets; we can only infer their existence by motion disturbances of their suns due to the planets' gravitational pull.

The fastest spacecraft launched from the earth at 16.62 kilometers per second picks up an additional 30 kilometers per second due to Earth's rotation. It would take 4.4 x 300,000: 47 = 28,000 years to get there. Such a trip exists only in our fantasy. We would have communication only every 8.8 years with the spacecraft after it lands.

We would need a human-friendly planet; it has recently been reported with great fanfare that scientists found a planet that may sustain life similar to that on Earth, but it is still about forty-five light-years from Earth. You can draw your own conclusion.

We can enjoy life here on earth as this is the best we can do for now, and it must be very disappointing to believers of extraterrestrial UFOs who seem to land on earth in their backyards quite often in their fantasies. Columbus made a risky but feasible trip; it lasted months, not years, and he could have turned back if it did not work out.

Based on these evaluations, we cannot find haven on any planet B, but humanity will not stop dreaming about it. Freeman Dyson wrote,

> The more I examine the universe and study the details of its architecture, the more evidence I find that the universe in some sense must have known that we were coming. There are some striking examples in the laws of nuclear physics of numerical accidents that seem to conspire to make the universe habitable.[339]

We are staying on this wonderful planet Earth for a while and should enjoy what it offers. About the stars, the great physicist Hans Bethe said, "Stars have a life cycle much like animals. They get born, they grow, they go through a definite internal development, and finally they die, to give back the material of which they are made so that new stars may live."[340]

Humanity has not been too accurate when it comes to predicting the future and the consequences of its actions. But every generation should commit to leaving the world a better place for succeeding generations.

[339] Freeman Dyson, *Disturbing the Universe* (New York: Harper & Row, 1979), 250.
[340] Hans A. Bethe, *The Road from Los Alamos: Collected Essays* (New York: Touchtone, 1991), 263.

The issue of global warming is tied to world politics, the environment, energy, food and water, cooperation, war, terrorism, and poverty. Differing economic interests create competition for resources among countries. Countries are being challenged by modernity in all its forms and by religious, philosophical, and moral issues. Nonetheless, it has the resources to address these issues.

Progress in science and technology may increase the wealth of some or most people and not affect the life of others. When the mass production of goods is outsourced to countries with low labor costs, that can create poverty, unemployment, and an uncertain future for many. Automation tilts the balance of power from labor to capital and the banks. Governments seem to be unable to deal with this problem. We face a dichotomy: a free, universal, borderless economy will produce goods at the most competitive prices to everybody's benefit. But if automation and robots that can be moved anywhere in the world are included, the deep problem no government seems to address is, What is the impact on the standard of living on American and European families when their jobs are being outsourced to countries with low wages and a lower cost of living and with automation provided by the advanced country?

When we look at the entire picture, we will conclude that the average American or European will lose. It is not a matter of skill, as the skills of people are being equalized with robots and training of people in underdeveloped countries. The high-tech jobs being created are of no use to people with high school diplomas or less. The manufacturing jobs are fewer and fewer due to automation, which is making products cheaper and of high quality. Compare today's automobile assembly lines to those in the sixties or earlier.

The concept of the assembly line put Detroit at the forefront of a manufacturing revolution. When the assembly line was adopted in other areas of manufacturing, the cost of goods dropped and the many employed in making them were able to afford them. The plight of Detroit today may be due to government, management, and labor incompetence, but the primary reasons are automation, outsourcing, and slow adoption of automation and understanding of the coming knowledge revolution. Postwar Japan and Germany adopted automation and paid more attention to quality and better labor relations; they were able to sustain growth and increase their market share of automobiles.

Automation is part of human progress and will be more so in the future; there is no going back to the horse-and-buggy days. Capital invested in automation displaces labor. Those having the capital invest in automation make more capital and reduce work done with labor. And the global flight of capital to safe places or to developed countries with more-transparent markets and opportunities leave poor countries in desperate situations.

There is much to do in this area to stop the robbing of wealth from citizens where it is created and being moved to tax havens. There has to be individual ethical responsibility and incentives to keep the wealth where it can develop the countries where wealth is produced. One can see the difference in countries that do not invest in knowledge as in Latin America and Africa versus Asia.

Knowledge enables people to foresee and address problems in a timely manner. Reforms are necessary to spread knowledge to underdeveloped countries. The developed countries try to help the undeveloped world when war, disease, and hunger break out, but it is much cheaper to take timely preventive measures earlier with education before things get bad and out of control.

Immense progress is reported in so many areas, but we hear about crises: unemployment and work instability, monetary crises such as the 2008 banking collapse, the rise of national debt, corruption (legal inequities or otherwise), soaring health costs, political instability, human migration, vestigial religious fundamentalism, world hunger, and environmental deterioration. Unfortunately, we have not found a prefect scientific economic system yet; there are too many variables and inadequate models, but we are still trying. Modern economists are trying to teach the rest of us that economics is a science, but that's a doubtful supposition. Unlike with scientists, you can pose a problem to two economists and get two or more conflicting answers.

Some of the major causes of the issues discussed come down to insufficient education in critical thinking and specialization of knowledge. What is the solution for these problems? Gaining knowledge and excellence, leading by example, disseminating information and education, further developing clean, renewable energy, and reducing war and thus the chances of nuclear war.

We have sufficient technical knowledge to address the problems now, and we will gain more in the future. We must concentrate on excellence, will, and educational information through the media and the Internet. A world informed about the issues is the greatest power. This is just as important as technical knowledge. We all need to exercise sincere self-knowledge, analysis, and evaluation to attain the greatest good.

In his *Study of History*, A. J. Toynbee wrote, "So close is the correlation between technological advancement and moral decline that the appearance of the former may be used as the ground of accurate forecasting of the latter."[341] His comments are valid—pure technological advancement does not necessarily mean advancement in knowledge and virtue (i.e., morality). Does it bring justice, equality, liberty, fellowship, and peace? Technology can be great when it is affordable and available to many, not just a few. Technology can benefit and harm humanity, so it must be accompanied by knowledge and wisdom. As Heraclitus stated, "Learning many things does not teach understanding."

Knowledge by itself does not bring progress; the application of knowledge does that. Knowledge can provide salvation, but it can also create problems.

We have the technical knowledge to address all the major issues today and create a better world tomorrow. By studying the past, we search for the jewels, the

---

[341] Robert Nisbet, *History of the Idea of Progress* (Basic Books, 1980), 6.

great achievements, but also the follies; that will help us to plan for the future using intellectual knowledge based on rationality rather than emotion.

The world is facing major problems: economic instability and a widening inequality between rich and poor, wars and threats of wars, terrorism, overpopulation, food shortages in some regions, and a deteriorating environment. Constantly increasing numbers of people, modern amenities, and higher living standards require more energy.

Cecil Rhodes (1853–1902), the father of Rhodesia, today's Zimbabwe, said this during the time of expansion and exploitation.

> We must find new lands from which we can easily obtain raw materials and at the same time exploit the cheap slave labor that is available from the natives of the colonies. The colonies would also supply a dumping ground for the surplus goods produced in our factories … Why should we not form a secret society with but one object … the bringing of the whole world under British rule, for the recovery of the United States, for making the Anglo-Saxon race but one Empire? What a dream, but yet it is probable; it is possible.[342]

Things have changed since Rhodes's times. There are hardly any colonies now. New nations, even those with many natural resources, lack the excellence required of their people and their governments. They suffer from ineffective government, corruption, and poverty. The overall problem is the low general knowledge of the population. It takes a long time to develop institutions and schools to raise the general knowledge level of the public so democratic institutions can be developed and human conditions improve. Knowledge leads to development of excellence in government. One can examine the development of Europe. It took a long time to develop to the level it is today—general prosperity prevails along with functional governments. European nations live in peace today, and they seem to have broken the twenty- or thirty-year cycles of internal strife and wars.

We will discuss how knowledge affects people and how affordable, renewable, and nonpolluting energy can do it. We must concentrate on saving our planet. If global warming increases, we can experience a runaway effect with unpredictable results and a short time to reverse it if that is even possible. We cannot chance that. We have fifty years to solve the energy problem, but we must start now. It is not easy, but we must do it for we have no choice.

---

[342] http://www.brainyquote.com/quotes/quotes/c/cecilrhode534426.html#cHhFOxMPP VxHi7WA.99.

ENERGY AND ALTERNATIVES

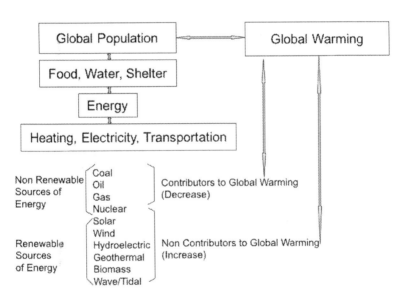

Diagram 2. Global Population, Global Warming, and Energy Interrelationships

ENERGY BACKGROUND

Diagram 2 shows how the various types of energy sources are in four sectors for use in electricity production for residential, industrial, and commercial areas and transportation. Energy is produced from renewable or nonrenewable sources. The chart shows these complex interrelationships.

All renewable sources—solar, wind, hydroelectric, geothermal, biomass/

waste, wave/tidal—are not contributors to global warming and hardly affect the environment. Of all the nonrenewable sources, only nuclear does not contribute to global warming. The rest of the nonrenewable—fossil fuels, coal, oil and gas—contribute to global warming.

Energy is the most dominant driver of all human activities; it serves all human needs, affects all industrial activity and products, and is the major driver of the basic human needs for food, water, and shelter. Developing low-cost and renewable energy will allow us to solve the global warming and environmental degradation issues. We can provide the world with sufficient water and food, and that can stop people from starving, migrating, and causing national and international problems. Nations would not go to war for water rights and energy sources such as oil over which wars are becoming rather frequent. In addition, energy plays a most important role in the economy in terms of imbalance of payments, economic uncertainty, wars, and their impacts.

Energy is the ability to do work, and it comes in many forms: kinetic, potential, thermal, electric, magnetic, nuclear, chemical, and others. It is used in industry, transportation, and homes. The biosphere—plants and animals—live in a symbiosis using the sun's energy, water, and soil nutrients to grow. Humanity's actions can interfere with this symbiosis.

Having abundant, inexpensive energy, humanity could produce all the water needed through desalination processes. An adequate water supply can make deserts bloom and supply food to an increased population. If land is scarce, hydroponic agriculture can be used to grow food. Hydroponics is the method of growing plants using mineral nutrient solutions in water, and it requires less space than do traditional agricultural practices. Thus, energy, water, and life are interdependent with energy being the main source. Low-cost energy is a major factor in powering agriculture, industry, and transportation and makes economies very competitive.

With the splitting of the atom and the creation of nuclear weapons, we also gained the know-how to exploit the atom for peaceful purposes. The United States' 108 nuclear reactors produce about 20 percent of its electricity. There are more than 400 nuclear reactors worldwide, producing about 15 percent of world's electricity.

There have been some major nuclear plant accidents around the globe and some near meltdowns such as at Chernobyl, Fukushima, and Three Mile Island. These accidents, especially the one in Fukushima, prompted the Japanese government to shut down all their nuclear plants. Germany will have phased out all its nuclear plants by 2022. At present, in the United States, the used nuclear material has been stored in the nuclear reactors themselves since the beginning of operations. Nuclear waste is highly radioactive and dangerous for thousands of years. Terrorism and the possibility of a dirty nuclear bomb are additional negatives for nuclear energy.

Nuclear energy did not prove as cost effective or as risk free as was originally hoped. Though there was euphoria at the onset of the production of power through the development of nuclear energy, people now fear it and have a very negative attitude toward it. Lewis Strauss, the chairman of the US Atomic Energy Commission, evoked a utopian future in a 1954 speech to the National Association of Science Writers.

> It is not too much to expect that our children will enjoy in their homes electrical energy too cheap to meter, will know of great periodic regional famines in the world only as matters of history, will travel effortlessly over the seas and under them and through the air with a minimum of danger and at great speeds, and will experience a lifespan far longer than ours as disease yields and man comes to understand what causes him to age.[343]

Strauss's prediction did not materialize. Electricity from fission-powered nuclear plants is not and will not be "too cheap to meter" unless major innovations decrease costs and a safe and cost-effective way is found to store practically for thousands of years the radioactive waste from nuclear plants.

When oil, coal, and natural gas created by the sun's energy millions of years ago are used as sources of energy, carbon dioxide and other harmful byproducts are released and pollute the environment. Thousands of people die from pollution-related causes every year, and more suffer from respiratory diseases. Moreover, all mining processes, especially oil production from shale, fracking for oil and gas, and coal mining, are negatively affecting the environment. Strict regulations need to be enforced to avoid oil spills, to reduce carbon dioxide emissions, and to prevent the contamination of soil and water.

The low cost of wind and solar energy has had many effects already in the marketplace. In the United States, wind and solar power produce about 8 percent of our electricity, and we have been experiencing double-digit increases yearly. The use of natural gas has exploded due to its low cost and fracking technology. Coal is on the decline; it hit 30 percent, an all-time low. Many old and inefficient coal plants are closing, and no new coal plants are being built in the United States. The high cost of electricity derived from coal is due partly to environmental regulations.

---

[343] Lewis Strauss, *Speech to the National Association of Science Writers*, New York, September 16, 1954.

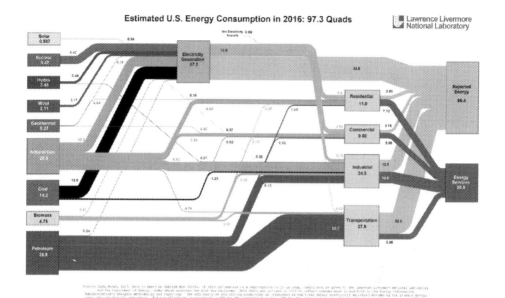

Diagram 3. Lawrence Livermore Flow Chart Showing the Estimated U. S. Energy Use for 2015.

Diagram 3 shows the estimated US energy use for 2016 and the complex interrelationships between the energy sources and in what sectors the different types of energy sources are used for the United States. Similar charts are for other countries. The chart shows the following:

- Nuclear power is used exclusively to produce electricity.
- Coal is used primarily for electricity production with very small amounts used for industrial purposes.
- Natural gas is used in all four sectors: electricity production for the residential, commercial, industrial, and transportation sectors.
- Oil is used primarily for transportation in the form of gasoline or diesel and industrial uses. A tiny amount is used for electricity production. Air and sea transport use 100 percent oil.

Fast, efficient trains have made major strides in moving people and relieving pollution and car congestion. Many countries have moved to superfast trains powered by electricity. There is no near-term solution for airplanes to use anything other than 100 percent oil-based kerosene, but other areas of transportation can switch to electricity. This is all a matter of cost, congestion, environmental factors, government policies, information, and human inertia.

Switching from one source to another cannot happen overnight; it takes time to build up infrastructure and related investments and to make technological breakthroughs. Most European and Asian countries have almost all their trains electrically powered.

Based on the above, we need to switch to renewable sources of energy for these reasons.

1. Fossil fuels are exhaustible.
2. There is no contribution to global warming from renewable sources.
3. We can achieve a clean environment.
4. It makes economic sense now and more so in the future with more technology advances.
5. The technology is available now and is cost effective.
6. It reduces the need to import oil and lessens the possibility of wars for resources.
7. It provides economic stability as there are no price fluctuations as seen in the oil market.
8. It reduces the causes of war and their associated expense.

We will be on our way to solving the global warming problem if we first concentrate on eliminating the use of coal for electricity production. This will be one of the greatest steps in reducing global warming and pollution as it is the greatest producer of CO_2. We also have to reduce our dependence on oil for ground transportation. This can be done with small, energy-efficient cars and electric cars with greater battery capacity.

For every kilowatt-hour produced using coal, the detrimental effect on global warming is twice that of the use of natural gas. In the meantime, inexpensive natural gas can provide a buffer in producing electricity for any shortfall situations.

SOME ENERGY FACTS

In 2015, the United States generated about 4,060 billion kWh (kilowatt-hours) of electricity, or 4,060 TW (terawatts=10^{12} watts). About 67 percent of the electricity generated came from fossil fuels—coal, natural gas, and petroleum—and 33 percent came from coal.[344]

In the United States, electricity accounts for 37.5 percent of all energy consumed. Electricity-producing plants are 32.3 percent efficient; a third of the energy is used, but the rest is wasted as heat. Cars, in comparison, are about 20 percent efficient.

---

[344] EIA, U. S. Energy Information Administration

THE PLAN

The switch to renewable sources can take place in two phases. The first phase from now to 2030 concentrates on reducing the use of the heavy polluters—coal and oil. The second phase, from 2030 to 2050, can address natural gas and nuclear energy. By meeting the 2030 goals, the second phase will be rather easier as technology will have advanced especially in the battery-storage area. It will require building more capacity for solar and wind energy primarily and geothermal and wave/tidal energy secondarily.

The present nuclear plants in the United States will be almost all be gracefully retired as they will have completed their lifecycles. New technology may be introduced to make them safer. Fusion energy may be feasible for the latter part of the twenty-second century.

Phase one is presented here in detail; a plan for the second phase can be completed later after assessing phase-one progress and after technology advances.

The plan for the first phase is this.

1. Increase energy production with solar, wind, geothermal, biomass, and waste as per diagram 2.
2. Reduce substantially or eliminate all coal-produced electricity by 2030. This will eliminate 1,364 million metric tons of carbon yearly, 71 percent of the total associated with electricity generation (2015). Coal is the most polluting source of energy in the electricity sector. For 2015, a total of 1,925 million metric tons of carbon were produced by electricity generation.
3. Reduce use of natural gas as the market allows. Natural gas produces 530 million metric tons of carbon yearly. This is 28 percent of the total associated with electricity generation (2015).
4. Require that all utilities buy extra electricity produced by solar houses at a fair price as is already happening in some European countries. This will induce homeowners to install larger solar systems for their own use and sell the excess to utility companies. Solar energy is produced at times of high electricity demand and uses otherwise unused roof space.
5. Continue energy conservation programs that include better insulation for houses and the use of solar water heaters. Require that all new houses have solar panels and a solar water heater where sun is plentiful.
6. Doing the above by the year 2030, we will move from 34.9 to 82 percent carbon-free electricity as shown in table 1. The remaining 18 percent will be produced by natural gas, which is not as harmful as coal.

7. Additional costs savings derived from health and climate changes due to emissions of greenhouse gases from fossil fuels are not included, but these benefits will be substantial.

The plan can be applied more globally with local adjustments due to resources available and local climate.

California moved its energy goal from 33 percent renewable by 2025 to 50 percent by 2030 as it is making great progress. Germany is up to 30 percent renewable without the benefit of the great amounts of sunshine the United States enjoys. China has almost doubled its use of solar and wind power installed compared to the United States.

The plan presented can be started now with the goals detailed. It is realistic and flexible; no rash decisions need to be made too early, and it can be modified if an improvement or breakthrough occurs in battery technology.

US OIL AND ELECTRICITY CONSUMPTION

The world's production of electricity is estimated to be 23,000 billion kWh.[345] The United States has about 4.7 percent of the world's population but consumes about 17.64 percent of the world's total electricity output. The total daily world production of oil is about 92 million barrels, about 33 billion barrels per year; US daily oil consumption is about 18.5 million barrels, about 20 percent of the world's production.

Contrary to the drum-beating politicians who say that the United States is becoming energy independent, it still imports about 9 million barrels of oil per day, about 10 percent of the world's usage. All the oil we use goes to the transportation sector (trucks, airplanes, railroads, ships), for the production of chemicals, and a minor quantity for heating. A very insignificant amount is being used for electricity production.

The world's proven oil reserves including shale deposits are estimated to be about 1,200 billion barrels. This means that at the present daily consumption of 92 million barrels, we have enough to last about thirty-six years. The consumption of oil keeps increasing as more cars are being produced.

The United States has a little less than 4.7 percent of the world's population but uses about 24 percent of the world's energy resources. Our GDP is also about 24 percent of the world's GDP. If the rest of the world used energy at the same rate as does the United States, the demand for energy would increase by a factor of about four to about 132 billion barrels of oil yearly. Theoretically, we would run out of oil in about eleven years. This will not happen soon as the GDP of the world is not about to get to the US oil consumption level anytime soon, but these are very scary

[345] https://yearbook.enerdata.net/world-electricity-production-map-graph-and-data.html

numbers. If we found 50 percent more oil, that would be enough to last for only fifty-four more years.

The oil supply has increased with use of fracking techniques in drilling and extracting, and that has led to a reduction of oil imports to the United States. Let's not ignore that before the 2008 economic crisis, oil hit $146 per barrel. Cheap oil just prolongs the long-term problem of postponing action and gives a false sense of security to people who do not switch to renewable sources of energy.

Oil is required for the production of chemicals, and there is no other alternative at this time for that purpose just as there is no alternative to oil to produce airplane fuel. The status quo will end up being a major issue for the airline industry.

The greenhouse effect is constantly getting worse with the increase of the use of fossil fuels. Is world climate instability lately telling us something? Why take a chance?

THE GOOD NEWS

America can cut down the use of oil by at least 50 percent in less than eight years and not have to import any. We will have a cleaner environment at little if any inconvenience. Our balance of payments will improve, and jobs will be generated locally; all that capital required now to pay for imported oil will stay here. We waste so much energy by our use of gas-guzzling modes of transportation, and we pollute the air. It was not long ago that we did not know leaded gas was harmful.

In the last ten years, three great technical advances in solar energy, wind energy, and battery advances for electric cars and energy storage surprised even the experts. These advances drove costs down and will do more so in the future as economies of scale improve, as higher volume production takes place, and as further incremental technological improvements and breakthroughs occur especially in battery technology.

Solar and wind energy costs have dramatically decreased, and installations are increasing with double-digit growth. Mass production will decrease the cost of batteries for electric cars. These areas are becoming Main Street, not simply fashionable projects for the environmental elite. It pays to invest in solar, wind, and electric cars instead of continuing with the traditional ways of doing things. One can see the annual increases of solar and wind energy production and the number and variety of electric car production. We need to look at the numbers carefully and objectively.

RENEWABLE ENERGY REVOLUTION

The renewable energy revolution started; it is gathering speed, and nothing can stop it. We are witnessing the dawn of a new era in energy production that will provide cheap energy for electric cars and trains. Our thermonuclear reactor 92 million miles away, our sun, has been feeding all that energy to us since our planet was formed. The sun has been responsible for the creation of our fossil fuels and wind. We used them and will use them for a while, but the sun can become our major, inexhaustible energy source. Nuclear energy was the first major energy source not derived from the sun. The human intellect finally created the knowledge to harness this immense source of energy effectively and competitively with fossil fuels.

Grid parity occurs when an alternate energy source can generate and provide power at a cost that is less than or equal to the price of power from the electricity grid. This means that energy produced by wind and solar is economically attractive and commercially viable for the first time in the nation's history, and it can compete with the rest of the existing fossil fuels and nuclear energy. Solar and wind energy have reached that point for most of earth's regions, and this is causing to the fossil-fuel energy production what the transistor did to the vacuum tube in the 1950s. This is being achieved without counting the government incentives, though they were critical at the inception stage. The government incentives will be phased out in about four years, by 2021. By that time, the cost of wind and solar energy will have been further reduced, and incentives will have run their course.

To give some quantitative numbers, we need to define some terms. The leveled cost of electricity (LCOE) is the cost of electricity that is estimated when all the original capital investment, maintenance, cost of capital, and fuel is included. Since solar and wind systems require low maintenance and do not use any fuel, it comes down to capital investment. Thus simply, the LCOE is calculated by dividing the original cost by the total amount of electricity produced over the system's lifetime.

LCOE includes all the up-front cost for building a plant, finance costs, interest expense, fixed operation and maintenance, cost of fuel, and the life of the plant. The price of a solar system consists of the solar panels, wiring, converter, installation, and licensing and inspection fees. These prices have fallen over the last five years. The price of panels fell over 70 percent in these five years down to around $0.5. For a large utility system, the total cost of installation is under $1.6 per watt.

Solar prices have undergone an unprecedented downward fall between 1990 and 2010, when the price of electricity from these sources dropped about twenty-five times. This rate of price reduction is accelerating; between late 2009 and 2016, the wholesale cost of solar modules dropped approximately 75 percent. Economies of scale in the production chain, continuous improvements of solar cell efficiencies, and market size have led to lower construction and installment costs.

Wind energy has experienced cost reductions as well. Larger windmills' rotor diameters, taller towers, improved blade efficiencies, and economies of scale were the major driver of this cost reduction.

Solar modules are usually warranted for twenty-five years with minor degradation during that time of about 20 percent. In California for example, with average of five hours of sun per day, a one-kilowatt system will produce over that twenty-five years 45,625 kWh not including limited degradation. The total cost of installation of the entire system is around $3,000; that means the cost of electricity is about 6.6¢ per kWh, less than what consumers pay. Cost estimates for large industrial and utility sites are less than $2,000 per kWh with a corresponding cost of electricity of about 4.4¢ cents per kWh. All these prices do not include any government subsidies. With the subsidies, the cost becomes much lower.

The Greentech Solar Report by Julia Pyper (January 14, 2015), stated,

> Solar Is Cheaper Than the Grid in 42 of the 50 Largest US Cities … According to a new report by the North Carolina Clean Energy Technology Center, backed by the SunShot Initiative, a fully financed solar PV system costs less than the energy purchased from a residential customer's local utility in 42 of the 50 largest cities in the United States.[346]

In 2014, the rooftop PV (photovoltaic) system has reached parity in over ten states in the United States; Deutsche Bank predicts solar grid parity in all fifty US states by 2016.

According to *Fortune* magazine (January 12, 2016), the US solar industry grew dramatically in 2015 and is expected to continue to do so in 2015. By the end of 2016 Its ranks grew to 240,000 workers and by the end of 2017 the number is expected to surpass 300,000. The coal industry now employs fewer than 70,000 workers the report noted.

Besides being clean, solar energy has the advantage of being produced during peak demand hours.

There are integration costs associated with intermittent renewable energy, but unlike fossil fuels, wind, solar, and many other renewables costs are zero. Wind-power technology has rapidly evolved. Turbines are much larger, growing from an average of 1.2 MW to today's 8-MW turbines, and a few companies are working on 10-MW turbines. These large turbines are better suited for offshore operations.

The newer turbines with improved blades can wring more electric power out of the wind (especially at lower wind speeds) than older turbines could. The combination of greater output and greater capacity nearly offsets the materials and labor cost increases that plague traditional resources.

The great advantage of the wind and solar installations are numerous.

- Quick installation. One advantage of solar and wind production systems is that once decisions are made, financing is easier as the time for the cash

---

[346] http://www.greentechmedia.com/articles/read/report-solar-is-cheaper-than-the-grid-in-42-of-the-50-largest-us-cities.

flow to start is short. Once the licensing is completed, the assembly starts and the installation takes weeks or months. Once sections of the system are finished, they can be turned on and start producing electricity. It is not like a coal or nuclear plant that takes from two to about eight years to complete.

- No more despoiling the earth as fossil-fuel plants do with mining, transport, drilling, and air pollution associated with coal, oil, and natural gas.

- When the useful life of renewable energy facilities is over, they can be easily dismantled; the material can be recycled and the area easily restored. One has to compare this with a fossil-fuel plants and nuclear plant where the land has to be restored. And nuclear waste must be dealt with for centuries.

- Minimal maintenance is required.

- Energy security and lower bills.

- Solar and wind energy production, unlike fossil-fuel electricity plants, uses hardly any water (cleaning panels and blades only).

- Residential solar panel installments will really increase if local utilities compensate solar producers of energy at prices closer to those they charge their consumers. This will help consumers maximize the energy produced and give them some additional income from their roofs.

- Battery storage costs are coming down; that will help consumers especially in sunny areas to store energy and use it for charging their electric cars.

- More freedom, personal control, good jobs, lower bills, good returns, energy security, renewable energy, diversification, clean industry, cleaner air.

GOAL

The energy revolution—we can call it evolution—is occurring as a gradual transition to renewable energy. The initiative blueprint will allow the world to decrease its reliance on coal over time while investing increasingly in renewables—solar, wind, and geothermal. The numbers in table 1 show how the United States can complete the transition and eliminate coal use for electricity by 2030.

Energy Source	2016 Average Production 460 GW, Installed Capacity	2016 Usage Percent	2030 Average Capacity 460 GW	2030 Usage Percent	Additional Watts	Investment in Dollars per watt	Investment in Billions of Dollars	Percent Yearly Increase
Hydropower	31.28	6.8	7	7				
Solar	40	1.7	440	20	400	1.25	500	20
Wind	83	6.4	305	20	222	1.25	278	7.9
Geothermal	1.38	0.3	14	3	12.4	4.5	56	
Biomass	6.44	1.4	9	2	2.76	1.5	4	
Total Renewables	76.36	16.6		52				
Nuclear	89.24	19.4		18				
Gas	150.88	32.5		30				
Oil and gases	3.22	0.5		0				
Coal	151.8	33		0				
Grand Total	460	102.5		100			837	
Average investment per year is $72 billion								

Table 1. Recommended Plan for Carbon Reduction by 2030 and Elimination of Coal and Oil for Electricity Production.

Table 1 shows how we can address the electricity issue, reduce carbon emissions, and eliminate the use of coal by 2030. We start with a 13.3 percent production of electricity using renewables and end up with 52 percent. If nuclear energy is included, carbon-free energy will be 70 percent by 2030. We assume the total power generation requirement will stay constant. Any increase in the overall energy should be strictly handled by renewable energy as it is the cheapest source. Coal-produced energy will be gradually reduced as renewable energy is building up. Solar energy used for charging electric cars should be done with additional home solar installations over and above that shown in the table. As the chart shows, we start with 36 percent of carbon-free sources and end up with 70 percent carbon-free sources.

Table 1 shows where we are today and where we want to be by 2030. The cost for this transition will be $837 billion over the next thirteen years. The yearly cost for this transition is $77 billion, about 0.4 percent of the 2015 GDP. A large amount of this will be recovered from lowered costs of production, job creation, growth, and reduction of the defense budget.

The evolution is already going on, and we need to accelerate it. The federal government can be very helpful in making available land particularly in the Southwest, where there is plenty of sunshine. In the meantime, we should stop investing in coal plants and retire them as they reach the end of their lifetimes and as more renewable energy comes online.

The data above assume that energy use remains constant; that requires that we increase our energy efficiency until 2030. This is all about using our electricity wisely so we get more done with less electricity. This can occur as we increase the efficiency of appliances and home insulation.

There is no technological barrier to achieving the goals by 2030. Since grid parity has been achieved already, the road will become smoother as volume production, technology improvements, and long-term planning make it easier for further efficiencies and price reductions.

AREA REQUIRED FOR SOLAR AND WINDMILL INSTALLATIONS

The sun's energy incident on the earth's surface is about one thousand watts or 1 KW per square meter (10.76 square feet). That means that if we use a panel that has 20 percent efficiency, we will capture about 200 watts in that one-square-meter area. The 20 percent efficiency is nominal at this time; higher efficiency systems are in production, and more than 26 percent efficiency has been demonstrated in the laboratory.

If we use lower efficiency panels, they will require more space; on the other hand, panels with higher efficiency are more expensive. The cost is always evaluated on a per-watt basis so the numbers can be compared with other sources of energy and various efficiency solar panels.

It is estimated that the land required to power the entire United States with solar energy would be 11,500 square kilometers (4,250 square miles), equivalent to less than 3 percent of California. This includes the efficiencies in the system, the extra area being used by utility access to the system, and an average of five hours per day of sunlight. The roofs of residential and commercial buildings could contribute a great amount of the needed area. And other renewable sources of energy could be used; that would further reduce the area needed.

The above estimates do not include home rooftop installations. This will be of great benefit as no productive land would be used and if utilities were forced to buy the extra energy generated at a reasonable price. This will maximize the home solar energy production and earn some extra income for the homeowner. The US Department of Energy's National Renewable Energy Laboratory (NREL), has found that the potential for the US building rooftops for solar photovoltaic (PV) systems could generate about 42 percent of national electricity sales.

Large department stores and industrial facilities are installing rooftop systems because the cost is negligible. The same applies to companies with large data centers as they want to move to carbon-free electricity.

Two types of solar energy are being used.

1. Photovoltaic (PV) panels are about 15–22 percent efficient. Continuous high-level research will substantially increase further efficiency and decrease costs. This type of system can be used for house rooftops, industrial and commercial buildings, or large utility plants. An increase of efficiency reduces the panel cost per watt and reduces the cost of installation for a given size system. A typical system has a twenty-five-year life with an end-life production being 80 percent of its initial level. A typical rooftop system is usually 2–10 kW.

2. Concentrated Thermal Power (CSP) utilizes mirrors to concentrate the sun's energy and boil water; steam powers turbines to generate electricity. The advantage of this method is that the hot water keeps going until it eventually cools and electricity production stops. CSP systems can be built as hybrids for twenty-four-hour operation as they can use natural gas to create steam during hours of no sunshine. CSP systems are used for large, utility-scale installations.

LCOE costs for either system—photovoltaic or CSP—is about the same; the cost of CSP slightly higher.

The space required for windmills is rather negligible. Very small amounts of land are used, and if farmland is used, farmers can supplement their income by renting small areas of their farms for the windmills.

The total wind energy capacity installed in the United States by the end of 2016 was 83 GW. In the last ten years, there has been growth from 6.64 to 65.9 GW for an average yearly growth of 25.8 percent.[347]

COSTS OF SOLAR AND WIND ENERGY

The press is full of articles about how wind and solar energy is cheaper than fossil fuel–produced energy. "Solar Is Cheaper Than Electricity from the Grid in 42 of 50 Largest U.S. Cities" (January 16, 2015), was written by Anastasia Pantsios of ECOWATCH.

> Now a new report called Going Solar in America, prepared by the North Carolina Clean Energy Technology Center with the support of the U.S. Department of Energy's SunShot Initiative, shows how the plummeting costs of going solar could already make it the more economical choice for energy consumers in 42 of the U.S.'s 50 largest cities. It found that in those cities, a fully financed solar system would cost average residential consumers less than they would pay for electricity from their current local utility.

> New York and Boston topped the list, in large part because the cost of electricity from the grid is very expensive there. The top ten, is rounded out by Albuquerque, San Jose, Las Vegas, Washington D.C., Los Angeles, San Diego, Oakland and San Francisco. High local energy costs also account for California cities filling half the top ten slots … However, our analysis shows that, in 46 of America's 50 largest cities, a fully-financed, typically-sized solar PV system is a better investment than the stock market, and in 42 of these cities, the same system already costs less than energy from a residential customer's local utility.[348]

In its report Cheap Natural Gas: Fracturing Dreams of a Solar Future, Lux Research stated that utility-scale solar power was poised to become cost competitive with natural gas by 2025. The report evaluated the leveled cost of energy (LCOE) for unsubsidized solar, hybrid solar/gas technologies, and natural gas till 2030 under various future natural gas price scenarios and was spread across ten parts of the world.

[347] American Wind Energy Association
[348] http://ecowatch.com/2015/01/16/solar-cheaper-than-grid/.

The study assumed a delay in shale gas production due to antifracking policies in Europe, a 39 percent decrease in utility-scale system costs by 2030, and high capital costs in South America.

The report concluded that the leveled cost of energy for unsubsidized, utility-scale solar globally will be only about $0.02/kWh above the price of power produced by combined cycle gas turbines by 2025. Ed Cahill, an associate at Lux Research and the lead author of the report, said,

> On the macroeconomic level, a "golden age of gas" can be a bridge to a renewable future as gas will replace coal until solar becomes cost competitive without subsidies. On the micro-economic level, solar integrated with natural gas can lower costs and provide stable output.[349]

Costs of installations for utility scale solar is around $1.5–$1.8 per watt for a twenty-five-year system and an 80 percent deterioration at the end. Wind energy installation costs are less than $1.5 per watt.

So right now, wind and solar power is cheaper than grid electricity due mostly to subsidies. These subsidies are important for the solar industry due to various factors such as natural resistance to the change to solar energy; incentives are required to overcome this resistance and until rooftop PV systems become a norm.

"In the areas where natural resources are not available in abundance and in areas where PV systems are not common, incentives are required by solar installers to make solar energy competitive. In sunniest regions, the looming reduction in the federal solar tax credit may not pose as a problem but can be a big hindrance in emerging market.

But eventually efforts should be made to phase out the subsidy because ultimately, it is this unsubsidized solar parity that matters. Places like southern California and New York are already at Unsubsidized Solar Parity and Germany is aiming to reach there soon. So, we can say that years down the line the only solar parity we will hear will be unsubsidized solar parity."[350]

The following article titled Solar and Wind Energy Start to Win on Price vs. Conventional Fuels tells it all.[351]

> For the solar and wind industries in the United States, it has been a long-held dream: to produce energy at a cost equal to conventional sources like coal and natural gas. That day appears to be dawning. The cost of providing electricity from wind and

---

[349] http://www.altenergy.org/renewables/solar/.
[350] http://www.altenergy.org/renewables/solar/
[351] *New York Times*, November 23, 2014

solar power plants has plummeted over the last five years, so much so that in some markets renewable generation is now cheaper than coal or natural gas …

In Texas, Austin Energy signed a deal this spring for 20 years of output from a solar farm at less than 5 cents a kilowatt-hour …

And, also in Oklahoma, American Electric Power ended up tripling the amount of wind power it had originally sought after seeing how low the bids came in last year.

"Wind was on sale — it was a Blue Light Special," said Jay Godfrey, managing director of renewable energy for the company. He noted that Oklahoma, unlike many states, did not require utilities to buy power from renewable sources. "We were doing it because it made sense for our ratepayers," he said.

According to a study by the investment-banking firm Lazard, the cost of utility-scale solar energy is as low as 5.6 cents a kilowatt-hour, and wind is as low as 1.4 cents. In comparison, natural gas comes at 6.1 cents a kilowatt-hour on the low end and coal at 6.6 cents. Without subsidies, the firm's analysis shows, solar costs about 7.2 cents a kilowatt-hour at the low end, with wind at 3.7 cents.

What about the subsidies for renewable energy? Fossil fuels receive a great number of subsidies. According to the Brookings Institute, "eliminating the 12 subsidies for fossil fuels in the U.S. would save $41.4 billion over 10 years without increasing fuel prices, reducing employment, or weakening U.S. energy security."[352]

According to the Washington Post, "fossil fuels received $550 billion in subsidies worldwide last year. That's 4x more than renewables."[353]

[352] Brookings Institute, February 2013, http://bit.ly/1h3mDhB.
[353] *Washington Post*, November 2014, http://wapo.st/1v7RVLf.

ELECTRIC CARS

The United States can cut the consumption of oil by half, improve the quality of air, help reduce carbon emissions, and eliminate the need for imported oil with knowledge and decisiveness now.

The list below shows what we can do. It will take some time for industry to switch and adopt, but consumers can force the issue. We can switch to smaller and hybrid electric or all-electric cars. We can produce all the electricity we need from renewable resources. It does not mean that gas cars will be eliminated; but doubling the mileage of small gas, diesel, and electric cars, we can cut oil consumption in half.

1. All electric cars can use renewable energy. Many all-electric and hybrid cars are in production, and more are in the planning stage. Practically every automobile company has one. Some all-electric cars have more than a 200-mile range.

2. Switch to smaller, fuel-efficient cars, and carpool.

3. Switch to diesel cars, which are 37 percent more efficient than equivalent gasoline-driven vehicles. Diesel car emissions have been improved substantially. Over half the new cars sold in Europe have diesel engines.

4. Switch to small diesel hybrid cars for additional energy efficiency that make more than fifty miles per hour.

5. Switch to hybrid or all-electric cars. The lifecycle costs of electric cars are competitive with gasoline cars and will become more so in the future as battery costs drop with improvements in technology, volume production increases, and increases in the price of oil.

6. Per the Center for Automotive Research, "Maintenance costs for electric drive vehicles are as much as 50 percent lower than traditional gasoline vehicles, thanks to fewer fluids to change, significantly reduced brake wear due to regenerative braking, and far fewer moving parts."[354]

7. Having small all-electric cars for commuting in an eighty-mile range or more will cover 90 percent of commuters. A very high percentage of people have two cars; they could use gas/diesel cars for longer trips. It is cheaper to rent a gas car for a long trip than having an extra car that requires additional insurance, maintenance, and space.

8. Electric cars reduce oil imports.

9. Electric cars reduce global warming and air pollution.

10. Electricity used for cars can be produced primarily at home in most cases by solar energy. This leads to zero pollution and no global warming. Electricity

---

[354] Center for Automotive Research, http://bit.ly/LO7he8 and US Department of Energy, http://bit.ly/QBLmGY.

is produced in power plants with about 32 percent efficiency versus 20 percent efficiency for a gasoline-powered car.

11. Companies can build more charging stations with solar and wind produced energy.

12. Make it mandatory for power companies to install 100 percent time metering in houses. This will increase energy savings and better stabilize the electrical grid demand by reducing the difference between day high and early morning low demand for electricity.

13. Utilities should be required to pay at the going rate for extra electricity being produced by homeowners with solar energy installations. This will be an incentive for homeowners to install larger solar energy systems on their roofs that produce more electricity than they consume. This has already been implemented in many European countries. In addition, this uses otherwise unused surfaces.

The highest demand for electricity is between 12:00 p.m. and 4:00 p.m.; the lowest demand occurs between 2:00 a.m. and 6:00 a.m. Electric utilities have to produce electricity using expensive natural gas during the high-demand hours. One of the major advantages that solar energy has is that it is produced when demand is the highest, between noon and 5:00 p.m.

Wind energy is produced at random; it depends on the weather usually more in the winter than in the summer, and more at night than during the day. There have been occasions when more wind energy was produced in a large local area than was demanded. This can be solved with more-robust, higher capacity, electric transmission systems, investment in battery storage systems or water pumping storage stations, and the use of the energy for powering desalinization plants. Water demand is increasing, and more desalination plants will be required in the future in dry areas and small islands. (This is covered in the resources section.)

BATTERIES

Besides the two major pillars—wind and solar—batteries constitute the third pillar of renewable energy. The first two pillars broke records by producing energy cheaper than fossil fuels could. Battery costs are going down and becoming more cost competitive. Battery technology is on a learning curve, but technology and volume will make them cheaper. People will start a major transition from the internal combustion cars to electric cars, and wind and solar energy will be able to be stored and thus available at all times. Gas-produced energy can always be a backup. With cost-competitive batteries, the ground-transportation sector can move away from fossil fuels.

Batteries and their associated costs are the key drivers of the development of electric cars and a crucial part of the future of solar and wind energy. Batteries can store electricity during peak production and dispense it at times when there is no sunshine or wind. Thus, the battery can become a double sword when it comes to renewables. It reduces carbon emissions from the production of electricity and the transportation sector, which is the biggest carbon contributor.

Though battery costs are a bit high right now, research taking place will drive costs down. The present costs are about $200–$300 per kWh, but that could get down to $125–$150 per kWh by 2017. All-electric, mass-produced cars have been announced to have the capacity of about 50 kWh and a range of over 220 miles in the US and European markets. The battery cost is about $145 per kilowatt hour; an electric car with a 50-kWh capacity battery will have a range of about 220 miles (354 km). When battery costs are reduced by 50 percent, the costs of the car will go down and its range will increase as the cars will be sold with higher-capacity batteries.

All-electric or hybrid cars with ranges of less than eighty miles are in production; they are ideal for most commuting. In the future, as electric cars proliferate, there will be more charging stations, and more-advanced technology will reduce charging times. Tesla has been making major strides in providing quick and abundant charging stations throughout the country.

The most key specifications for the car batteries besides costs are high power density per pound and high cycle endurance. There is a great need to drive battery costs down not only for the sake of electric cars but also for storing solar and wind energy. There is also a growing demand in many underdeveloped countries for battery usage for off-the-grid solar and wind energy storage where central grids are unreliable or nonexistent. Electricity that cannot be stored can be put to use in desalination plants; the world is heading for a water as well as an energy shortage crisis.

The existing battery technology with some increase in volume and some innovation can replace most new cars let's say by 80 percent by 2030. In addition, the same battery technology can be used to store solar or wind electricity for backup and in remote areas; this will further increase volume and drive battery costs down. Massive production of electric cars and some battery innovations can drive the cost of the battery to about $150 dollars per kWh. That would drive the cost of a 40-kWh battery to about $6,000. More than 90 percent of commuters can be using a car with a 40-kWh battery and with a range of about 140 miles. Traveling longer distances can be accommodated with fast recharging times—about thirty minutes.

Today, the total life costs of an electric car are less than that of the equivalent gasoline automobile. Hybrid cars provide an intermediate solution for those with longer commutes and city driving. There is a lifetime cost risk of the battery, but this will be reduced when the costs of recyclable batteries are reduced.

The combination of solar-produced electricity for electric cars and the savings involved in not importing oil has the additional effect of eliminating pollution caused by the power plant producing electricity. The effects on clean air and the cost of importing foreign oil outweighs by far any additional upfront costs of the electric cars.

The United States is importing about 10 million barrels per day at $100 per barrel—a cost of $365 billion dollars per year. Every investment dollar we make in producing electricity locally for electric cars creates jobs at home and saves dollars that go overseas for importing foreign oil.

HOME ENERGY EFFICIENCY

Listed below are some actions that can be taken to switch to renewable and clean energy.

1. Home heating should be done with natural gas. It is efficient and cleaner than oil heating. All new homes should be heated by gas. If they have a solar system, they can use the extra electricity for heating. When cheap batteries become available, it makes sense to have an all-electric house, all renewable energy, and zero carbon emissions.
2. Replace all incandescent lighting with LEDs preferably.
3. Refrigerators older than twenty years use too much energy to be cost effective.
4. Electric utility companies should be obligated to buy all extra energy that consumers are generating from residential solar installations at a competitive rate as is done in some European companies.
5. National, uniform codes for installation, permits, and inspections will further reduce installation costs. The cost of solar for home installations in Germany is less than that in the United States for this reason. There is too much paperwork and too much variation in regulations from state to state in the United States.

There is a real push for commercial buildings and industrial sites to go solar. Because of the economies of scale, the cost of installation per watt is less than that for residential applications.

Businesses, which consume large amounts of electricity, invest in their own solar or wind energy farms so they produce cheaper, clean, and renewable energy. Companies such as Apple, Google, Walmart, Ikea, and others are already leading the way to a carbon-free energy environment. I believe they are doing it not only to be environmentally friendly but also because it makes economic sense.

China was late in entering the renewable energy revolution, but it became the world leader in producing renewable energy in less than five years. It leads the world in solar and wind energy capacity with extensive year-to-year growth.

ENERGY AND WAR

Energy and access to it have been the cause of wars. A high percentage of our defense budget goes for a large military to keep the lines of oil flowing. The recent wars in Iraq, Afghanistan, Libya, and other Mideast countries are directly or indirectly connected to oil. In addition, we prop up unpopular regimes and we draw the wrath of their citizens. Iran is another case of constant friction as it is a major oil producer and partially control the Strait of Hormuz, the entrance to the Persian Gulf. Gen. Wesley K. Clark, former supreme allied commander, Europe, from 1997 to 2000, claimed in a speech given in 2007 that America underwent a "policy coup" at the time of the 9/11 attacks. He revealed that right after 9/11, he was privy to information contained in a classified memo: "US plans to attack and remove governments in seven countries over five years: Iraq, Syria, Lebanon, Libya, Somalia, Sudan and Iran." At the Pentagon, he was told, "We learned that we can use our military without being challenged. We've got about five years."[355]

Energy consumption, besides being the key driving factor of the GDP, also impacts the environment and thus the quality of life.

In the last twenty years, a consensus has developed that drastic action must be taken in the use of energy and cut CO_2 emissions. However, two larger factors will make this agreement and its effects minuscule: the increase in population and the increased energy needs of underdeveloped and developing nations. It is projected that the daily usage of oil will increase to 128 million barrels per day by 2030 up from 94 million today. This by itself will more than wipe out the benefits gained from the move to renewable sources. We all read about the monthly increases of over a million new cars on the road in China, India, and other countries. These cars are not replacement cars as in the United States, thus oil consumption will increase dramatically.

The following statistics are alarming. The United States, with 4.7 percent of the world's population, uses 24 percent of the daily oil production, of about 92 million barrels. If the rest of the world was to use the same amount as the United States, the world's daily oil production must be increased to 414 million barrels, an increase of 500 percent.

Estimates are that the total known world's oil reserves are approximately 1,200 billion barrels. At the present daily rate of consumption, 92 million barrels, that will last thirty-six years. If the entire world was to use oil at the same rate as the United States, it will last about six or seven years. But oil consumption is increasing.

---

[355] http://www.salon.com/2007/10/12/wesley_clark/

The yearly US cost of imported oil is about $200 billion depending on the price of oil. This cannot be sustained for very long without a dollar collapse as we keep borrowing this amount or printing more dollars. The time for change is now. Fracking techniques are not environmental friendly, and fracking will only postpone the day of reckoning. We should use the time to improve renewable energy technologies.

What if the known oil reserves are wrong and they are double? Still, the time for change is now as it takes years and years to make the transition. A massive education program on renewable energy would be very helpful.

So much effort is put into endless discussions especially during election campaigns on drilling into the most environmentally sensitive areas such as Alaska so we can enjoy driving our SUVs on borrowed money. If we discover 10 billion barrels, we will go through that in 1.3 years at the rate of 20 million barrels per day. And it would take at least ten years before the first drop of gasoline got into our tanks. It is hard to sound an alarm, but we should bear in mind that if the world is not prepared for oil becoming scarce, its cost will skyrocket; without energy, the world economic order will collapse.

For the world to continue with economic development and increase GDPs, its energy sources must satisfy two requirements: they must be from renewable sources and environmentally friendly. If either of these two requirements is not met, we will run out of energy altogether or the environment will deteriorate to the point that life will be threatened. In the environmental threat, the greenhouse effect is the most serious. It threatens not only the environment; it can also produce a calamity of events and threaten life itself.

Renewable energy and electric cars is the answer. We cannot say, "We do not have money for solar and wind energy, but we have money for war."

NUCLEAR FUSION

Our sun is an immense nuclear fusion reactor; hydrogen atoms fuse under immense temperature and pressure to produce helium atoms and provide us free, safe, and constant light, which consists of photons. This photon energy is responsible for life in our planet, solar, and wind energy. The sun is a finite mass that uses tons of matter daily; it will run out of matter in approximately 5 billion years. It will then die along with the earth.

We have been able to duplicate the sun's fusion process in making the hydrogen bomb, which is an uncontrollable explosion used for destructive purposes. Our dream and ambition is to duplicate the fusion taking place in the sun but under controlled conditions. It is the ultimate goal and will be the greatest achievement of the humanity. For controllable and sustainable fusion to take place, extremely high pressures and temperatures are required without melting the containers that enclose this extremely hot and pressurized gas-plasma. If this were to become reality, it would generate cheap, clean, and inexhaustible energy as in the sun that will last as long as the sun exists. Research is being done now, and billions are being spent, but our ambition and dreams are greater than the challenge. However, the practical implementation is far in the future.

WATER

Water is a precious good, and its existence or scarcity determines the standard of living of people across the world. If we have plentiful energy, we can solve the water problem as three quarters of the globe is covered with water. Cheap and plentiful energy can be used in desalination plants to produce drinking water. Energy makes up half the operating costs of desalination plants.

The largest desalination plant the western hemisphere, in Carlsbad, California, cost $1 billion and went into operation in December 2015. The plant will serve San Diego County with the capacity of 50 million gallons of fresh water daily, about a tenth of the county's total water use. It is heralding a new era in US water use. It is the most technologically advanced seawater desalination plant. The cost of the water is about twice the cost of water from the region's largest water wholesaler. In absolute numbers, it costs about half a cent to produce a gallon of drinking water at the plant. Considering the alternatives, that is reasonable.

With experience, cheaper energy, and further technology innovations, the price of such desalinization plants can be reduced and can make them more environmentally friendly. Right now, about sixteen desalination plants are in the plans along the California coast.

WORLD POPULATION

With the world, a war began that will end with the world, and not before:
the war of man against nature, of spirit against matter, of liberty against
fatality. History is nothing but the story of this endless struggle.[356]

AWARENESS OF THE PROBLEM

There are about 7 billion people in the world today, twice the number of 1970,
and that number is expected to reach about 9.3–10 billion by 2050. People live longer
thanks to progress in medicine and increases in food production.

Economic development typically involves improvements in a variety of indicators
such as education and literacy rates, health care conditions, life expectancy, and
poverty rates. The gross domestic product (GDP) is the market value of all final
goods and services a nation produces yearly. If we take the GDP as the key indicator
of economic development, looking at national statistics, we can see that the energy
usage of a nation is proportional to its GDP. GDP does not consider important
aspects such as leisure time, environmental quality, freedom, social justice, and other
quality-of-life issues.

GDP VS. PER-CAPITA INCOME—RICH VS. POOR.

In his classic book *An Essay on Population* (1798), Thomas Malthus (1766–1834)
described one of the greatest problems facing the world.

---

[356] Jules Michelet, *Introduction to World History*, trans. Flora Kimmich (1831).

The power of population is indefinitely greater than the power in the earth to produce subsistence for man. Population, when unchecked, increases in a geometric ratio. Subsistence increases only in the arithmetic ratio. A slight acquaintance with numbers will show the immensity of the first power in comparison of the second.[357]

As late as 1950, most people around the world lived as the ancients had. They had no electricity, cars telephones, and limited indoor plumbing. They had not benefited from the industrial age. Now, entire regions of the world have all these goods, and some skipped the industrial age altogether. They moved to the postindustrial age of the service economy and the information age. A personal computer today has capabilities unthought-of forty years ago; it can include all the functions of television, music recorder/player, send/receive e-mail instantly, entertainment, and so on. Yet most people do not participate in the creation and dissemination of knowledge. They occasionally and passively watch TV or read what is happening in more-developed countries. Their education level remains low.

There are visible signs of nature abuse such as local pollution in many areas. The worldwide media report that environmental problems are getting worse as populations increase. Here is just a sample of these problems:

- deforestation—loss of jungle forests around the equator
- contamination of soil and air resulting in the extinction of species
- erosion of topsoil and overuse of chemical fertilizers
- overfished oceans
- depletion and contamination of ground water
- nuclear waste and other toxic substances
- lack of clean water, resource depletion, epidemics, and migration
- breakdown of the ozone layer

Many of these problems are due to the use of nonrenewable energy sources. Yet invisible and the most dangerous of them all is the problem of global warming hovering over the planet. The planet's average temperature has increased over 2 degrees C in the last century.

In the last two centuries, the overpopulation problem was relieved by immigration and colonization. Millions of people moved to new territories such as Australia, New Zealand, and North and South America. The new territories needed labor, and the immigrants fulfilled that need. Now, industrial and farm automation has substantially reduced the need for manual labor. There is a south-to-north economic hemisphere migration, legal and illegal, that causes many problems. Wars

---

[357] T. Malthus, *On Population* (New York: Modern Library, 1960), 9.

in the Middle East and North Africa put additional pressure on southern Europe with the thousands of refugees who flee wars and conflicts in North Africa, Syria, Iraq, Afghanistan, and Pakistan.

Malthus observed that the increase of population was necessarily limited by the means of subsistence: "That population does invariably increase when the means of subsistence increase. And that the superior power of population is repressed, and the actual population kept equal to the means of subsistence, by misery and vice."[358] He meant that sooner or later, the population would be checked by famine and disease and lead to what is known as a Malthusian catastrophe.

As a cleric, Malthus saw this situation as divinely imposed to teach virtuous behavior.

> Yet in all societies, even those that are most vicious, the tendency to a virtuous attachment is so strong that there is a constant effort towards an increase of population. This constant effort as constantly tends to subject the lower classes of the society to distress and to prevent any great permanent amelioration of their condition.[359]

Paul Kennedy, referring to the time of industrialization, stated,

> The British people escaped their Malthusian trap via three doors: migration, agricultural revolution and industrialization. It is equally important to notice, however, that this escape was not very common. Certain countries-Belgium, Germany and the United states-imitated the British practices, ... increased productivity, wealth and standard of living. Other countries such as Ireland were not able to solve.[360]

T. S. Aston stated,

> The central problem of the age ... how to feed and clothe and employ generations of children outnumbering by far those of any other time.[361]

> By the 1840's starvation and immigration had reduced population by about one-fifth ... Industrialization and modernization

---

[358] Ibid., 52.
[359] Ibid., 14.
[360] P. Kennedy, *Preparing for the Twenty-First Century* (New York: Random House, 1993), 10.
[361] T. S. Aston, *The Industrial Revolution, 1760–1830* (Oxford, 1968), 129.

certainly caused problems in Western societies, but they paled in comparison with the lot of those who increased their numbers without passing through the industrial revolution.[362]

Around sixty years ago, the population of the big countries in the Middle East and vicinity—Egypt, Iran, Turkey—had about 20 million people each; they now have about 80 million each, and that number is increasing at a high rate. The same is repeated in Latin America, Africa, and Asia except in China, Japan, and Korea.

Malthus's theory was correct for primitive societies at his time, but it is not as applicable today. Modern medicine has reduced or wiped out many epidemic diseases. Famines are rarer as poor areas have more access to food through the transfer of surplus food from rich areas. Today, Malthus's theory of population control has a rather small or insignificant effect. We live in a wired world in which the instant an earthquake occurs or a famine or a disease breaks out, the world becomes aware immediately and responds. Food is rushed in quickly by international assistance organizations and philanthropists to fight malnutrition or starvation and epidemics.

These epidemic diseases must be fought locally before they spread via today's advanced transportation system. In addition, when an epidemic breaks out, all types of worldwide medical institutions rush in to study it and develop the antidote to squelch the disease.

WHAT CAN BE DONE?

With the Malthusian rule not working, we are left with only some challenging but powerful choices: education, knowledge, and development.

The evidence is overwhelming that education leads to lower fertility, stabilization of population, and increased prosperity. This has already happened in developed countries that have experienced decreases in population.

Examples abound about all the progress humans have made in increasing food production and the new wealth that fed an increased number of mouths. In addition, overpopulation creates more pollution, which has detrimental effects on the environment. The earth can sustain a much higher population than today's, but we need to take a breather and catch up with alternative renewable energy supplies.

I believe that the following is a practical and effective way of informing and educating people worldwide.

1. Start massive information programs to inform and educate people about the perils of overpopulation. The standard of living will not increase if the

---

[362] Ibid., 11.

population increases. The Internet can play a major role in this endeavor. Obviously, it cannot happen overnight.

2. The Internet can be used to spread massive amounts of knowledge for education and development. Funding projects for some energy developments and Internet access will have a highly beneficial effect on the underdeveloped world.

3. Start intensive programs and investments on alternate, renewable energy sources. The good news is that some countries have taken major steps in addressing this issue, but much more needs to be done.

4. Governments must address the economic gap between rich and poor, an overall climate of pessimism, and unemployment and its consequences. Economic development is a must.

INTERNET

The Internet can spread knowledge and education anywhere on earth. It has been in widely use since around 1990, and its increase has been spectacular. The Internet has had a major influence in how information is generated and transported. Just as the printing press had an immediate and positive impact on civilization, the Internet will do so to at least the same if not a greater degree. There is no better medium for the propagation and dissemination of knowledge. Its use just started to be felt, but it is only fifteen years old in wide use. The Internet cloud with its data banks has become the depository of practically all knowledge not only for books and text but for pictures, X-ray and MRI records, and all types of information such as news, business, correspondence, advertisements, etc.

Information on the Internet moves instantly around the world, and people from any place on earth can access this depository of knowledge. However, access to it is an issue with most of the undeveloped countries.

Computer processing power and memory storage costs are diminishing. Numerous devices from computes to tablets and telephones with the computing power of a PC are sitting idle for most of the time. People may be poor, but they do not lack cell phones.

Entire libraries are digitized and exist in this depository of information. The searching and classification techniques are being perfected. Instantaneous translation is available now and is still being perfected. We may be the same world as before, but we have a common information base.

In modern times, we have seen the power of the Internet helping topple several Arab regimes by providing instant communication among protesters or revolutionaries. The Internet along with the telecommunication system makes it feasible for governments to listen to phone calls, determine where the caller is, and record all e-mails and all other information and sites one visits. Companies also gather a lot of information from Internet users. Privacy is being reduced, but despite all these issues, the benefits far outweigh the risk.

We are still at the dawn of the Internet Age. Humanity has not been a good predictor of near- and long-term effects of previous inventions on society, and it will be the same with the Internet. So far, we see bookstores, record stores, newspapers, and traditional mail being substantially reduced or going out of business. The Internet enables remote banking and shopping, global commerce flourishes, and competition increases. Instant communication aids outsourcing immensely. Personal services are being negatively impacted. Operators, secretaries, and phone-assist jobs are reduced or being outsourced to cheap labor countries.

However, we will need to adjust the ways we do things. Will all this knowledge really make a difference? I believe yes. Knowledge will bring more excellence and the ability to make politicians and the masses to make better political decisions to improve all lives. It will limit dogmatism and increase knowledge, progress, and happiness. Knowledge and prosperity will bring additional material goods that will provide hope for those living in misery.

These issues have been with us for a long time, but there is something alarming about them now and in the immediate future. The growing population requires more and more energy, and that leads to environmental deterioration.

According to IEA World Energy Outlook of 2011, the major problem of people without access to electricity is in sub-Sahara Africa, India, and the rest of developing Asia and Latin America, with 586 million, 668 million, and 30 million people respectively. By 2030, there will be 645 million, 375 million, and 10 million respectively

Today's industrialization, robotics, scientific breakthroughs, the globalized economy, and overnight air transportation to practically everywhere on the globe destroy jobs in far greater numbers than they did in the past. Production is gradually transferring to cheaper labor countries. As an example, shipping construction moved from Japan, to Korea, and then to China in about forty years. Most semiconductor chip assembly moved from United States to Japan, to Korea, the Philippines, Malaysia, and on to China in about twenty years.

In addition, major structural problems are created by capital, the mover of the world's economy, rather than labor. This along with automation caused wealth to move from the poor to the rich. Global inequality soared; 1 percent of the population has about 50 percent of the world's wealth.

Developing countries are also participants in global warming and local wars; the issues can be best addressed by the following:

- advanced and rich countries providing leadership
- population control being seen as a worldwide issue
- stopping energy needs increasing at a rate driven by increasing populations
- sharing technology
- cooperation in the world to conquer energy and population growth

6

WAR

Minds, nevertheless, are not conquered by arms, but by love and generosity
—Spinoza[363]

The thought that we're in competition with Russians or with Chinese
is all a mistake, and trivial. We are one species, with a world to win.
There's life all over this universe, but the only life in the solar system
is on earth, and in the whole universe we are the only men ... We
are living in a world in which all wars are wars of defense.
—George Wald[364]

HISTORY OF WARS

In this chapter, I will discuss past wars through the writings of historians and great minds and set the background for a discussion of the reasons for wars and the deaths, misery, and other problems they bring. By examining their causes and reviewing the past, we can come up with some promising solutions for the future.

There has been recorded warfare on earth since ancient times when various hordes started moving around for better land for food, for plunder, and colonization.

Homer's *Iliad*, written around the eighth century BC, is the first detailed historical account of war, the Trojan War between the Greeks and Trojans that took place around 1200 BC.

---

[363] Benedictus de Spinoza, The Selected Works of Baruch de Spinoza, XI.

[364] George Wald, from speech given at an antiwar teach-in at the Massachusetts Institute of Technology on March 4, 1969: "A Generation in Search of a Future," ed. Ron Dorfman for *Chicago Journalism Review* (May 1969).

Herodotus, the father of history, provided a description of the Persian wars that took place in the fifth century BC. He described the famous battles of Marathon and Thermopylae, the naval battles of Salamis and Mycale, and the battle of Plataea. In the first masterpiece of Greek prose, he wrote *Histories* to remind the generations to come of the causes and the events that took place and the destruction the war caused and offer a description of the civilization at the time.

He stated in his introduction to *Histories*,

> This is the display of the inquiry of Herodotus of Halicarnassus, so that things done by man not be forgotten in time, and that great and marvelous deeds, some displayed by the Hellenes, some by the barbarians, not lose their glory, including among others what was the cause of their waging war on each other.[365]

After Herodotus, Thucydides, the other famous ancient Greek historian, described the Peloponnesian War (431–404 BC). This war sapped the creativity of Athens and was one of the reasons its golden age ended.

Thucydides was concerned with the causes of war, the verification of his sources, and lessons for the future. He stated,

> And with regard to my factual reporting of the events of the war I have made it a principle not to write down the first story that came my way, and not even to be guided by my own general impressions; either I was present myself at the events which I have described, or else, I heard of them from eye-witnesses whose reports I have checked with as much thoroughness as possible … but if it be judged useful by those inquirers who desire an exact knowledge of the past as an aid to the interpretation of the future, which in the course of human things must resemble if it does not reflect it, I shall be content. In fine, I have written my work, not as an essay, which is to win the applause of the moment, but as a possession for all time. To the question why they broke the treaty, I answer by placing first an account of their grounds of complaint and points of difference, that no one may ever have to ask the immediate cause which plunged the Hellenes into a war of such magnitude.[366]

Thucydides described the dehumanization of war:

---

[365] Herodotus, trans. A. D. Godley (Cambridge: Harvard University Press, 1920).

[366] Thucydides, *The Peloponnesian War* (London: J. M. Dent; New York: E. P. Dutton Kagan), 5.

"In peace and prosperity, states and individuals have better sentiments, … but war takes away the easy supply of daily wants, and so proves a rough master, that brings most men's characters to a level with their fortunes."[367]

He reminded us that even in the barbarity of war, some humane rules need apply: "You should not destroy what is our common protection, namely, the privilege of being allowed in danger to invoke what is fair and right."[368]

Thucydides described the horror and the total destruction of the Athenian expedition in Syracuse.

> This was the greatest Hellenic achievement of any in this war, or, in my opinion, in Hellenic history; at once most glorious to the victors, and most calamitous to the conquered. They were beaten at all points and altogether; all that they suffered was great; they were destroyed, as the saying is, with a total destruction, their fleet, their army, everything was destroyed, and few out of many returned home. Such were the events in Sicily.[369]

General George Marshall, President Truman's secretary of state and former chief of staff, noted that nobody could think of the problems of the 1950s unless he had reflected on the fall of Athens in the fifth century BC.

> I doubt seriously whether a man can think with full wisdom and with deep convictions regarding certain of the basic issues today who has not at least reviewed in his mind the period of the Peloponnesian War and the fall of Athens … there were no nuclear weapons, no telecommunication, no guns and gunpowder … the logistics of the war were primitive, yet twenty hundred years later one of the most distinguished leaders of America, military and political affairs found Thucydides indispensable to his thinking.[370]

Voltaire took a tragic view of history: "History in general is a collection of crimes, follies, and misfortunes, among which we now and then meet with a few virtues, and some happy times: as we sometimes see a few scattered huts in a barren

[367] Ibid.
[368] Thucydides, *The Peloponnesian War*, trans. John H. Finley (New York: Modern Library, Random House, 1951), book 5.7, 331.
[369] Ibid., book 8.7, 488.
[370] Winks, *History of Civilization*, xxx.

desert."[371] And Voltaire commented on war in his *Dictionary*: "War is the greatest of all crimes and yet there is no Aggressor who does not color his crime with the pretext of justice."[372] Voltaire held that belief was the cause of crimes: "As long as people believe in absurdities they will continue to commit atrocities."[373]

In his *Political Observations*, James Madison wrote,

> Of all the enemies to public liberty, war is, perhaps, the most to be dreaded because it comprises and develops the germ of every other. War is the parent of armies; from these proceed debts and taxes ... known instruments for bringing the many under the domination of the few ... No nation could preserve its freedom in the midst of continual warfare.[374]

The famous English poet Shelley provided some human follies as excuses for war.

> Every epoch, under names more or less believable, has deified its peculiar errors; Revenge is the naked idol of the worship of a semi-barbarous age; and Self-deceit is the veiled image of unknown evil, before which luxury and satiety (fullness) lie prostrate.[375]

American essayist Ralph Waldo Emerson (1803–1882) was concerned about the power man posed at his time and expressed this prophetic thought: "Don't trust children with edge tools. Don't trust man, great God, with more power than he has until he has learned to use that little better. What a hell we should make of the world if we could do what we would!" [376] Emerson would be outraged today at the power we have acquired since and the number of so many destructive weapons we have used or stored in arsenals.

Although war has been glorified, Solzhenitsyn (1918–2008), the famous novelist and Nobel Prize winner, brought up the other, real dimension of war.

> No war is ever a way out. War is death. A war is terrible not because of advancing troops, houses on fire and bombings. A war is terrible in that it subordinates all that is thinking to the

---

[371] Boorstin, *Seekers*, 190.
[372] Durant, *History of Philosophy*, 318.
[373] *Civilization's Quotations: Life's Ideal*, ed. R. A. Krieger (Algora Publishing, 2002), 150.
[374] James Madison, *Political Observations*, 1795.
[375] http://www.academia.edu/16687076/A_Short_History_of_Literary_Criticism.
[376] R. W. Emerson, *Adventures of the Mind*, *The Saturday Evening Post* (New York: Vintage, 1960), 200.

legitimate power of stupidity. … Although, to be fair, this is the way things are here even without a war. [377]

Napoleon (1769–1821) was a master on the battlefield. He fought many wars and won most but the most critical. He led his nation into multiple notorious battles and temporarily conquered most of Europe and Egypt. He invaded Russia and was ultimately defeated by superior Russian tactics and the Russian winter. His loss at Waterloo was decisive; he was exiled, and he never returned to France alive. France paid a terrible price for his misadventures. Indeed, he may have learned his lesson based on his statement on war above. He made the famous statement on war: "There are two powers in the world, the sword and the mind. In the long term, the sword is always beaten by the mind."[378]

Napoleon was not alone. Throughout history, many other leaders have done their part in conquering and taking revenge via war or due to pure megalomania or insanity. Historians describe the causes, campaigns, battles, losses and gains, and the aftermath. We cannot be sure about all the truths, but we are sure of the aftermath of the great campaigns.

The Persians attacked Greece and were finally defeated at Salamis. The Athenians went to Sicily and were destroyed. Alexander the Great reached the Hindus River. Hannibal crossed the Alps with his elephants to fight Rome, which eventually prevailed around 183 BC. Tamerlane came to eastern Turkey and conquered it, but his empire fell apart after his death in 1405.

The Mongols captured all China and got all the way from Mongolia to western Europe and had more land under their control than any other nation in history. The crusaders reached the Holy Land multiple times and were finally defeated in the Ninth Crusade. The Turks besieged Vienna twice but were finally defeated in 1683.

Multiple European countries colonized parts of Africa, North and South America, and Asia. They were eventually forced to leave or abandon their colonies due to sheer exhaustion.

Physicist Max Born pondered the implications of atomic weapons.

It seems to me that the scientists who led the way to the atomic bomb were extremely skillful and ingenious, but not wise men. They delivered the fruits of their discoveries unconditionally into the hands of politicians and soldiers; thus, they lost their moral innocence and their intellectual freedom.[379]

---

[377] A. Solzhenitsyn, *The First Circle*, 1958.
[378] B. N. Moore and K. Bruder, *Philosophy, The Power of Ideas* (Mountain View, CA: Mayfield, 1990), 1.
[379] http://faculty.humanities.uci.edu/bjbecker/RevoltingIdeas/lecture20.html.

Gilbert Murray commented on continuous wars and peace.

> I start from the profound conviction that what the world needs
> is peace. There has been too much war, and too much of many
> things that naturally go with war; too much force and fraud, too
> much intrigue and lying, too much impatience, violence, avarice,
> unreasonableness, and lack of principle … But the world is not
> merely threatened by the prospect of future wars. It is filled with
> wars now … Wars caused by rivalry for the possession of colonies
> and rebellions, caused in colonies by unjust exploitation.[380]

In his book *How War Begun*, Mumford Lewis described nuclear war.

> The most formidable threat we confront, perhaps, is the fact that
> the fantasies that governed the ancient founders of civilization have
> now become fully realizable. Our most decisive recent inventions,
> the atom bomb and the planetary rocket, came about through
> a fusion of secular and "sacred" power, similar to their ancient
> union. Without the physical resources of an all-powerful state
> and the intellectual resources of an all-knowing corps of scientists,
> that sudden command of cosmic energy and interplanetary space
> would not have been possible. Powers of total destruction that
> ancient man dared impute only to his gods, any mere Russian
> or American air force general can now command. So wide and
> varied are the means of extermination by blast and radiation
> burns, by slow contamination from radioactive food and water,
> to say nothing of lethal bacteria and genetic deformities that the
> remotest hamlet is in as great peril as a metropolis. The old factor
> of safety has vanished …

> What is more disturbing than our official reversion to the lowest
> level of barbarism in war is the fact that even after the last war only
> a minority of our countrymen seems to have reflected on the moral
> implications of this practice of total extermination as a moral and
> acceptable means of overcoming an enemy's resistance. There is
> nothing in our code now to distinguish us from moral monsters
> of Genghis Khan. If we are willing to kill 100,000 people with
> one blow by random genocide, as in Hiroshima, there is nothing

---

[380] Gilbert Murray, *The Problem of Foreign Policy*, Internet, 1921.

to keep us from killing 100,000,000-except the thought that our countrymen may be massacred in equally large numbers.[381]

Our own military leaders have wryly admitted that in any large-scale war neither side can hope for a victory; indeed, they have not the faintest notion of how such a war, once begun, might be ended, short of total extermination for both sides. Thus, we are back at the very point at which civilization started, but at an even lower depth of savagery and irrationality. Instead of a token sacrifice to appease the gods, there would now be a total sacrifice, merely to bring an end to our neurotic anxieties.[382]

Albert Schweitzer made his Declaration of Conscience speech that was broadcast to the world over Radio Oslo; he pleaded for the abolition of nuclear weapons. He ended his speech with, "The end of further experiments with atom bombs would be like the early sunrays of hope which suffering humanity is longing for."[383]

WHAT IS WAR?

Most of our history books are devoted to wars. Some people were glorified by war, many were killed, and some became rich. Wars of colonialization brought wealth to the colonizers at first, but eventually, most colonies had to be abandoned as too costly to keep. Very few countries if any benefited from wars in the long run, especially in modern times.

Wars corrupt people and governments especially when they last too long. The costs and casualties rise, and the original purposes and promises do not prove out with the passage of time.

The results of the Vietnam, Afghanistan (Russian and American invasions), and Iraq wars testify to the fact that the reasons for starting wars can blur and be disputed. Alliances shift among the people one supports, and armaments get into the wrong hands. War produces too many casualties and immense costs, and the people stop supporting it.

In ancient times, Heraclitus wrote, "War is the father and the king of all … war is universal, and strife is justice"[384]

Per Carl von Clausewitz (1780–1831), a nineteenth-century Prussian general

---

[381] Lewis Mumford, *How War Begun, Adventures of the Mind, The Saturday Evening Post* (New York: Vintage Books, 1960), 195.

[382] Ibid., 199.

[383] A. Schweitzer, *Bulletin of Atomic Scientists*, June 1957.

[384] Heraclitus, c. 500 BC.

and military theorist, said, "War is the continuation of policy by other means" and "Everything in war is simple, but the simplest thing is difficult."

Gilbert Murray described war this way.

> To others who fought in the trenches or drove a tank or shut a remote missile and those on the receiving end war is one of the following: mud, filth, cold, rain, snow, heat, fear, death, maiming, gassing, blown up, bombed, hunger, starvation, atrocities, looting, rape, run over, pillage, kidnap, madness, torture, extortion, manipulation, mutilation, drowning, vandalism, refuges, radiation and leukemia, human suffering and whatever worse the human animal contrived.[385]

In 1929, Erich Maria Remarque (1898–1970) described the horrible experiences of German and French soldiers in trench warfare during World War I.

> This book is to be neither an accusation nor a confession, and least of all an adventure, for death is not an adventure for those who stand face to face with it. It will try to tell the story of a generation of men, even though they may have escaped the shells, were destroyed by the war.[386]

Yet there were no lessons learned, and ten years later, the world plunged into the worst war ever, World War II, and ended with the nuclear bombing of Hiroshima and Nagasaki.

War has been conducted with different strategies according to the equipment and technology at the time. Wars have been waged with stones, sticks, daggers, mace and axes, javelins, darts, slings, swords, pikes, hand-to-hand combat, knives, lances, bow and arrow, horses, ships, armor, shields, and helmets, mercenaries, and fortifications. Gunpowder and canons made fortifications obsolete, and tanks made trenches obsolete. Earth, sea, and air weapons dazzle the mind. Guns, hand grenades, machine guns, airplanes, different types of missiles, radar, battleships, submarines, torpedoes, aircraft carriers, helicopters of all kinds, balloons, drones, communications, and infrared cameras for night fighting.

Nuclear weapons were attached to missiles that could be launched from the ground or the sea or from the air. The Cold War created a climate of competition and terror, and we live in the present environment with thousands of nuclear bombs being pointed in every direction.

Small, portable tactical missiles as well as antiaircraft and antitank missiles can

---

[385] Gilbert Murray, *Problem of Foreign Policy.*
[386] Erich Maria Remarque, *All Quiet on the Western Front*, 1929.

be launched by all types of carriers including even pickup trucks and drones. Since World War II, technology has revolutionized war by creating massive amounts of destructive power. And all this exists in a world full of increased terrorism. The miniaturization of weaponry has greatly increased the power of terrorists.

But the results of wars have not changed much. The Vietnam War and the war in Lebanon showed that strength does not guarantee victory however victory is defined. Limited wars of this type and recent wars in the Middle East show that even small numbers of weapons can be very effective in wars and terrorism.

At present, we see a lot of terrorism, which is not unlike guerilla warfare. It is based on hit-and-run tactics and killing innocent civilians regardless of the threat of being killed or captured. Terrorists gather, fight, and disperse. They use terror tactics to gain local support and recruits. Regular armies have a hard time dealing with enemies that appear and then disappear. Drones controlled from miles away are no match for boots on the ground.

Nuclear weapons have become very small; nuclear material in dirty bombs is one of the biggest threats civilization faces today. A catastrophic, all-out war will cause mutual annihilation, but how can we protect ourselves from terrorists' dirty bombs? With so much nuclear material and so many weapons lying around, the laws of probability say that accidents and terrorist activities could increase considerably.

Napoleon's wars, the Franco-German War of 1870–71, and World Wars I and II ended in disaster for the aggressors. Germany's capitulation to the Allies and Russia led to the split of Germany into East and West and the European split into Communist East and the Democratic West.

With the participation of the great powers directly or indirectly, the civil war in Vietnam went on for over twenty years. The French and the United States spent men and wealth and left with nothing to show for it.

Throughout most of history, nature had been responsible for most human deaths caused by earthquakes, tsunamis, volcanoes, floods, hurricanes, and famines. But in the twentieth century, humanity itself caused many more deaths than did nature—187 million—through wars, massacres, civil wars, persecutions, and policy-induced famines.[387]

Since the end of World War II, despite the Cold War and minor wars in various parts of the globe, the world has had the longest period of peace.

The first conclusion about all major wars is that all invasion campaigns ended up in disaster for the invaders. The small wars in which the great powers participated had the same result: high casualties, high costs, and an amount of built-up hate that spreads terrorism now and in the years to come. Religious fervor and intolerance add to this hate.

Recently, religious and civil strife is being resurrected in more areas than just the Middle East. Killings and terror resembling those of the Middle Ages and carpet

---

[387] Rees, *Our Final Hour*, 25.

bombing and destruction in Gaza resembling the leveling of Dresden in World War II occurs periodically. Terrorism has reached America and Europe at the hands of outsiders but also at the hands of local sympathizers. Americans and Western Europeans are fighting on the side of people who no one can define precisely and with shifting loyalties in Iraq and Syria.

The second conclusion is that the Cold War remained cold. The mutually assured destruction (MAD) deterrence doctrine has worked so far. But one wonders how long it will last with nine nations possessing nuclear weapons and the continuous friction among the superpowers for control of Eastern Europe.

The third conclusion is that advanced technology to kill and maim has been spread in three directions: large atomic weapons with the capability of killing hundreds of millions, powerful tactical weapons in the hands of small countries, and weapons of terrorism available to small groups whether government controlled or terrorist organizations with or without religious motivations. These terrorist groups act on their own or in cooperation with similar ideological and or religious groups. People born in Europe or in the United States who are sympathetic or filled with religious fervor go and fight in the Middle East and commit atrocities there or locally.

THE RISK OF NUCLEAR WAR

Undoubtedly, nuclear weapons pose the greatest threat. During the Cuban missile crisis in October 27, 1962, the United States and the Soviet Union came to the brink of nuclear war. On that day, the American destroyer USS *Beale* began dropping depth charges on the nuclear-armed Soviet Submarine B-59, which was lurking near the US blockade line around Cuba. "The charges were nonlethal warning shots intended to force B-59 submarine to the surface, but the submarine's captain mistook them for live explosives."[388] Convinced he was witnessing the opening salvo of World War III, the captain angrily ordered his men to arm the sub's lone nuclear-tipped torpedo and prepare for attack.

The misunderstanding could have resulted in disaster if not for a contingency measure that required all three of the Soviet submarine's senior officers to sign off on a nuclear launch. The Soviet captain was in favor, but Vasili Arkhipov, B-59's second in command, refused to give his consent. After calming the captain down, Arkhipov coolly convinced his fellow officers to bring B-59 to the surface and request new orders from Moscow. The submarine eventually returned to Russia without incident, but it was over forty years before a full account of Arkhipov's lifesaving decision finally came to light. Despite all the immense destructive power the world possesses and all this planning and fail-safe systems, it came down to one man who saved it from its insanity.

[388] http://www.history.com/news/history-lists/5-cold-war-close-calls;

The historian Arthur Schlesinger Jr., one of President Kennedy's aides during the Cuban missile crisis, said,

> This was not only the most dangerous moment of the Cold War. It was the most dangerous moment in human history. Never before had two contending powers possessed between them the technical capacity to blow up the world. Fortunately, Kennedy and Khrushchev were leaders of restraint and sobriety; otherwise, we probably wouldn't be here today.

Robert McNamara, the US secretary of defense at the time and later on during the Vietnam War, wrote,

> Even a low probability of catastrophe is a high risk, and I don't think we should continue to accept it … I believe that was the best managed cold world crisis of any, but we came within a hairbreadth of nuclear war without realizing it. It's no credit to us that we missed nuclear war-at least we had to be lucky as well as wise … It became very clear to me as a result of the Cuban missile crisis that the indefinite combination of human fallibility (which we can never get rid of) and nuclear weapons carries the very high probability of the destruction of the nations.[389]

In another case,

> On December 5, 1965, a group of soldiers were pushing an A-4E fighter plane onto an elevator abroad the USS Ticonderoga, an aircraft carrier about 70 miles off the coast of Japan. The plane's canopy was open … The deck rose as the ship passed over a wave, and one of the sailors blew a whistle, signaling the pilot should apply his brakes. The pilot did not hear the whistle. The plane started rolling backwards. The sailor kept blowing the whistle; other sailors yelled, "Brakes, brakes," and held on to the plane. They let go as it rolled off the elevator into the sea. In an instant, it was gone. The pilot, his plane, and a Mark 43 hydrogen bomb vanished.[390]

---

[389] Rees, *Our Final Hour*, 26–27.
[390] Eric Schlosser, *Command and Control, Nuclear Weapons, the Damascus Incident and the Illusion of Safety* (Penguin, 2003), 312.

In another incident, on January 25, 1995,

> The lunch of a small research rocket launched by Norway prompted a warning at the Kremlin that Russia was under attack by the United States. Russian nuclear forces went on full alert. President Boris Yeltsin turned on his "football" retrieved his launch codes. And prepared retaliate. After a few tense minutes, the warning was declared a false alarm. The weather rocket had been launched to study the aurora borealis, and Norway had informed Russia of the trajectory weeks in advance.[391]

There have been many other incidents described in detail by Eric Schlosser in his book *Command and Control, Nuclear Weapons, the Damascus Incident and the Illusion of Safety.*[392]

In addition, five Cold War "close call" incidents have been described by Evan Andrews.[393]

The United States is a rather organized state and an open society in which many incidents and accidents described above come to light and are debated. If the United States has had so many mishaps, how many have other nuclear-possessing countries had? The answer may not be so pleasant!

But the nuclear race continued despite the fact that neither side achieved superiority as if the goal had been not just to kill but also to make the bodies of the enemy more radioactive after the nuclear exchange. All was in vain; as McNamara said, "Virtually every technical innovation in the arm race has come from the US. But it has always been quickly matched by the other side."[394]

It was not long that the United States and the Soviet Union developed a single missile carrying multiple warheads that targeted independent targets. These were called MIRVs for Multiple Independent Reentry Vehicles. On March 23, 1983, under President Ronald Reagan, the Space Defense Initiative (SDI) program nicknamed Star Wars was initiated. The goal of this program was to develop a sophisticated antiballistic missile system to prevent missile attacks from other countries specifically the Soviet Union. It sounds like a dream on paper. The system was to include high-tech antimissile lasers, high-energy particle beams, and antimissile systems both space and ground based. The program was abandoned after costing over $30 billion without much to show for it.

The cost of the SDI program is controversial. According to Stephen Schwartz, "Since President Ronald Reagan launched SDI in 1983—which is when many people

---

[391] Ibid., 478.
[392] Ibid.
[393] http://www.history.com/news/history-lists/5-cold-war-close-calls. October 16, 2013.
[394] Rees, *Our Final Hour*, 29.

erroneously believe US work on missile defenses actually began—the amount is $209 billion."[395]

There were concerns of the system being in violation of the ABM treaty, of sparking an intensive arms race with no end in sight, possible miscalculations of the parties, the overall system effectiveness, and budgetary concerns.

One can very likely defend against one or a few incoming missiles, but defending against a rain of thousands of real and additional thousands of fake missiles would be an impossible task. And how can one defend against nuclear cruise missiles fired from enemy submarines lurking twelve miles off the mainland coast and flying close to the ground and striking coastal cities in less than five minutes? This arms race insanity continued with those for and those against for a long time until the Soviet Union collapsed and the fears subsided. Nature reveals its secrets equally to all people with good or bad intentions.

In an editorial in *Scientific American* (June 2001), the editors stated,

> Regarding strategic missile defense, researchers' best guess is that a reliable system is infeasible. The burden of proof is now on the proponents of missile defense. Until they can provide solid evidence that a system would work against plausible countermeasures (decoys), any discussion of committing to building one - let alone meeting a detailed timeline - is premature. It is one thing for a software company to hype a product and then fail to deliver; it is another when the failure concerns nuclear weapons, for which "vapor-ware" takes on a whole new, literal meaning. ... It would be nice to be perfectly sure about everything, to get 365 vacation days a year and to spend some of that time on Mars. But we can't confuse wants with facts. As Richard Feynman said, "Science is a way of trying not to fool yourself."

Per Wikipedia, on Strategic Defense Initiative,

> Physicist Hans Bethe, who worked with Edward Teller on both the atom and hydrogen bombs at Los Alamos, claimed a laser defense shield was unfeasible. He said that a defensive system was costly and difficult to build yet simple to destroy, and claimed that the Soviets could easily use thousands of decoys to overwhelm it during a nuclear attack. He believed that the only way to stop the threat of nuclear war was through diplomacy and dismissed the idea of a technical solution to the Cold War, saying that a defense shield could be viewed as threatening because it would

---

[395] Stephen Schwartz, *The Real Price of Ballistic Missile Defenses*, April 2012.

limit or destroy Soviet offensive capabilities while leaving the American offense intact. In March 1984, Bethe coauthored a 106-page report for the Union of Concerned Scientists that concluded "the X-ray laser offers no prospect of being a useful component in a system for ballistic missile defense."[396]

Living under the threat of a nuclear holocaust is bad enough, but living under a false impression that one side has full protection and can wipe the other side off the face of the earth defies rationality; history teaches us that there have always been ferocious and powerful men who did all the unspeakable harm they could. But the threat still remains from the thousands of nuclear missiles.

Referring to the great risk of these problems Sir Rees said,

> Humanity is more at risk than any earlier phase in its history. The wider cosmos has a potential future that could be even be infinite. But will these vast expenses of time be filled with life, or as empty as the first Earth's sterile seas? The choice may depend on us, this century.[397]

Some say the Cold War and the stockpile of weapons kept the peace. But both sides have built all types of weapons. The stockpiles include small tactical nuclear weapons to be fired from long-range cannons, from cruise missiles, large nuclear weapons to be carried by bombers, ICBMs, MIRVs, ship missiles, and submarines. Tens thousands of nuclear and thermonuclear bombs were built by the United States and Russia and a smaller number of the other seven countries with such nuclear capabilities in spite of their cost to their peoples. The largest H-bomb ever exploded at a test site had strength of 55 million tons of TNT, more than 4,000 times the power of the Hiroshima bomb. Large H-bombs can devastate a city the size of Chicago, and the number of them can cover practically every small city. In addition, the devastation from nuclear weapons is not only from instant death, destruction, and the radiation that lingers for a long time but also the destruction of the infrastructure of power and transportation grids and the famine that will follow. In addition, the so-called nuclear winter that will follow may have long-term negative effects on the atmosphere that causes unparalleled freezing due to clouds of dust as happens with large volcanic eruptions.

The rogue states are an entirely different problem. Getting hold of nuclear matter and making dirty bombs is another difficult issue.

The world must establish strict security control of nuclear reactors and their

---

[396] *Union of Concerned Scientists. Space-Based Missile Defense: A Report by the Union of Concerned Scientists* (Cambridge, MA, 1984).
[397] Rees, *Our Final Hour*, 188.

nuclear material facilities so there will be no diversion of nuclear material to any terrorist group or rogue state.

Ploughshares Fund states, "As long as nuclear weapons exist, the chances of survival of the human species are quite slight." Every study of long-term risk analysis supports Noam Chomsky's claim. Ploughshares estimates there are 19,000 warheads in the world today, 18,000 of which are in the hands of the United States and Russia. Whatever the exact numbers are the American/Russian nuclear arsenals are the only ones capable of totally destroying all human life. As security analysts Campbell Craig and Jan Ruziicka pointed out, "Why should Iran or North Korea respect non-proliferation when the most powerful states lecturing them possess such enormous arsenals?"[398]

French writer André Malraux (1901–1976) famously declared that the twenty-first century "will be spiritual or it will not be at all."

Man attains knowledge that sometime transcends his capacity to predict or control it. His loss of control in the case of war may become highly explosive and expand with unpredictable results. In the case of nuclear war, once it starts, no one can predict how to control it till all the weapons are used up or its consequences. But most can agree its consequences will be more destructive than humans have experienced before, and our civilization, if humans survive, will resemble that of the Stone Age.

What has gone wrong? With all this technology around, shouldn't we begin to reevaluate our values in some of the areas of technology?

At the dawn of the twenty-first century, the world was shocked by the 9/11 terrorist attacks, and a cloud of discouragement enveloped humanity as acts of unprecedented terrorism took place. Wars to kill perpetrators were started; wars occurred in Afghanistan, and incursions were made into Pakistan, Iraq, Yemen, and Somalia. The Arab Spring involved civil wars in Egypt, Libya, Tunisia, and Syria. Eventually, Bin Laden was eliminated, but Iraq was split into three factions, and terrorism is on the increase. Hundreds of thousands have been killed, and more than $1 trillion has been spent on fighting terrorism.

There have been terror hits by religious terrorist zealots in the United States, Russia, Spain, England, France, and Belgium in the West and most countries in the Middle East between Libya and Pakistan.

In Iraq, interventions by the United States and its allies for "regime change" and WMD (weapons of mass destruction) that were never found if they ever existed left the country split in at least three factions, and it is in a disastrous situation with a very uncertain future. The war resurrected old religious differences in the wider area of the Muslim world and has made the Middle East a burning fire. It is in the worst shape it has been for the last hundred years. Wars inflamed by religious fervor,

[398] http://www.theguardian.com/commentisfree/2012/oct/27/vasili-arkhipov-stopped-nuclear-war.

poverty, and the availability of twentieth-century killing guns spread destruction and destabilization to emerging countries in the area. The Palestinian-Israeli conflict is still going on with collapsed peace talks and no peace in sight. And a new type of terrorism has turned its ugly head in Europe by local sympathizers; Europeans are going to the Middle East to fight with ISIS, a sect that brought back barbarism and brutality.

The problem with the terrorism is that after a while, it turns to a civil war and all terror becomes legitimized under the flag of security or religion, and violence and chaos reign. The great powers may have learned their lesson: intervention leads nowhere. But human arrogance and the desire to do some good cannot always be controlled. The hate generated from these wars lasts for many generations on all sides.

First Russia and later America and its allies left Afghanistan with a shaky government and a questionable future. Libya and Syria were involved in internal civil and tribal wars, great powers intervened with heavy bombings, and both countries are in shambles and face a grim future. Egypt and the Arabian Peninsula all the way to Yemen and parts of central West Africa are not in the most stable position either with internal religious strife, wars, and terrorism.

And with ISIS, Syria and Iraq are afire. Russian and Turkish involvement has exacerbated the situation. Millions of refugees from war-torn countries are flooding neighboring countries, and millions try to escape to the safety of Europe risking their lives in crossing the Mediterranean and the Aegean. Drone bombings in Pakistan, Yemen, Somalia, and Syria seem to be a continual state of affairs.

World public opinion and outcry somehow prevents carpet bombing of cities as in World War II, but it still takes place whether against terrorists or insurgents. Regardless of advanced technology, boots on the ground are required for street fighting while tanks and machine guns are the predominant forces used to capture and hold territory; that makes battles deadly for soldiers and civilians alike. The lesson has been learned; no one is willing to commit boots on the ground.

Humanity gets into a mode in which rationalism is pushed aside and manipulation by certain fundamentalist ideas or special interest groups takes over. Manipulation by certain media is being rationalized with the rationalization of bias doctrine playing a major role. Rationalization of bias is the doctrine of making up one's mind on doing something that he wants and then rationalizes it. An example of it is the Iraq War. Some people wanted to get rid of Saddam Hussein and concocted all kinds of reasons to justify it such as Iraq possessing WMDs, oil, posing a threat to Israel, supporting terrorism, etc.

We rushed into the war. Hardly any questions were asked about casualties, the length of the war, proof of WMDs, and the cost. And the answers were of the most optimistic kind—estimates put the cost at a couple of hundred million dollars at most. Certain media were preaching daily the war propaganda. There was no question of America's capability of toppling Saddam; that did not take long.

We deposed Saddam, but the country is in shambles; it is split into four fighting groups and has an unstable government. The arrogance of power showed its ugly head. Unilateral actions without UN consent, miscalculations on the cost and time, and lack of proper congressional oversight created one of the biggest disasters in modern times. Iraq was destabilized, and we have yet to see the end. Even the pope called the war immoral and illegal, but voices of reason and constraint were overpowered by the loud sounds of the trumpets of war.

James Mann of the *Los Angeles Times* (February 6, 2015) stated,

> At the top of the list was the war in Iraq. Bush and his advisors badly misjudged what it would entail. They overestimated the international support the United States would be able to obtain for military action. They asserted before the war that American troops would need to stay in Iraq for no more than a couple of years. The administration's public estimate before the war was that it would cost less than $100 billion; instead, it cost $2 trillion. Intended originally as a short-term demonstration of American power and influence, the Iraq war over the longer term brought about the opposite. In its unhappy aftermath, Americans became increasingly cautious, more reluctant to become involved overseas. Overall, the war will go down as a strategic blunder of epic proportions, among the most serious in American history.

> The short-term benefits proved dubious at best, but the harmful long-term consequences were incalculable, both for the federal government and, more importantly, for American society … and the Senate's recent report on enhanced interrogation techniques makes current judgments on that dark era even harsher than they would have been otherwise. Torture is torture, and no passage of time will change the moral judgments on that.

We spent lives and treasure, and then it was time to make an inglorious withdraw having achieved an uncertain result and leaving a split Iraq mired in a civil war.

We have not learned a single lesson from the past. Invasions are quick and thoughtless, and no precise figure was estimated for the duration of war and the cost in lives and treasure.

In his book *The Arrogance of Power*, former senator William Fulbright (1905–1995) and chairman of the Foreign Relations Committee warned the public about American tendencies to too easily intervene in affairs of other nations.

Power tends to confuse itself with virtue and a great nation is particularly susceptible to the idea that its power is a sign of God's favor, conferring upon it a special responsibility for other nations—to make them richer and happier and wiser, to remake them, that is, in its own shining image. Power confuses itself with virtue and tends also to take itself for omnipotence. Once imbued with the idea of a mission, a great nation easily assumes that it has the means as well as the duty to do God's work.[399]

MODERN WARFARE

The literature is full of descriptions of inventions for war that would be beneficial and lower costs, death, and destruction. Yet they turned out to be futile guesses as the horror of wars increased.

In a sermon in 1621, John Donne advocated the view that weapons might be turned to human benefit.

So by the benefit of this light of reason, they have found out Artillery, by which wares come to quicker ends than heretofore, and the great expense of blood is avoided: for the numbers of men slain now, since the invention of Artillery, are much less than before, when the sword was the executioner.[400]

We have seen the results since; cannons have become much bloodier.

The point about deterrence later appeared among Alfred Nobel's ideas. In 1891, he commented on his dynamite factories by saying, "Perhaps my factories will put an end to war sooner than your congresses: on the day that two army corps can mutually annihilate each other in a second, all civilized nations will surely recoil with horror and disband their troops."[401] Nobel did not live long enough to experience the horrors of World War I and see how wrong his invention proved to be. Dynamite is great to break rocks and make roads for the benefit of humanity, but it was too tempting to use it in war. It proved once more that technology knowledge without wisdom is dangerous.

In his 1903 lecture "The Discovery of the Future," H. G. Wells praised humanity's achievements and what was coming.

---

[399] J. W. Fulbright, *The Arrogance of Power* (New York: Random House, 1966), introduction.
[400] J. Donne, *Sermons of John Donne*, vol. 1, ed. George R. Potter and Evelyn M. Simpson (University of California Press, 1957), 359.
[401] https://www.nobelprize.org/alfred_nobel/biographical/articles/tagil/

We are in the beginning of the greatest change that humanity has ever undergone. There is no shock, no epoch-making incident— but then there is no shock at a cloudy daybreak … It is possible to believe that all the past is but the beginning of a beginning, and that all that is and has been is but the twilight of the dawn. It is possible to believe that all that the human mind has ever accomplished is but the dream before the awakening …

For all the folly, blindness, and pain of our lives, we have come some way from that. And the distance we have travelled gives us some earnest of the way we have yet to go. Why should things cease at man? Why should not this rising curve rise yet more steeply and swiftly? There are many things to suggest that we are now in a phase of rapid and unprecedented development.[402]

Gilbert Murray witnessed the horrors of World War I and wrote in his book *The League of Nations and the Democratic Idea in 1918,*

The next European war, if it ever occurs, will surpass in horror anything that the world has known. It will be to this War as this War has been to the old wars of our fathers, which now seem but small things, strangely chivalrous and ineffective and almost merciful.[403]

His predictions were justified beyond any doubt by the horrors of World War II. Former President Dwight Eisenhower saw enough war as the supreme commander of the allied liberation of Europe. In his "The Chance for Peace" (April 16, 1953), he challenged America to protect its interests in the world while recognizing the limits of brute military power.

A nation's hope of lasting peace cannot be firmly based upon any race in armaments but rather upon just relations and honest understanding with all other nations … Every gun that is made, every warship launched, every rocket fired signifies, in the final sense, a theft from those who hunger and are not fed, those who are cold and are not clothed.

---

[402] Wells, *The Discovery of the Future,* Internet.
[403] Gilbert Murray, *The League of Nations and the Democratic Idea* (1918).

Eisenhower cautioned us,

> In the councils of government, we must guard against the acquisition of unwarranted influence, whether sought or unsought, by the military–industrial complex. The potential for the disastrous rise of misplaced power exists, and will persist. We must never let the weight of this combination endanger our liberties or democratic processes. We should take nothing for granted. Only an alert and knowledgeable citizenry can compel the proper meshing of the huge industrial and military machinery of defense with our peaceful methods and goals so that security and liberty may prosper together.[404]

Eisenhower also commented on the morality of nuclear war.

> No matter how well prepared for war maybe we may be, no matter how certain we are that within 24 hours we could destroy Kuibyshev and Moscow and Leningrad and Baku and all the other places that would allow the Soviets to carry on war, I want you to carry this question home with you: Gain such victory and what do you do with it? Here would be a great area from the Elbe to Vladivostok and down through Southeast Asia torn up and destroyed without government, without its communications, just an area of starvation and disaster. I ask you, what the civilized world do about it? I repeat there is no victory in any war except through our imaginations, through our dedications, and through our work to avoid it.[405]

The introduction of nuclear weapons led to a race for nuclear supremacy as if there ever can be one up. In 1949, at the dawn of nuclear development, Albert Einstein (1879–1955) commented on nuclear power.

> Since I do not foresee that atomic energy is to be a great boon for a long time, I have to say that for the present it is a menace. Perhaps it is well that it should be. It may intimidate the human race into bringing order into its international affairs, which, without the presence of fear, it would not do … I do not know with what weapons World War III will be fought, but World War IV will

[404] Wikipedia.
[405] S. D. Sagan and K. N. Waltz, *The Spread of Nuclear Weapons* (New York and London: W. W. Norton, 1995), 61.

be fought with sticks and stones. (From 1949 interview in Liberal Judaism)

Some years later, President Kennedy realized the danger of nuclear war: "Mankind must put an end to war, or war will put an end to mankind."

MODERN WARFARE AND THE CLASH OF CIVILIZATIONS

Besides nuclear war, the world in the last forty-five years has endured two different types of war; the first is the modern, electronic conventional war, and the second is terrorism prompted by the clash of civilizations.

The modern electronic war started at 2:00 p.m. on October 6, 1973. The Egyptians launched war against Israel on Yom Kippur, the holiest day in the Jewish calendar. In broad daylight, the Egyptian army crossed the Suez Canal and moved rapidly into Sinai. The Israeli army and air force, known as one of the best in the world, had to retreat, due to surface-to-air and antitank missiles. Big tank battles followed until a cease-fire that went into effect on October 25, 1973. The negotiations ultimately resulted in the 1978 Camp David Agreements and the peace treaty between Egypt and Israel in 1979. What were the differences between and the previous wars?

- Both sides were about equivalent in tactical weapons: tanks, airplanes (in which Israel had superiority), and troops.
- Egypt was able to defend its army from the superior Israeli air force, which proved ineffective due to surface-to-air missiles.
- The Israeli fortifications on the east side of the canal were taken out quickly, with the:
  Rocket propelled grenades, shoulder fired, antitank, reusable, unguided,
  AT-3 Sagger manual command, wire guided antitank missile,

The portable antitank weapons and the surface-to-air missiles made a big difference in the battlefield.

Since the 1973 Yom Kippur war, all these electronic weapons have become deadlier, better guided, smaller, and cheaper. I call them CPGMs for compact, precision-guided Munitions. CPGMs are inexpensive; practically every soldier can carry one. They can be used against tanks, airplanes, and small boats. CPGMs can be produced in large quantities at a cost of thousands of dollars each. Big platforms such as tanks, airplanes, and ships cost millions. Because CPGMs are small and portable, they must be securely stored and away from the hands of terrorists as they can cause severe damage.

Man fought battles with swords and sometimes on horseback. Then fortifications provided safety until gunpowder came into play. Trench warfare or "mad and stupidity war" as some call it providing safety from machine guns but not from tanks and airplanes.

Machine guns, tanks, airplanes, and ships were the main weapons of World War II. Now, wars can be fought with battalions of people fighting with machine guns, antitank weapons, and low-altitude antiaircraft missiles. The navy can use small and fast attack boats with multiple missiles. Tanks are heavy, expensive, noisy, and require an immense logistics supply line. Movable truck-mounted missiles can take care of high-altitude aircraft.

Drones can provide excellent, up-to-date mapping information and even firepower upon command or with remote missiles.

Small, portable weapons may not be the appropriate for all cases, but they constitute an element to be considered depending on the enemy's inventory, military technology, and manpower strengths.

Terrorism is caused by the clash of civilizations. In his famous book *The Clash of Civilizations and the Remaking of World Order*,[406] Samuel Huntington provided a description of nine civilizations making up the world post-1990: the Western, Latin American, African, Islamic, Sinic, Hindu, Orthodox, Buddhist, and Japanese civilizations.

Multicultural, multiracial, and multireligious societies are spreading all over the planet. Countries' borders are all mixed up. Royalties and creeds are not coinciding. Economic differences constitute an additional factor. Peoples' loyalties and religious zealotry across this entire spectrum are divided and not always predictable.

For the last fifteen years, we have seen a level of violence due to terrorism caused by the amalgam of people we discussed above. Killings of people in massive scale in theaters, trains, stadiums, airports, and streets are too common. The world is in turmoil as terrorism causes fear, anxiety, and death and prompts the spending of billions for security the world over. War is taking place in the Middle East, and crimes of revenge take place in the western hemisphere; they are unpredictable, random, and extreme. Guns, explosives, airplanes, and now cars and trucks are being used as weapons.

Some reconciliation among the entire spectrum of differences must occur so the world may find some of the past's tranquility.

---

[406] S. P. Huntington, *The Clash of Civilizations and the Remaking of World Order* (Touchstone, 1996).

WAR AND PEACE

Plans for peace are not new as wars have been a continuous curse on humanity as far back as written history and beyond.

The war and peace issue and how to prevent war have been greatly discussed subjects for many centuries as they continue to be today. Back in the sixteenth century, Erasmus, one of the greatest minds of the Renaissance, was very concerned about the stability of peace in the midst of what was to come of the religious strife that was to break out with the Reformation, which had just started. He proved very prophetic based on what took place in the century that followed. In 1517, he personified peace, and in one of his most important writings, "The Complaint of Peace," he condemned what was about to take place: religious war, with the participation of the church.[407]

Erasmus wrote on peace and war,

> As Peace, am I not praised by both men and gods as the very source and defender of all goods things? What is there of prosperity, of security of happiness that cannot be ascribed to me? ... the most criminal of all causes of war is the desire for power. When certain princes see power slipping from them because a general peace has lent them expendable, they stir up war to remain in power and oppress the people. Others are unable to find a place in peaceful society.[408]

In 1761, Rousseau published his "Perpetual Peace" as his first essay; in it, he wrote,

> Never did the mind of man conceive a scheme nobler, more beautiful, or more useful than that of a lasting peace between all the peoples of Europe. Never did a writer better deserve a respectful hearing than he who suggests means for putting that scheme in practice ... I see in my mind's eye all men joined in the bonds of love. I call before my thoughts a gentle and peaceful brotherhood, all living in unbroken harmony, all guided by the same principles, all finding their happiness in the happiness of all.[409]

---

[407] Erasmus, *The Essential Erasmus*, trans. J. Dolan (Mentor-Omega Book, 1964), 176.

[408] Ibid., 177.

[409] Jean-Jacques Rousseau, *A Lasting Peace through the Federation of Europe and the State of War (1756)*, trans. Charles Edwyn Vaughan (London: Constable, 1917).

Jean-Jacques Rousseau continued his war evaluation.

> Firmly convinced as I am that nothing on this earth is worth
> purchase at the price of human blood, and that there is no more
> liberty anywhere than in the heart of the just man, I feel, however,
> that it is natural for people of courage, who were born free, to
> prefer an honorable death to dull servitude.[410]

R. Dubos pessimistically pointed out, "Technological problems have rarely
solved social problems in the past, nor are they likely to do so in the future"[411]

KANT AND PEACE

Kant felt that war was the greatest obstacle to morality and that the preparation
for war is the greatest evil; therefore, we must renounce war. "The morally practical
reason utters within us its irrevocable veto: *There shall be no war.*" [412]

In the treaty of Basel, Prussia ceded France territory west of the Rhine so it could
partition Poland with Russia and Austria. Kant was so indignant at this that he wrote
Perpetual Peace (1795) as a just treaty that could be signed by nations. He stated six
preliminary propositions to be taken immediately for a perpetual peace among states.

1. "No treaty of peace shall be held valid in, which there is tacitly reserved
   matter for a future war.

2. No independent states, large or small, shall come under the dominion of
   another state by inheritance, exchange, purchase, or donation.

3. Standing armies shall in time be totally abolished.

4. National debts shall not be contracted with a view to the external friction
   of states.

5. No state shall by force interfere with the constitution or government of
   another state.

---

[410] Rousseau, *Conscience is the Social Contract voice of the soul.*
[411] R. Dubos, *Reason Awake: Science for Man* (New York and London: Columbia University Press, 1970), 96.
[412] I. Kant, *The Science of Right*, conclusion

6. No state shall, during war, permit such acts of hostility which would make mutual confidence in the subsequent peace impossible: such are the employment of assassins, poisoners, breach of capitulation, and incitement to treason in the opposing state."[413]

Three additional articles provide for not only a cessation of hostilities but also a foundation on which to build a peace.

1. "The civil constitution of every state should be republican.

2. The law of nations shall be founded on a federation of free states.

3. The law of world citizenship shall be limited to conditions of universal hospitality." [414]

LEO TOLSTOY AND PEACE

In his masterpiece *War and Peace*, Leo Tolstoy provided a very detailed description of Napoleon's invasion of Russia and a philosophical view of the cause of war, the conduct and thoughts of war, its aftermaths, and its miserable results on our bodies, minds and souls. Here are some of his thoughts.

> How can patriotism be a virtue … when it requires of men an ideal exactly opposite to our religion and morality- an admission, not of the equality and fraternity of all men-but of the dominance of one country or nation over all others? … Tell people that war is an evil, and they will laugh; for who does not know it? Tell them that patriotism is an evil, and most of them will agree, but with a reservation. "Yes," they will say, "wrong patriotism is an evil; but there is another kind, the kind we hold." But just what this good patriotism is, no one explains.[415]

In *Christianity and Patriotism*, he discussed the propaganda used by governments to drum up support for wars. It is as current today as it was back in 1895 and before the holocausts of twentieth-century wars.

---

[413] I. Kant, *Perpetual Peace,* Section I, Internet
[414] Ibid.
[415] Leo Tolstoy, *Patriotism, or Peace?* trans. Nathan Haskell Dole (1896).

In all history there is no war which was not hatched by the governments, the governments alone, independent of the interests of the people, to whom war is always pernicious even when successful. The government assures the people that they are in danger from the invasion of another nation, or from foes in their midst, and that the only way to escape this danger is by the slavish obedience of the people to their government. This fact is seen most prominently during revolutions and dictatorships, but it exists always and everywhere that the power of the government exists. Every government explains its existence, and justifies its deeds of violence, by the argument that if it did not exist the condition of things would be very much worse. After assuring the people of its danger the government subordinates it to control, and when in this condition compels it to attack some other nation. And thus, the assurance of the government is corroborated in the eyes of the people, as to the danger of attack from other nations.[416]

Emerson provided a philosophical description of war and peace.

If peace is to be maintained, it must be by brave men, who have come up to the same height as the hero, namely, the will to carry their life in their hand, and stake it at any instant for their principle, but who have gone one step beyond the hero, and will not seek another man's life;—men who have, by their intellectual insight or else by their moral elevation, attained such a perception of their own intrinsic worth, that they do not think property or their own body a sufficient good to be saved by such dereliction of principle as treating a man like a sheep.[417]

NUCLEAR WAR

The Pastoral Letter on War and Peace approved by the Catholic Bishops of America stated,

In concluding this summary, we respond to two key questions often asked about this pastoral letter: Why do we address these matters fraught with such complexity, controversy and passion? We speak as pastors, not politicians. We are teachers, not technicians.

---

[416] Leo Tolstoy, *Christianity and Patriotism*, vol. 20, 44, Internet, 40.
[417] Ralph Waldo Emerson, *The Complete Works*, vol. 11.

We cannot avoid our responsibility to lift up the moral dimensions of the choices before our world and nation. The nuclear age is an era of moral as well as physical danger. We are the first generation since Genesis with the power to threaten the created order. We cannot remain silent in the face of such danger. Why do we address these issues? We are simply trying to live up to the call of Jesus to be peacemakers in our own time and situation.

What are we saying? Fundamentally, we are saying that the decisions about nuclear weapons are among the most pressing moral questions of our age. While these decisions have obvious military and political aspects, they involve fundamental moral choices. In simple terms, we are saying that good ends (defending one's country, protecting freedom, etc.) cannot justify immoral means (the use of weapons which kill indiscriminately and threaten whole societies). We fear that our world and nation are headed in the wrong direction. More weapons with greater destructive potential are produced every day. More and more nations are seeking to become nuclear powers. In our quest for more and more security we fear we are actually becoming less and less secure.[418]

The letter condemned any strategy to use nuclear war as the destruction would be immense.

We see with increasing clarity the political folly of a system which threatens mutual suicide ... To believe we are condemned in the future only to what has been the past of U.S.- Soviet relations is to underestimate both our human potential for creative diplomacy and God's action in our midst which can open the way to changes we could barely imagine.[419]

REASONS FOR WAR

After all the history of so many world disasters, one would think that starting a war could become a major cause for present and future calamities. However, the thinking is that we somehow can afford it and it is worth it to restore our honor. But

[418] *A Pastoral Letter on War and Peace by the National Conference of Catholic Bishops*, May 3, 1983, Internet.
[419] Ibid.

the reason is revenge. Military power might hardly be an advantage to those trying to kill the parties responsible for terrorist atrocities. More than likely, killing terrorists will also result in many civilian and other noncombatant deaths.

Gilbert Murray justified the importance of the League of Nations.

These things are not fancies. They are real forces and full of power, which no wise statesman will overlook or forget to reckon with. The building of a League of Nations is not an affair of emotion; it is a work of reason, of patience, of skill in international law and statesmanship; but those who have faith in the work will be helped forward by these hopes and longings ...

Human skepticism and human inertia are powerful forces, but these things are surely stronger ...

The broken treaty, the calculated ferocity in Belgium and Northern France, the killing of women and non-combatants by sea and land and air, the shelling of hospitals, the treatment of wounded prisoners in ways they had never expected; all the doctoring of weapons with a view to cruelty; explosive bullets; the projectile doctored with substances which would produce a gangrenous wound; the poisoned gases; the infected wells. It is the same method throughout. The old conventions of humanity, the old arrangements which admitted that beneath our cruelties, beneath our hatreds there was some common humanity and friendliness between us, these have been systematically broken one after another ...

This is not the time to make any definite proposals. Civilization has still many slave trades to abolish. The trade in armaments is perhaps the most oppressive of all, but there are others also, slave trades social and intimate and international; no one can tell yet which ones and how many it may be possible to overthrow. But there is one thing that we must see. This war and the national aspiration behind the war must not be allowed to fall into the hands of the militarists. I do not say that we must not be ready for some form of universal service: that will depend on the circumstances in which the war leaves us. But we must not be militarized in mind and feeling; If I may speak more personally, there is none of my own work into which I have put more intense feeling than into my translation of Euripides' "Trojan Women," the first great denunciation of war in European literature.[420]

Norman Angell, the 1933 Nobel Peace Prize winner, made a point about international cooperation, peace, and rationalism as the keys to peace.

> The final chapter of The Great Illusion presents a convincing plea for a change in foreign policy from that of a war policy to one of international cooperation and peace. If this is not made, war, he says, will be inevitable. The fact that we are living in a world of international interdependence makes it imperative that we organize the international community of nations accordingly, basing the community on the common interests, which bind nations together, relinquishing the principle of isolated national defense, providing collective security through common effort by erecting an international authority, which can replace the prevailing international anarchy.

> Norman Angell speaks to the intellect. He is cool and clear. He has a profound belief in reason and in rationalism. He is convinced that at long last reason will prevail when we succeed in sweeping away the mists of illusion and intellectual error.[421]

Tolstoy had faith on man's education saying,

> One would expect that with the spread of education and the increased intercourse of nations, the enormous growth of the public press, and the absence of all danger from foreign invasion, the illusion of patriotism would be more and more difficult to maintain and would finally become an impossibility.[422]

Tolstoy told us how we get involved in wars.

> The government assures the people that they are in danger from the invasion of another nation, or from foes in their midst, and that the only way to escape this danger is by the slavish obedience of the people to their government. This fact is seen most prominently during revolutions and dictatorships, but it exists

---

[420] Gilbert Murray, *Faith, war, and policy; addresses and essays on the European War*, Internet.
[421] http://www.nobelprize.org/nobel_prizes/peace/laureates/1933/press.html.
[422] Paul Borger, *Christianity and Patriotism: with pertinent extract from other essays*, Internet.

always and everywhere that the power of the government exists. Every government explains its existence, and justifies its deeds of violence, by the argument that if it did not exist the condition of things would be very much worse. After assuring the people of its danger the government subordinates it to control, and when in this condition compels it to attack some other nation. And thus, the assurance of the government is corroborated in the eyes of the people, as to the danger of attack from other nations.[423]

GLOBAL MILITARY EXPENDITURES

According to the SIPRI (Stockholm International Peace Research Institute), the following chart shows the military expenditures of top five countries.

The 15 countries with the highest spending account for over 81 percent of the total;

The USA is responsible for 39 per cent of the world total, distantly followed by the China (9.5 percent of world share), Russia (5.2 percent), UK (3.5 percent) and Japan (3.4 percent)

Indeed, compare the military spending with the entire budget of the United Nations.

The United Nations and all its agencies and funds spend about $30 billion each year, or about $4 for each of the world's inhabitants. This is a very small sum compared to most government budgets and it is less than three percent of the world's military spending. Yet for nearly two decades, the UN has faced financial difficulties and it has been forced to cut back on important programs in all areas, even as new mandates have arisen. Many member states have not paid their full dues and have cut their donations to the UN's voluntary funds. As of December 31, 2010, members' arrears to the Regular Budget topped $348 million, of which the US owed 80%.[424]

---

[423] Leo Tolstoy, *Christianity and Patriotism (1895)*, vol. 20, 44.
[424] http://www.globalissues.org/article/75/world-military-spending.

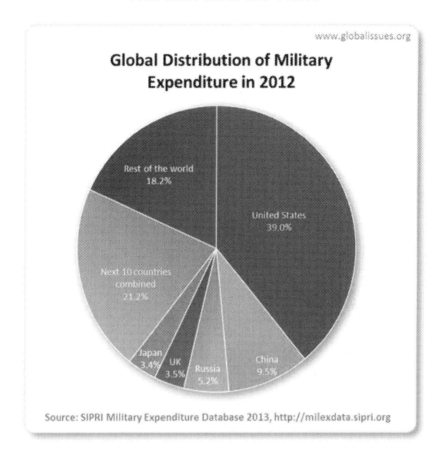

Diagram 4. SIPRI (Stockholm International Peace Research Institute) the military expenditures of top five countries.

The following are some comments by the *New York Times* (October 8, 2014), and former President Obama. Mr. Obama, his supporters said, is a "gloomy realist" who has learned history's lesson: that American military power, no matter how great in relative terms, is ultimately of limited utility in conflicts that are, at their root, political or ideological in nature.

With today's technology and terrorism, there have been no clear-cut wins and no clear borders. One may capture land, but in the long run, if the local population is uncooperative and is using violence and terrorism, where is the victory? Where is the victory? Where is the morality?

Many times, we take sides trying to help the "good side"; we bomb, we kill innocents as part of the collateral damage, but we make no long-term peace. Most of the time, the people we supported switched sides, and the outcome was not the expected one. What remains are hate, poverty, and destruction-feeding revenge that are ready to explode at the first chance. The successes the West has had after so many wars and interventions are very few and highly negative if one considers the total cost. The total cost is not the cost of war itself only; it is the continuous military spending that so much President Eisenhower warned us about.

A civilization cannot be without peace. As discussed previously, Whitehead set the qualifications for an advanced civilization: truth, beauty, adventure, art, and peace. He added,

> Peace as the Harmony of Harmonies which calms destructive turbulence and completes civilization. Thus, a society is to be termed civilized whose members participate in all five qualities-Truth, Beauty, Adventure, Art, Peace.[425]

War brings civilization to a standstill if not to a retreat.

We can see in modern history with the wars in Vietnam, Afghanistan, and Iraq what its cost is for societies. We rush into wars without considering the outcome and the ultimate cost. Good intentions are not enough. Everyone senses continuous anxiety and sadness; they think something is missing and something can always get worse. The return of caskets of the fallen is a constant reminder.

Wars are unpredictable; they can be fought to an end, but no victor will emerge. The Middle East is a great example of an area where temporary military wins by great powers end up in destruction and chaos for the locals who still have to violently settle differences among themselves.

Judging from recent history, there is not much world cooperation for peace, and there is much distrust among the great powers; there is no obedience to the United Nations charter and no long-term, rational planning not only for the avoidance of war but for the ending of war and its consequences. Everyone seems to know how to start one, but no one seems to know how to end one.

The famous astronomer Carl Sagan said, "Every thinking person fears nuclear war, and every technological state plans for it. Everyone knows it is madness, and every nation has an excuse."[426] Along these lines, George Wald added, "Nuclear weapons offer us nothing but a balance of terror, and a balance of terror is still terror." [427]

It seems that the climate prevailing for starting a war is hair-trigger militarism, the type that created the quagmires of Iraq and Afghanistan. And in modern times, based on recent experience, we hear of some terrorist or a wedding being blown up

---

[425] Whitehead, *Adventures of Ideas*, 283.
[426] Carl Sagan, *Cosmos* (New York: Random House, 1980), 320.
[427] George Wald - *A Generation in Search of a Future,* Speech, http://www.elijahwald.com/generation.html

from halfway around the world by a drone. And the war and the building up of hate continue.

The ending of World War I sowed the seeds for World War II. The recent wars were not too different. The instability and turmoil in the Middle East and oil triggered the wars still going on inside Iraq and its neighbors.

With the slightest provocation, there is a response always with the sword and more likely with an unprecedented violence at a disproportionate level. With today's technology and tactical weapons, the number of crimes committed by such blind responses is out of order; they kill civilians. We hear of all the precision weaponry with needlepoint accuracy and yet, schools, religious sites, and hospitals are hit and written off as collateral damage. Intentional or unintentional reasons make little difference to victims. By the time the response is over, the level of anger, outrage, threats and cry for revenge escalates and the cycle of violence repeats.

Many people would agree that our recent leaders could not match the intellectual power of Dwight Eisenhower or George Marshall.

Shouldn't we listen to Eisenhower's and Marshall's cautions?

WHAT WE CAN DO?

- We must eliminate and or reduce causes of conflict. Negotiating for peace sometimes seems a waste of time, but rushing into war is worse. A good outcome is not warranted; a wishful victory may turn into a calamity despite the immense amount of blood shed and wealth spent.

- We must make ourselves and the rest of the world if possible independent of oil or other critical supplies that cause wars. The continuous need for oil causes conflict or possibly war. We constantly hear that the great defense budgets are to keep the oil trade routes open. Now that renewable wind and solar energy are competitive with fossil fuel–based energy, we must spend the money to build these resources, have clean air, and never run out of sun and wind energy.

- Spend resources on peaceful projects that will make countries independent of oil.

- The yearly United Nations budget for helping underdeveloped countries is about $30 billion where the yearly world budget for armaments and defense is $1.3 trillion. Imagine if that amount were spent to improve lives. In just one year, one could build a quarter of the world's electricity capacity using renewable energy or fifty subway systems around the world.

- The costs of maintenance, service, and eventual replacement of nuclear weapons is ongoing. Weapon reductions and eventual elimination will wipe out these costs.

- Though the dismantlement of nuclear weapons is occurring in some countries, nuclear weapons development continues in others. Whether and when the various nations of the world can agree to stop this development is uncertain. But individual scientists can still influence this process by withholding their skills.

- Start disarmament talks for reduction and eventually complete elimination of nuclear weapons. If we do not get rid of nuclear weapons, they will become a cause for a first strike to wipe them out by some crazy ruler.

A project of addressing the issues of war and global warming is not a social experiment involving difficult human problems. In cases of war, if the great powers provide humanitarian aid and intervene militarily only to avert genocide, famine, and epidemics, we will have made progress.

Nuclear weapons made war obsolete between major powers during the cold war and up to now, but it can lead to Armageddon—total holocaust among the major powers—if they get involved in nuclear war. If one nation uses one or a few nuclear weapon against an opponent, the opponent will eventually respond the same way. Thus, the logic of having nuclear weapons is wrong and suspect at best.

Hans Bethe (1906–2005), Nobel Prize–winning physicist, found the energy source of the stars and campaigned for nuclear disarmament. He said,

> If we fight a war and win it with H-bombs, what history will remember is not the ideals we were fighting for but the methods we used to accomplish them. These methods will be compared to the warfare of Genghis Khan who ruthlessly killed every last inhabitant of Persia ... I call on all scientists in all countries to cease and desist from work creating, developing, improving and manufacturing further nuclear weapons - and, for that matter, other weapons of potential mass destruction such as chemical and biological weapons.[428]

---

[428] Hans A. Bethe, *The Road from Los Alamos: Collected Essays* (New York: Touchtone, 1991), 17.

The great powers should simply stay out of conflicts, use diplomacy, and provide humanitarian aid only; the past results of other responses have been disastrous. We do not need interventions; we should spend some of the defense budget money on becoming energy independent.

We can assist underdeveloped nations through technical development and humanitarian assistance; that is how we make friends. When we join sides with warring nations, we make enemies and increase violence, terrorism, and revenge.

I shall recall former senator Fulbright's concluding statements made in his book *The Arrogance of Power*, published in 1966 in the middle of a frightening Cold War.

> The kind of foreign policy I have been talking about is … intended quite literally to conserve the world-a world whose civilizations can be destroyed at any time if either of the great powers should choose or feel driven to do so. It is an approach that accepts the world as it is, with all its existing nations and ideologies, with all its existing qualities and shortcomings. It is an approach that purports to change things in ways that are compatible with the continuity of history and within the limits imposed by a fragile human nature … that we make our own society an example of human happiness, that we go beyond simple reciprocity in the effort to reconcile hostile worlds-has been based on two major premises: first, that, at this moment in history at which the human race has become capable of destroying itself, it is not merely desirable but essential that the competitive instinct of nations be brought under control; and second, that America, as the most powerful nation, is the only nation equipped to lead the world in an effort to change the nature of its politics.
>
> If we accept this leadership, we will have contributed to the world "an idea mankind can hold to." Perhaps that idea can be defined as the proposition that the nation performs its essential function not in its capacity as a power, but in its capacity as a society, or, to put it simply, that the primary business of the nation is not itself but its people …
>
> If we can bring ourselves so to act, we will have overcome the dangers of the arrogance of power. It would involve, no doubt, the loss of certain glories, but that seems a price worth paying for the probable rewards, which are the happiness of America and the peace of the world.[429]

---

[429] Fulbright, *Arrogance of Power*.

We do not have to deal with the same problems now as at the time Fulbright drew his conclusions. However, the overall problems persist, and nations are not too different, as we have seen many wars, instability, and a substantial growth in worldwide terrorism. We need to make friends by helping nations. War has been tried. It does not work.

EPILOGUE

Love responsibility. Say: "It is my duty, and mine alone, to save
the earth. If it is not saved, then I alone am to blame."[430]

I discussed the history of the human progress and the two main problems
the world is facing—global warming and nuclear war. These problems are a cloud
hanging over humanity; they may end all human life on our beautiful and perhaps
unique planet. I discussed knowledge—knowledge of goodness and wisdom, virtue,
and solutions to problems.

In every crisis, as the Chinese say, there is an opportunity. Let's take this
opportunity to cooperate and establish unity among all nations to solve the global
warming problem by switching to renewable sources of energy and abolish all war,
especially nuclear weapons. We can switch from perpetual war to perpetual peace.

We live in a critical period in humanity's history, and we must temper our
effect on nature and other human beings that can be disastrous. As we gain more
knowledge, we will be that much more capable of doing so; it makes technical,
economic, and moral sense.

The moral virtue and intellectual honesty of the Socratic "know thyself" is
indispensable; in the words of St. Paul, "Love … takes no pleasure in wrongdoing,
but rejoice to the victory of truth; sustains, believes, hopes, endures, to the last" (1
Corinthians 13:4–8). We need to keep knowledge of the goodness in mind and let
virtues determine the universal values of humanity.

It is all about knowledge, virtue, love, and hope for humanity to preserve human
life on earth permanently. We need to change ourselves through the acquisition of
knowledge and consequently excellence and happiness; we can prove wrong what

---

[430] Nikos Kazantzakis, *The Saviors of God: Spiritual Exercises*, trans. Kimon Friar (1960).

Tolstoy wrote: "Everybody wants to change the world, but no one wants to change himself."

Kant recognized and stated the limits of human reason. In his *Critique of Practical Reason*, he stated something that was inscribed on his tombstone.

> Two things fill the spirit with ever new and increasing wonder and awe, the more often and the more continuously I contemplate them: the starry sky above me and the moral law within me … The first begins from the place I occupy in the external world of sense … unbounded extent … and limitless times … the second begins from my invisible self, my personality … in a world which has true infinity.[431]

This is Kant's testimony of the unknown and immense universe and the deep unknown of one's soul. It has been over two hundred years since Kant spoke these words. We still look at and study the faraway stars; we know more about them now than humanity knew in Kant's time, but do we know more about our own minds and hearts?

In his book *The Saviors of God*, Kazantzakis stated,

> Your first duty, in completing your service to your human race, is to feel within you all your ancestors. Your second duty is to throw light on their onrush and to continue their work. Your third duty is to pass on to your son the great mandate to surpass you.[432]

Here are questions we all should ask ourselves: Did we make life better for our children? Are we leaving the earth in peace and its environment better, cleaner, and sustainable for our children without using up all of the earth's resources? Are we leaving the earth empty of destructive weapons that can blow up earth's life in hours? If the answer is yes, we will have done our duty. We will have made progress. And according to Ernest Hemingway, "There is nothing noble in being superior to your fellow man; true nobility is being superior to your former self."

The human spirit reached a high plateau in ancient Greece, but it stood rather still for about a thousand years. It went into an intellectual recession for a millennium, was rekindled in the Renaissance, and has continued in an upward trend since. But the light still shines with the same pattern: high technical progress on one side and low ethical standards on the other. Can we change the pattern and make uniform progress in both areas? Can we continue to gain technical knowledge but also

---

[431] I. Kant, *The Critique of Practical Reason*, Encyclopedia Britannica, vol. 42 (Chicago: Great Books 1952), 360.
[432] Kazantzakis, *Saviors of God*.

elevate our spirits and stop the vicious cycles of war, stop global warming, and save the planet?

About sixty years ago, the great philosopher Bertrand Russell stated,

> The state of mind which I have been trying to describe is what I mean by wisdom, and it is undoubtedly more precious than rubies. The world needs this kind of wisdom as it has never needed it before. If mankind can acquire it, our new powers over nature offer a prospect of happiness and well-being such as men have never experienced and could scarcely even imagine. If mankind cannot, every increase in cleverness will bring us only nearer to irretrievable disaster. Men have done many good things and many bad ones. Some of the good things have been very good. All those who care for these good things must hope, with what confidence they can command, that in this moment of decision the wise choice will be made.[433]

And as an ancient Greek inscription states, "The aim of mankind should be to tame the savageness of man and make gentle the life of the world."[434]

I would add to that, "And, man, be kinder to our planet!"

H. G. Wells said, "Human society never has been quite static, and it will presently cease to attempt to be static."[435] As technology changes, the risks to the earth become magnified, and we need to address these risks before it is too late.

I will adopt the optimism of Marquis de Condorcet and his belief in the ultimate endurance and perfectibility of humanity, to act wisely: "Nature has indissolubly united the advancement of knowledge with the progress of liberty, virtue, and the natural rights of man. Prosperity will dispose men to humanity, to benevolence, and to justice."[436]

Technology for renewable energy can take care of global warming. It can enhance civilization globally by elevating underdeveloped countries. In addition, it will stop energy from becoming a casus belli, a pretext or cause for war.

Let us move forward. Let us make the earth, the true Garden of Eden, so much better with permanent life and the abolition of nuclear weapons. Let us live with knowledge, virtue, and happiness. Knowledge may not save us, but we cannot be saved without knowledge.

---

[433] Bertrand Russell, *Adventure of the Mind*, 305.
[434] Edith Hamilton, *The Lessons of the Past*, 84.
[435] H. G. Wells, *Delphi Collected Works*, Internet.
[436] Marquis de Condorcet, *Sketch of a Historical Picture and the Progress of the Human Mind* (1794).

INDEX

M

MAD 196, 208
Magellan 69, 74
Maintenance 32, 164, 166, 173, 220
Malthus 180, 181, 182, 183
Marcus Aurelius 42, 47, 50, 51, 52, 53, 119
Mark Anthony 40
Marquis de Condorcet xiii, 8, 72, 225
Marquis Mirabeau xvi
Martin Luther 69, 79, 142
Martin Luther King Jr 142
Martin Rees 100, 149
Matthew 52, 53, 56, 115, 120
Matthew Arnold 52, 53
Medieval xx, 60, 61, 62, 63, 65, 66, 67, 69,
    70, 75, 95
Meditations 51
Memory 3, 6, 7, 9, 10, 26, 41, 84, 85, 88,
    107, 130, 184
Michael Faraday 95
Michelangelo 68, 69, 75
Michel Eyquem de Montaigne 81
Microscope 82
Middle East xi, xxi, 4, 62, 143, 182, 183,
    195, 196, 201, 202, 208, 218, 219
Miguel de Cervantes 69
Mike Salvaris xvi
Military Expenditures 216, 217
Milky Way 2, 43, 151, 152
Miltiades 37
Minoan 5, 7
MIRVs 198, 200
Modern Period 67, 75, 81, 85
Modern Times 26, 43, 45, 61, 62, 68, 81,
    83, 86, 95, 101, 104, 113, 119, 120,
    134, 184, 193, 203, 218
Montesquieu 89
Morality xix, xxi, 16, 18, 26, 28, 32, 52,
    53, 66, 78, 84, 85, 91, 92, 103, 104,
    114, 116, 117, 121, 140, 142, 147,
    148, 154, 206, 210, 211, 217
Morals xii, xvii, xix, xxi, 14, 17, 19, 22, 25,
    26, 27, 29, 32, 33, 35, 40, 41, 45,
    47, 49, 51, 52, 54, 92, 94, 103, 104,
    110, 113, 115, 116, 117, 120, 121,

123, 125, 128, 129, 132, 138, 140,
    142, 147, 153, 154, 191, 192, 203,
    212, 213, 223, 224
Mozart xi, 82
Muhammad 62
Mumford Lewis 192

N

Nagasaki 97, 194
Napoleon 131, 191, 195, 211
Neolithic Age 1, 2, 4, 5
Neoplatonism 49, 54, 126
Neutrons 94, 97, 98
New Testament 75, 76, 115, 118, 119
Newton xi, xxiii, 2, 80, 82, 85, 86, 88, 89,
    95, 139
Niccolò Machiavelli 75
Nicomachean Ethics 104, 105, 108, 112,
    119, 124, 125, 129
Niels Bohr xxiii
Nietzsche xviii, 23, 24, 81, 82
Nobel 13, 190, 204, 215, 220
Noncumulative Knowledge xv, xxii,
    xxiii, 135
Norman Angell 215
North Africa xi, 182
North Korea 143, 201
Novum Organum 73, 74, 87, 137
Nuclear Fusion 178
Nuclear reactors 157, 200
Nuclear War xii, xiv, 142, 150, 154, 192,
    196, 197, 199, 201, 206, 207, 212,
    213, 218, 220, 223

O

Odyssey 10, 14, 15, 16, 123
Oil xiv, xxi, 69, 95, 142, 144, 157, 158,
    159, 160, 161, 162, 163, 166, 167,
    173, 175, 176, 177, 178, 202, 219
Old Testament 46
Olympia xx
Oratory xix, xx, 12
Origen 56
Ostrogoths 48, 58

Q

Quadrividium 58

R

Rackham Routledge 28, 118
Raphael 69, 75, 93
Rationale 22, 127
Rationalism 22, 83, 88, 117, 202, 215
R. Dubos xxi, 87, 100, 210
Reason xiii, xix, xxi, xxiv, 4, 8, 13, 18, 21,
    22, 23, 24, 25, 28, 32, 36, 39, 41,
    46, 48, 51, 52, 63, 77, 79, 83, 84,
    88, 91, 93, 100, 104, 105, 106, 107,
    112, 113, 114, 116, 122, 125, 130,
    134, 135, 137, 142, 176, 203, 204,
    210, 214, 215, 224
Reasons for War 213
Reformation xiii
Religion xvii, xxii, 15, 18, 53, 54, 55, 59,
    60, 62, 68, 91, 116, 119, 139, 140,
    202, 211
Renaissance xi, xvii, xx, 6, 11, 26, 31, 40,
    58, 60, 62, 64, 67, 68, 69, 70, 71,
    73, 74, 75, 76, 77, 78, 79, 81, 83,
    93, 101, 111, 119, 131, 209, 224
Renewable xiv, 143, 144, 145, 154, 155,
    156, 157, 160, 161, 162, 163, 165,
    166, 168, 169, 171, 172, 173, 174,
    176, 177, 178, 183, 184, 219, 220,
    223, 225
Republic 25, 32, 78, 92, 108, 124
Residential 156, 159, 165, 169, 170, 176
Resources xii, xiii, xiv, xv, xxi, 3, 82, 105,
    107, 142, 143, 144, 145, 150, 153,
    155, 160, 162, 165, 171, 173, 174,
    192, 219, 224
Revolution xi, xii, 45, 46, 86, 91, 94, 95,
    100, 131, 144, 146, 163, 182
Rhetoric 12, 106, 107, 122
Richard Falckenberg 70
Robert McNamara 197
Robert Nisbet xv, 154
Roger Bacon 63, 85

Roman xviii, 10, 23, 40, 41, 42, 46, 48,
    49, 50, 55, 57, 58, 59, 60, 61, 62, 67,
    68, 70, 73, 75, 79, 87, 127
Romance 9
Romans 19, 20, 26, 37, 46, 47, 48, 49, 59,
    101, 139
Ruskin xix, xx
R. Winks 58, 89, 90

S

Schopenhauer xviii, 115, 116
Schweitzer xvii, xviii, xix, 193
Science xi, xxi, 12, 17, 34, 61, 65, 87, 93,
    100, 101, 158, 199, 210
Scientific revolution 73, 89
Seneca 47, 48, 49, 50, 53, 109, 110,
    127, 139
Silk Road 64
Sir Rees 150, 200
Slavs 19
Social Contract 91, 210
Society xi, xiv, xvi, xvii, xviii, xix, xxi,
    xxiii, 4, 5, 11, 18, 20, 25, 26, 27, 32,
    38, 55, 60, 61, 66, 67, 88, 100, 112,
    113, 117, 121, 129, 140, 141, 146,
    149, 155, 182, 185, 198, 203, 209,
    218, 221, 225
Socrates xii, xvii, 18, 20, 24, 25, 26, 27,
    28, 29, 30, 31, 34, 35, 36, 37, 41,
    42, 54, 55, 105, 106, 111, 117, 118,
    119, 124, 131, 132, 133, 135, 136,
    138, 139
Solar panel 161, 164, 166, 169
Solar system xxii, 2, 68, 74, 80, 82, 87, 99,
    151, 152, 164, 170, 176, 187
Solzhenitsyn 190, 191
Sophocles 17, 37, 60
Space xxi, 2, 10, 11, 23, 43, 61, 74, 100,
    152, 157, 161, 168, 169, 173,
    192, 198
Space Defense Initiative (SDI) 198
sphere xvii, 21, 23, 43, 44
Spinoza xviii, 82, 84, 85, 88, 89, 113,
    114, 187
St. Ambrose 56

234

Stars 2, 18, 43, 45, 57, 80, 96, 97, 98, 152, 220, 224
Stoa 41, 42, 50
Stoicism 41, 42, 47
Stone Age. xx, 201
St. Paul xii, 56, 118, 119, 223
Sumeria 5
Summa Theologica 111, 126
Summum bonum 26, 113

T

Technological progress xii, 101, 144
Technology xiv, xxiv, 61, 144, 146, 147, 154, 165, 170, 187, 225
Temperance 20, 21, 26, 27, 33, 41, 52, 107, 108, 109, 118, 121, 123, 126, 127, 128, 129, 131
Ten Commandments 20, 118
Tertullian 59
Thales 19, 24, 86
Theatre 12
Themistocles 37
Theodore Gaza 70
Theogony 16
The Prince 75
Thermal 157
Thomas Aquinas 26, 35, 63, 111, 119, 126, 139
Thomas Jefferson 89, 114, 125
Thomas More 76
Three Mile Island 157
Thucydides 12, 37, 38, 39, 188, 189
Timothy Ferris 43
Titian 69, 75
Trivium 58
Truth 21, 22, 23, 25, 26, 27, 28, 29, 36, 48, 52, 54, 56, 63, 81, 87, 90, 93, 103, 111, 123, 124, 126, 132, 137, 147, 218, 223
Turgot 7, 8, 89
Turks 19, 59, 61, 63, 70, 78, 191

U

United Nations xii, 144, 216, 218, 219

Universe xi, xiii, xxiii, 1, 2, 18, 19, 23, 35, 41, 43, 80, 93, 96, 97, 98, 99, 100, 150, 152, 187, 224
Utopia 76

V

Vandals 48, 59
Vasari 69, 79
Vasco da Gama 69, 74
Vice 84
Victor Hugo xi, 82
Vikings 59
Virtue xi, xii, xiii, xiv, xv, xix, xxi, xxiv, 7, 8, 15, 16, 18, 20, 25, 26, 27, 28, 29, 30, 34, 41, 47, 48, 51, 52, 58, 65, 66, 76, 84, 91, 102, 103, 104, 105, 106, 107, 108, 109, 110, 111, 113, 114, 116, 117, 118, 119, 120, 121, 122, 123, 124, 125, 126, 127, 128, 130, 132, 133, 135, 136, 137, 138, 139, 140, 142, 145, 154, 204, 211, 223, 225
Virtue is aretê, ἀρετή. 116
Virtuous life 26, 29, 133, 140
Visigoths 19, 48, 59
Vitruvius 49
Voltaire 82, 89, 90, 91, 131, 140, 189, 190

W

Water xv, xxi, 12, 19, 23, 35, 45, 49, 64, 94, 142, 143, 145, 146, 151, 153, 157, 158, 161, 166, 169, 174, 175, 179, 181, 192
Wells 147, 148, 149, 204, 205, 225
Werner Jaeger 10, 14, 55, 117
Western civilization xx, 9, 11, 12, 14, 20, 34, 37, 40, 48, 53, 65, 140
William Fulbright 203
Wisdom xi, xx, xxi, xxii, 3, 9, 15, 16, 18, 19, 22, 26, 27, 28, 33, 41, 49, 54, 56, 73, 76, 78, 87, 91, 93, 105, 106, 109, 110, 119, 121, 123, 124, 125, 126, 127, 128, 130, 131, 132, 133, 134, 135, 136, 137, 147, 154, 189, 204, 223, 225

Printed in the United States
By Bookmasters